RISK BASED THINKING
2nd Edition

CERM Academy Series on Enterprise Risk Management

Greg Hutchins PE CERM
CERMAcademy.com
503.233.1012
800.COMPETE

HOW TO ORDER:

Cost is $89.00 per copy plus $6.00 Shipping/Handling in the U.S. Offshore orders are based on the form of delivery. Quantity discounts are available from the publisher.

Quality Plus Engineering
4052 NE Couch St.
Portland, OR 97232
USA

503.233.1012
800.COMPETE
800.266.7383
GregH@CERMAcademy.com

For bulk purchases, on your letterhead please include information concerning the intended use of the books and the number of books you wish to purchase.

TABLE OF CONTENTS

CHAPTER 1 - INTRODUCTION

CHAPTER 2 – NEW MANAGEMENT PARADIGM

CHAPTER 3 – RBT CONTEXT, FRAMEWORKS & DEFINITIONS

CHAPTER 4 – ISO 9001:2015 STANDARD

CHAPTER 5 - ISO 31000:2018 GUIDELINE

CHAPTER 6 – COSO ERM GUIDELINE

CHAPTER 7 – BUSINESS CASE FOR RISK

CHAPTER 8 – RISK BASED THINKING JOURNEY

CHAPTER 9 – EXECUTIVE MANAGEMENT

CHAPTER 10 - NEW QUALITY ORGANIZATION

CHAPTER 11 – CERTIFICATION BODIES

CHAPTER 12 – RISK BASED AUDITING

Questions **Page**

CHAPTER 13 - RISK ASSESSMENT TOOLS

CHAPTER 14 – RISK MANAGEMENT AND CONTROL

CHAPTER 15 – FUTURE OF QUALITY: RISK®

“Taking control of uncertainty is the fundamental leadership challenge of our time.”

Ram Charan

Attacker’s Advantage, 2015

CHAPTER 1:

INTRODUCTION

What is the key idea in this chapter?

The key idea in this chapter is Risk Based Thinking or RBT is an amalgam of 1. Risk based, problem solving and 2. Risk based, decision making®.

We feel so strongly about Risk Based Thinking (RBT) that we trademarked the expression: Future of Quality: Risk®. We believe that RBT will change the quality profession and all operational excellence professions.

What is your background in quality and risk management?

We have been in quality for more than 30 years. We go back to the Mil Q (predecessor of ISO 9001) and Mil I (inspection) days of quality. We have been involved with Enterprise Risk Management (ERM) for a dozen years and product risk (FMEA) for almost 30 years. A little more background may help.

- Founder and Principal Engineer with Quality + Engineering (www.QualityPlusEngineering.com), a Critical Infrastructure Protection: Forensics, Assurance, Analytics® engineering firm.
- Founder and Developer of Certified Enterprise Risk Manager® (CERM) Academy and family of risk management certificates.
- Founder of CERM Risk Insights™ emagazine (Insights.CERMAcademy.com) with a circulation of almost 30,000.

- Founder of 800Compete.com - buy American and source domestically consulting risk firm.
- Founder of WorkingIt.com - focused on automation and the Future of Work.
- Risk engineer and consultant for global companies on risk management, homeland security, and asymmetric warfare.
- Developer of *Future of Quality: Risk* slide deck that went viral on Linkedin.
- 9001, ISO 14001, and ISO 27001 risk management systems consultant.
- Lead instructor and consultant for one of the first North American Certification Bodies in 1987.
- Author of more than 20 books.
- Author of multiple risk based, auditing books, which have been approved by national authorities.
- Author of 100's of engineering, quality, and risk articles for ASQ, PMI, IEEE, IIE, QD, and many other journals.
- Author of best selling **ISO 9001** (translated into more than 8 languages).
- Author of **Value Added Auditing**™ - the first risk based, process auditing, and assurance book.

Lesson Learned: We have gone through a number of cycles in operations management, engineering, project management, supply management, ISO management systems, and quality. We have learned much. To share this knowledge, at the end of each question we provide a **Lesson Learned** profile of what works in Risk Based Thinking, risk assessment, risk management, and enterprise risk management.

Resource: Read '99 Quotes About Risk That Inspire You To Great Things'

Http://Insights.CERMacademy.Com/2014/06/52-99-Quotes-Risk-Inspire-Great-Things-Tyler-Tervooren/

Why did you write this book?

Twenty years ago, we wrote 4 best selling, ISO 9001 books. They were fun times. Quality was Job #1. W. Edwards Deming, Joseph Juran, Phil Crosby, and other quality gurus were considered quality management and general management authorities. We would give a quality or ISO talk and then walk away with 1 or more clients.

So why are we writing another book on quality and replowing a topic that has been written about extensively? The challenge is there is little information on Risk Based Thinking (RBT) addressing ISO 9001:2015 and ISO other management system standards. ISO: Risk Based Thinking is the first book on RBT and operational risk. This book in its second edition is the first update.

There are a number of additional reasons why we wrote this book:

- **Lack of consistency.** ISO definitions of key risk concepts are written broadly so they can be interpreted and used by a global audience. This is great, except the definitions can seem cryptic and not usable by the layperson. In this book, we explain risk concepts and their application with ISO 9001:2015 in a practical manner.
- **Cycles of quality.** Quality profession has gone through cycles, ISO 9001, Malcolm Baldrige National Quality Award, Six Sigma, lean, operational excellence, etc. We believe quality is going through a new cycle that incorporates RBT, risk management, and Enterprise Risk Management (ERM) processes. Many quality professionals know quality concepts and tools, but do not understand broader business concepts such as Enterprise Risk Management (ERM); Governance, Risk, Compliance (GRC); COSO ERM framework; and other new acronyms, which are explained fully in this

book.

- **Unique perspective.** We have been through previous cycles of operational excellence. We are firmly grounded in risk and ERM and can provide clues to the future of ISO 9001:2015 and other management systems.

- **Risk Based Thinking.** ISO has adopted the tagline Risk Based Thinking (RBT). RBT may become the basis for ALL ISO management system standards. If so, we provide tips and tools how to architect, design, deploy, and assure RBT.

- **Last person standing.** There is some truth to this assertion. Many experts who have been involved with quality from the Mil Q and Mil I periods are no longer practicing quality. Many quality professionals since the inception of ISO 9001 in 1987 have also retired. We provide critical context in the integration of quality and risk.

Lesson Learned: RBT is a major evolution in quality management. We believe you should start to integrate RBT into your management systems early on. It will make the transition easier to ISO 9001:2015 and may set the foundation for the transition to other ISO families of standards to risk.

Resource: Read 'How To Make Smarter Decisions' Http://Insights.CERMacademy.Com/2014/02/41-Get-Wrong-Greg-Hutchins/

What problem are you trying to solve in this book?

When we started writing this book, we thought key risk concepts would be applicable, consistent, and well defined in ISO risk standards. Wrong!

Why is this important? ISO 9001:2015 is one of the first major ISO standards revised to Annex SL, which we will discuss shortly. As well, the supporting standards such as ISO 31000:2018, the ISO risk management standard, have not been modified to be consistent across Annex SL, ISO 9001, and ISO 14001. The result is critical risk definitions and concepts are different. Also, key risk concepts are not well developed and are open to interpretation. This can create variability, confusion, and ultimately risk in application.

Lesson Learned: Consistency in standards development is the hallmark of quality interpretation and application. Hopefully, this book can provide some clarity about RBT and risk management so you can develop and apply consistent RBT practices in your organization.

Resource: Read 'Are You Managing Risk Or Is It Managing You' Http://Insights.CERMacademy.Com/2012/05/Are-You-Managing-Risk-Or-Is-It-Managing-You/

Why is there repetition in this book?

In this book, we emphasize and repeat critical concepts. Yes, this is intentional and not the result of poor editing. The same thing is stated and revealed in different ways from different perspectives. We want the information or answers to each question to stand alone. As well, we stress some key ideas so they are well understood and can be applied uniformly.

Also, we present ideas in a bulleted fashion so you can use them as a checklist.

Lesson Learned: It takes 3 repetitions at least for a new concept to be understood and applied. Many risk concepts are new to our readers. RBT is new to the ISO families of standards.

Resource: Read 'Because We've Always Done It That Way' 'Http://Insights.CERMacademy.Com/2014/01/37-Always-Done-Way-Mark-Moore/

Are the recommendations in this book a 'one size fits all' approach?

No. The ideas in this book should be adapted to an organization using the expertise of a Quality Management System (QMS) consultant with extensive risk management (RM) knowledge, skills, and abilities. As well, defer to the advice and suggestions of your Certification Body (CB). This advice will be crucial to your certification.

The responses in this book should be used as guidelines and are based on current knowledge and best practices. Many unanswered questions remain how companies will deploy Risk Based Thinking and how Certification Bodies will conduct risk based audits.

Lesson Learned: Do what works for you and your organization with the risk recommendations in this book.

Resource: Read '99 Quotes About Risk That Inspire You To Great Things'
Http://Insights.CERMacademy.Com/2014/06/52-99-Quotes-Risk-Inspire-Great-Things-Tyler-Tervooren/

Does the size or complexity of the organization change the responses to the questions?

ISO 9001:2015 was designed to apply to different organizations including U.S. and global; public and private; large and small; for profit and not for profit; product and service; and listed and not listed organizations (i.e. New York Stock Exchange). ISO 9001:2015 standard provides a common management system and process based approach that needs to be tailored to an organization.

The intent of the ISO certified organization is also critical. If an organization just wants its ISO 9001:2015 certification, then it must tailor and prioritize the ideas in this book. On the other hand if an organization wants to improve and implement world class risk management, then many ideas in this book are applicable.

Your context, maturity, and risk processes (capability) will require tailoring. So, we recommend you secure the assistance of a risk management systems expert to be your trusted advisor.

Lesson Learned: Understand the context of your ISO 9001:2015 certification and application. What is your ISO vision and mission? Do you simply want to get certified or improve operational excellence through risk management?

Resource: Read 'It's All Risky Business'
Http://Insights.CERMacademy.Com/2014/03/44-Risky-Business-T-Dan-Nelson/

What is Annex SL?

Annex SL defines the high level structure of ISO standards, provides identical core text, and provides key definitions that will be found in future and revised management system standards such as ISO 9001:2015, ISO 14001:2015, and others. This will ensure common understanding and implementation of management system standards. It is expected that 30% of all management system standards will have common language, numbering, and clauses. This will result in a number of benefits including: integrated certifications, consistency across management systems, and common application of RBT.

The International Organization for Standardization (ISO) is very good at developing consensus driven, harmonized, international standards. For example, ISO 9001 has been hugely successful. But, there has been a challenge. Each ISO standard is developed by a separate Technical Committee often independently of each other. The standards sometimes seem like standalone documents. ISO developed Annex SL to provide consistency within and harmony across its families of standards.

So when a new ISO management system standard is proposed or an existing standard is revised, a business case or justification study will be developed to address each of the following principles:

- **Market relevance.** Standard should add value and meet the needs of stakeholders. This is broader than satisfying customers. Impacted parties of the standard and important market needs are identified, so the standard can satisfy them.

- **Compatibility.** Potential conflicts, overlaps, and risks with existing or planned ISO standards are identified and reconciled.

- **Topic coverage.** Standard is appropriate and applicable to a broad stakeholder constituency. A number of sectors have developed harmonized ISO 9001 sector specific standards such as AS 9100 in aerospace. This has sometimes resulted in redundancy and confusion. Management system standards should have sufficient specificity or generality to eliminate or at least minimize sector specific standards

- **Flexibility.** Standard is sufficiently flexible so it allows an organization to innovate, differentiate, or compete beyond the requirements of the standard. Management system standards should be adaptable to any organization, product, or service within relevant sectors, across cultures, and be usable by organizations of any size.

- **Free Trade.** Standard encourages global free trade and does not provide any technical barriers to free trade. The purpose of ISO 9001 has always been to encourage open and free trade of goods and services.

- **Applicability of conformity assessment.** Standard allows for the demonstration of conformance through third-party certification. Conformity assessment is a hallmark of ISO standards development. The need for 1st, 2nd, and/or 3rd party conformity assessment is critical to validate implementation and verify compliance. ISO offers the structure of national mutual recognition agreements, national accreditations, Certification Bodies, and auditors who affirm compliance to the standard.

- **Exclusions.** Standard allows organizations to specify product test methods, performance levels, or other specific requirements. Management system standards should not specify product specific requirements, test methods, performance limits, or detailed specifications.

- **Ease of use.** ISO standards should be easily understood and applicable for use by any organization within any country within any culture.

If there is variation, inconsistency, or omission in the above principles, then the ISO standards development structure is at risk. **ISO: Risk Based Thinking** attempts to identify risks and offer constructive solutions.

Lesson Learned: Annex SL is a break through concept in ISO management systems because it encourages consistency, transparency, and conformity assessment. So, learn to love Annex SL. The document will make certification much easier for companies, consultants, and Certifications Bodies.

Resource: Read 'What Could Go Wrong?'
Http://Insights.CERMacademy.Com/2014/04/44-Go-Wrong-John-Millican/

How do you know the answers to the questions are accurate?

Great question. We have been through four iterations of ISO 9001 standards development. We have been involved with ISO 9001 since its inception in 1987. We have been on Technical Committee (TC) 176 that writes ISO 9001. We have written best selling books on ISO 9001. We have written dozens of ISO 9001 articles. We have assisted dozens of companies achieve certification. We know quality. We know risk.

Our responses are based on informed speculation. There will be critical issues that still need to be discussed and resolved in the standard. We also plan to revise this book yearly as companies mature their RBT system to risk management or Enterprise Risk Management.

Lesson Learned: We understand there will be more changes in other ISO management systems standards. So, stay flexible. For this reason, we wrote this book at a high level.

Resource: Read 'Don't Hear What I'm Not Saying'
Http://Insights.CERMacademy.Com/2014/05/49-Dont-Hear-Im-Saying/

Why do you refer to non ISO standards in this book?

Good question. This book is about ISO RBT, but we refer to non ISO standards. Why?

A number of risk concepts, definitions, and other issues have not been addressed in related ISO standards. So, we have provided additional context and explanations based on additional risk documents.

Another reason is certified companies may have different levels of risk maturity and capability. Companies starting their RBT journey may adopt, adapt, and deploy different risk management frameworks. Also, companies will develop different risk taxonomies to fit their specific context. They will then architect, design, deploy, assure, and improve their risk management systems differently based on their context. Also much like quality is a journey, risk management is a journey that starts with organizations adopting RBT and moving towards increased risk maturity and capability.

OK, why not simply defer to ISO 31000:2018 and other ISO risk guidance documents. ISO 31000 was first issued in 2009 and updated in 2018. ISO 31000:2018 addresses a number of issues coming out of ISO 9001:2015, but does not specifically address Risk Based Thinking.

ISO is also a consensus building, international organization that develops lowest common denominator standards applicable to everyone. Organizations may want to develop world class, operational risk management systems. This book can be used by the former and the latter.

Lesson Learned: We stress the hallmark of quality is consistency. Expect variances in ISO risk definitions and implementation until all ISO families of standards have been rewritten and integrated with the standardized requirements in Annex SL, which for some ISO standards are still five years away.

Resource: Read 'Latest ISO Certification Statistics'
Http://Insights.CERMacademy.Com/2013/11/30-Iso-Trends-Greg-Hutchins/

Why not quote long passages directly from ISO standards?

ISO standards are copyrighted, specifically have a ©. We respect and follow the letter and intent of intellectual property and copyright law. So, we defer to fair use to paraphrase limited parts of standards so they are understandable and usable by the layperson as well as by the expert quality risk practitioner. If we use a term or a brief section of the standard, we put it in quotation marks, refer to its origin, and defer to 'fair use.'

Your life will become simpler having access to the latest version of the standard. We strongly recommend all ISO certified companies, consultants, and interested parties purchase ISO 9001:2015, ISO 31000:2018, and other guidance documents listed in this book.

Lesson Learned: You may need multiple copies of the standards. Purchase licenses to the new families and updated ISO families of standards. The ISO license allows you to share the standards legally.

What are additional risk resources and references?

At the end of many responses in this book, you will find a **Resource** article, blog posting, or video. Type this link in your browser and it will take you to an important free resource.

Also, *CERM Risk Insights* is our weekly risk emagazine. The site has category listings you will find helpful.

Lesson Learned: Visit *CERM Risk Insights* for thousands of risk articles. The articles can be found at http://insights.cermacademy.com for additional information on RBT, risk assessment, risk management and enterprise risk management. You will find almost risk articles in the following helpful categories on the right side of the page:

- Careers@Risk™
- Cyber@Risk™

- Decisions@Risk™
- Design@Risk™
- ISO9001:2015@Risk™
- Life@Risk™
- Pharma@Risk™
- Process@Risk™
- Projects@Risk™
- Quality@Risk™
- Reliability@Risk™
- Software@Risk™
- Suppliers@Risk™
- Tips&Tools@Risk™

Resource: Visit Careers@Risk For Career Information. Http://Insights.CERMacademy.Com/Category/Careersrisk/

How can you access 'Resource' help quickly?

This book offers 100's of RBT and risk management resources. Read the ones that are appropriate to you.

Also, instead of entering the URL at the *CERM Risk Insights* for an article each time, just keep the page below open in your browser:

http://insights.cermacademy.com

Each time you want to read an article, enter the first few words of the **Resource** title in the Search box on the upper right side of the above URL and it will take you directly to the article. You will save time accessing the article.

Lesson Learned: if you need additional information after reading a response, search the **Resource** link in most questions or send us an email at GregH@CERMAcademy.com. Our team of risk engineers will get back to you shortly

Resource: Read 'VUCA's Impact On The Quality Profession'
Http://Insights.CERMacademy.Com/2013/04/11-Vucas-Impact-On-The-Quality-Profession-Greg-Hutchins/

How many companies are certified to ISO 9001:2015 and other management systems?

ISO does not really track who is certified. We know this seems strange. Individual CB's that conduct certification audits track their certificates. ISO plans to develop an integrated list of certified companies through its CERTO process.

However, It is believed more than 1.7 million companies are certified to some management system standard and somewhere between 1.1 to 1.2 million companies are certified to ISO 9001. And, it is estimated another 500,000 companies use ISO 9001 to self-certify, self-declare, or improve their processes. We currently do not know how many companies have transitioned to ISO 9001:2015 and other ISO risk based standards

Lesson Learned: The changes occurring in ISO 9001 and the other management system standards will impact many companies, whether they are certified, self certified, or using ISO standards to improve their operations.

Resource: Read 'U.S. Manufacturing Competitiveness At A Critical Crossroads'
Http://Insights.CERMacademy.Com/2014/10/62-Us-Manufacturing-Competitiveness-Critical-Crossroads-Stuart-Rosenberg/

CHAPTER 2:

NEW MANAGEMENT PARADIGM

What is the key idea in this chapter?

The key idea in this chapter is Risk Based Thinking (RBT) is a new management paradigm for ISO management system standards and is a disruptive concept. As well, the Baldrige Performance Framework, U.S. Government, and many companies are adopting Enterprise Risk Management (ERM) and RBT is the first stop in the ERM journey.

What is disruptive change?

Many organizations, associations, and standards are going through disruptive change and innovation. We believe this is occurring to ISO 9001:2015 and the other ISO families of standards.

So, what is disruptive innovation? Wikipedia defines 'disruptive innovation' as:

> "... innovation that helps create a new market and value network, and eventually disrupts an existing market and value network (over a few years or decades), displacing an earlier technology. The term is used in business and technology literature to describe innovations that improve a product or service in ways that the market does not expect, typically first by designing for a different set of consumers in a new market and later by lowering prices in the existing market."

As you read this chapter, look at some of the disruptive changes that ISO has created: RBT value proposition, direct management engagement, service differentiation as well as tangible product emphasis, process approach requirements, QMS verification beyond documentation, new forms of assurance, etc.

Lesson Learned: Read Clayton M. Christensen's books on disruptive innovation such as **The Innovator's Dilemma** and **The Innovator's Solution**. They will provide insights on what is occurring with ISO standards development, your organization, and even your career.

Resource: Read 'Future Of Quality'
Http://Insights. CERMacademy.Com/2013/03/Future-Of-Quality/

What is VUCA?

VUCA is an acronym standing for Volatility, Uncertainty, Complexity, and Ambiguity (VUCA). VUCA is the driver of disruptive change and disruptive innovation. VUCA is the new normal. RBT is a direct result of VUCA.

Just think of all the changes occurring in your company. Globalization. New regulations. Changing customers and product preferences. New competitive product offerings. New technologies. New business models. Product lifecycle compression. Risk based ISO standards. RBT.

Now, think of all the changes occurring in your life. New work. New jobs. New duties. New products. New technologies. Risk management. More schooling.

Lesson Learned: VUCA is one of the key business concepts over the next ten years. So, understand and incorporate the VUCA acronym into your vocabulary. The bottom line is change is no longer linear.

Resource: Read 'At The Intersection Of Change And Risk'
Http://Insights.CERMacademy.Com/2013/12/31-Intersection-Change-Risk-Mark-Moore/

What is a 'black swan' event?

Globalization has increased uncertainty and the probability of a 'black swan' event occurring. A black swan event is one that has a high consequence and relatively low probability. The challenge is low probability events are now becoming high probability events. Think floods, global warming, ebola, wars, earthquakes, flooding, tsunamis, forest fires, etc.

Uncertainty has become the new normal. One hundred year events now seem commonplace. We are finding natural events that should occur every hundred years occur more frequently and even yearly in some cases. Just think of global weather patterns. 2014 was the warmest year on record and 2015 had some of the highest storm and rain totals in recorded history.

Lesson Learned: Just read your local paper or watch a TV program. What is the common denominator of the program? Risk. The unknown, unknowable, or even unthinkable can occur, just think of September 11, 2001. While these events cannot be anticipated, these events can adversely impact an organization.

Resource: Read 'Disruptive Education Risks - It's Everywhere'
Http://Insights.CERMacademy.Com/2013/02/8-Disruptive-Innovation-In-Education-Its-Every-Where-Jerry-Brong/

What are business examples of VUCA and black swans?

Customer wants, needs, and expectations are increasing. Customers used to be the end user of a product or service and now 'interested parties' include stakeholders throughout the organization and throughout the world.

Globalization has resulted in international trading. In a global world with interconnected supply chains, business and operational risks can surface unexpectedly. And, companies are using extended supply chains to provide goods and services throughout the world in a just in time manner. The leaning of the supply chain implies one event can disrupt the entire value chain. For example, the loss of a single source supplier can rapidly impact a company and its supply chain potentially undermining the company's reputation and its financials.

An unknown, unforeseen, and low probability event from a small fourth or fifth tier supplier can adversely impact the final company whose brand can be jeopardized. Just think of the poor publicity resulting from the use of child labor in a fourth tier supplier.

Lesson Learned: VUCA and black swan events are counter intuitive and can call into question much lean, quality, and Six Sigma conventional wisdom such as single sourcing, offshoring, no buffer inventories, and just in time delivery – all of which add system risk. So, question your conventional wisdom regarding operational excellence. Also, expect and plan for the unexpected.

Resource: Read 'Qantas $3B Loss, Risk Is More Than Compliance' Http://Insights.CERMacademy.Com/2014/09/57-Quantas-3b-Loss-Risk-Compliance-Greg-Carroll/

Is VUCA creating opportunities (upside risks)?

Yes. Opportunities are called upside risks in ISO 9001:2015.

Innovative and risk taking companies are keenly aware that VUCA can also impact upside risk, such as investment opportunities and the costs of borrowing for capital projects and expansion. For example, each new startup with a new idea is an example of a risk taker seeing VUCA disruption as an opportunity to create value with new products and services in new markets.

VUCA is also creating new management paradigms on how to lead and manage. Investors are demanding higher levels of risk assurance and transparency from company managers. Companies are aware of their risks and are now managing through a risk lens. Government regulators are aware of risks and are evaluating company's exposures and risk-controls. Bond rating agencies, such as Standard & Poor's, rate company's Enterprise Risk Management (ERM) systems for effectiveness.

Volatility – New School Solutions	
Old School	**New School**
Is inwardly focused	Is outwardly focused
Accepts the status quo	Thinks about tomorrow's risks before they occur
Expects cause and effect relationships	Understands risk correlation is more common than causality
Process stability	Process innovation

Lesson Learned: We live in the age of VUCA disruption. Risk management is the preferred system to manage in VUCA time. See 'Old School' vs. 'New School' Management sidebars on the following pages.

Resource: Read 'Cultivating A Risk Paradigm Shift In Your Organization' Http://Insights.CERMacademy.Com/2013/03/10-Cultivating-A-Risk-Management-Paradim-Shift-In-An-Organization/

Is VUCA disrupting ISO?

Yes. Standards making organizations are being disrupted. In much the same way, ISO is innovating with RBT and risk requirements.

It seems ISO is innovating and developing a new business management system model based on RBT due to its changing marketplace and its uncertainty, specifically:

- ISO is facing economic and revenue pressures. ISO publicly stated it needed to adopt a new business model due to its changing standards development context. Why? More standards are available online at a reduced price or gratis.

- Multiple ISO management systems are being developed, such as for auto, aerospace, and other sectors. Diversity is creating more variation, uncertainty, and ultimately risk in standards development.

Uncertainty – New School Solutions	
Old School	**New School**
Clings to existing processes when they are unstable	Develops new stable and capable transforming processes
Relies of past solutions to solve today's problems	Recognizes opportunities to change processes and seeks to adapt
Wants known business objectives and plan to achieve them	Understands that objectives are fluid and flexibility is critical for success
'This too shall pass' attitude	Anticipates uncertainty to develop new or modify existing business model

- Customers want increased assurance beyond management systems certification including business and risk assurance. This is creating a market for multiple types and levels of assurance from commodity certification to business assurance to 'opinion' based attestation more commonly found in financial statements.

- Global standards emphasize public safety, health and risk criteria, specifically placing risk alongside quality or even replacing quality.

- Risk is becoming more prominent in government, public agency, and NGO operations, so contractors and consultants are developing risk management, assurance, and control programs.

- Management system certification is commodifying and losing brand value in developed countries. Management system certification may even commodify in developing countries, where significant certification growth has occurred over the last ten years.

- Credibility of third-party certifications is decreasing in sectors and in developed countries.

- More companies are self-certifying or self-declaring conformance to management system standards.

Lesson Learned: ISO 9001:2015 is the first disruptive standard coming out of Annex SL to respond to the above market changes.

Resource: Read 'Business Disruption Is Sweeping The World With Rapid Change'
Http://Insights.CERMacademy.Com/2014/09/58-Business-Disruption-Sweeping-World-Rapid-Change-Rick-Torben/

What is ISO's new tag line?

ISO developed a new tag line: Risk Based Thinking (RBT). We simplify this as RBT throughout this book. According to ISO, RBT consists of the following key concepts:

- RBT is a critical element of what organizations and people already do - automatically and even unconsciously.
- Risk has always been part of ISO 9001. ISO 9001:2015 now has explicit requirements that are integrated into the entire quality management system.
- RBT integrates preventive action.
- RBT is already part of the process approach that has been part of ISO 9001 since the 2000 revision.
- RBT incorporates positive - opportunity risk and negative - downside risk into its approach.[i]

As you read this book, you will see RBT has been part of quality and Six Sigma if we view RBT in terms of controlling variation or uncertainty.

Lesson Learned: RBT is a fluid concept, which will evolve. ISO is coming to terms with risk in QMS and other management system standards. ISO recognizes many ISO 9001 stakeholders are NOT ready for risk. Many countries voted down the Committee Draft (CD) and the Draft International Standard (DIS), while two - thirds or so approved them. RBT may also

Ambiguity – New School Solutionsılutions	
Old School	**New School**
Is uncomfortable with ambiguityıe context and environment sur-	Uses ambiguity to act and to innovateeholders and environmental
Seeks structure and direction	Is comfortable with fluid structuree
Attempts to understand the entire	and movement to solve a problem
Cannot identify the right problem	Has a feeling for critical issues,
to solve and starting point of the problem	frames them, and creates 'what if' scenariosies surrounding an issue

change as different families of ISO standards are updated or proposed.

Resource: Read 'What Does Risk Based Thinking Really Mean?' Http://Insights.CERMacademy.Com/2014/05/48-Risk-Based-Thinking-Really-Mean-T-Dan-Nelson/

Why did ISO adopt Risk Based Thinking?

We discussed VUCA is disrupting standards development. So, ISO has not formally announced why it decided to incorporate risk into its families of standards. We can only speculate. However, the following reasons may shed light on the question. The following is our speculation why ISO specifically adopted RBT:

One of the tenets of this book is ISO 9001:2015 reflects the macro changes occurring in today's economy and marketplace. What do we mean? When ISO 9001 came out in 1987, the focus was developing a proceduralized Quality Management System (QMS). It was a great idea for its time. Quality management, quality assurance, and quality control were essential to a company's competitiveness.

Almost 30 years later, the emphasis is how to address VUCA and manage in VUCA time. The ISO ecosystem is maturing. CB's, consultants, and other stakeholders are developing new business assurance and revenue models. The conventional wisdom is a new management paradigm is

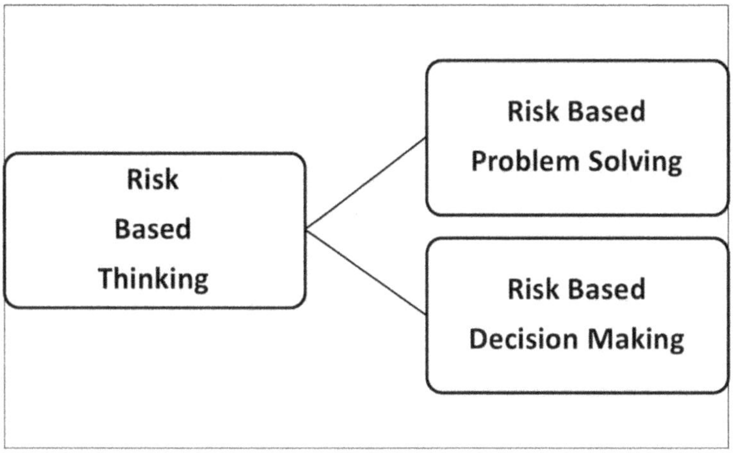

Figure 1: Risk Based Thinking Components

evolving around RBT, risk assessment, risk management, and ultimately Enterprise Risk Management.

Also, ISO has a number of interested parties who have new requirements. National standards organizations want ISO to standardize and incorporate risk. Accreditors want the international standards development process to be more consistent and harmonized so additional revenue can be generated. Global CB's want standards to incorporate risk management since many have embraced and rebranded into risk organizations. ISO consultants are seeing the commoditization of ISO consulting and want higher margins.

ISO decided it needed more consistency among its standards, hence the development of Annex SL. ISO needed to update its management system standards around a global theme that addressed VUCA, hence the development of RBT. ISO needed new revenue sources, hence a focus on developing a new business model that incorporated RBT or risk into its families of standards.

Lesson Learned: We believe ISO 9001:2015 is a good to great document. Why? It is moving conformity assessment to a higher level of assurance, rigor, professionalism, consistency, and clarity. It is moving conformity assessment beyond binary quality to a higher level of assurance based on risk assessment and risk assurance. And ultimately, the standard may be moving to a business management system.

Resource: Read 'Reinvent Or Die?
Http://Insights.CERMacademy.Com/2013/03/Reinvent-Or-Die-2/

How do you define Risk Based Thinking?

RBT is a good to great concept for ISO. However, there are problems.

RBT as defined and described by ISO is difficult to operationalize or audit. How do you operationalize or audit Risk Based Thinking? What evidence, artifacts, or data is the auditor going to find based on someone's thinking? So, how do you read someone's thoughts? Not unless you have taken and passed a Mind Reading 101 course, you cannot audit Risk Based Thinking.

However, you can audit Risk Based Thinking artifacts. For this reason, we define RBT (See Figure 1) as:

- Risk based, problem solving.
- Risk based, decision making.™

Why? Both of the above bullets are demonstrable, auditable, and offer verifiable evidence to a Certification Body of conformance, performance, and verification of risk-control effectiveness.

Lesson Learned: RBT is a good concept that needs to be operationalized and be auditable based on 1. Risk based, problem solving and 2. Risk based, decision making.

Resource: Read 'Fear And Caution Under VUCA'
Http://Insights.CERMacademy.Com/2013/03/Fear-And-Caution-Under-Vuca/

What is the value proposition for adopting Risk Based Thinking?

The standard writers called ISO 9001:2015 a 'significant revision.' The significance and impact of RBT in the revision was discussed and sometimes ferociously attacked during the development of the standard. Developed countries voted down the standard during the Committee Draft and Draft International Standard. However, these countries realized that RBT is not going away, so they closed ranks around ISO saying that RBT is good for countries and companies.

The commonly heard refrain from ISO standards community, CB's, auditors, and consultants goes something along the following, RBT will:

- Improve customer satisfaction.
- Assure consistency of goods and services.
- Establish a proactive culture of prevention and improvement.
- Establish a risk based culture, which successful companies can adopt in the face of VUCA disruption.

Lesson Learned: After sometimes vicious opposition, the ISO community is slowly coming to terms with RBT and Annex SL changes. So, start integrating RBT into your management system processes. It is the future of operational excellence including Six Sigma, quality management, and process management.

Resource: Read 'Business Model Innovation'
Http://Insights.CERMacademy.Com/Files/2014/01/Business-Model-Innovation-Extract1.Pdf

What is the essence of Risk Based Thinking?

RBT is a good idea, but it has to be defined better, operationalized, and ultimately be auditable. We discuss these ideas in great detail over the next 300 pages.

We migrated from quality to risk about a dozen years ago. We developed the 4P's™ model, which we believe can be used as the basis for RBT or specifically risk based, problem solving and risk based, decision making:

- **Proactive.** Proactive behavior refers to anticipatory, change oriented, and self-initiated management and leadership. In other words, proactive behavior involves acting in anticipation and advance of uncertainty or risk rather than just reacting. It means anticipating risk and taking control to mitigate risks. Taking control means architecting, designing, deploying, and assuring a context sensitive control environment. It also means making things happen rather than reacting, adjusting, or waiting for a threat or negative event to occur.

- **Preventive.** Prevention involves designing a control system and processes to keep undesirable events, threats, or risks from occurring or recurring. Prevention is based on the belief a risk is less imminent and perhaps acceptable to the organization.

- **Predictive.** Prediction involves anticipating events or threats before they occur. Systems and processes are in place to ensure business continuity and be able to meet business objectives.

- **Preemptive.** Preemption involves being able to forestall a threat or risk from occurring by being proactive in the face of risk. Preemption is based on the belief a risk is imminent, material, and consequential to the organization.

Lesson Learned: The above 4P's is our PDCA risk cycle. Use the 4P's in designing your RBT system of controls and treatment.

Resource: Read 'Proactive - Preventive - Predictive - Preemptive' Http://Insights.CERMacademy.Com/2013/03/Proactive-Preventive-Predictive-Preemptive/

Is ISO 9001:2015 moving to a business management system?

ISO 9001:2015 seems to be migrating from a QMS to a business management system. We may be seeing this in other ISO management system standards.

These changes are a critical change for the quality community and may point to a larger change occurring in the profession, specifically a move from traditional quality management, quality assurance, and quality control to risk management, risk assurance and risk-control.

Lesson Learned: Keep up with the changes occurring in ISO 9001:2015 and other ISO and even national standards. They are all incorporating some of risk management. Your future and career may depend on it.

Resource: Read 'Don't Hear What I'm Not Saying'
Http://Insights.CERMacademy.Com/2014/05/49-Dont-Hear-Im-Saying/

Is there evidence of reduced interest in quality and ISO 9001?

ISO standard developers saw the same data points as we did about reduced interest in quality. Quality was maturing. ISO 9001 QMS was perceived less as a competitive advantage or differentiator. CB's and consultants were getting squeezed on margin. The standard was not keeping up with the times. The developers decided to use ISO 9001:2015 as the mechanism to make the standard as well as other ISO families of standards emphasize RBT and risk management.

Lesson Learned: Study the Google Ngram data points in the **Resource** listed below. Risk management is becoming more critical to all organizations.

Resource: Future of Quality: Risk Management
http://insights.cermacademy.com/2012/05/future-of-quality-data-points-greg-hutchins-qualityrisk/

What does ISO recommend to facilitate the transition to RBT and risk?

ISO/TC 176, the developers of ISO 9001:2015, developed the following recommendations to facilitate the transition to RBT:

- Identify risks and opportunities in the organization.
- Analyze and prioritize the risks and opportunities in the organization.
- Plan actions to address the risks.
- Implement an action plan.
- Check the effectiveness of the actions.
- Continually improve.[ii]

As well, ISO has offered similar advice to companies adopting risk management for other standards.

Lesson Learned: The above recommendations are generic. A major reason for the **ISO: Risk Based Thinking** book is to offer more guidance for architecting, designing, deploying, and assuring RBT and risk frameworks.

Resource: Read 'Risk Decisions And Human Nature' Http://Insights.CERMacademy.Com/2013/06/17-Decisions-And-Human-Reliability-Uncertainty-Ed-Perkins/

Has risk always been a part of ISO 9001:2015?

ISO maintains risk has implicitly been a part of the standard since the ISO 9001:2015 revision. How? In the new standard, 'preventive action' has evolved to 'actions to address risk and opportunities.' This changes the Corrective Action – Preventive Action (CAPA) model. In the past, Preventive Action was implemented as a result of Corrective Action specifically to prevent the recurrence of the nonconformity.

Some quality authorities follow this logic: RBT has always been a part of the ISO management systems ethos since its inception in 1987 because Statistical Process Control (SPC) deals with the control of process variation. And, the control of process variation is all about risk management. Since it was always implicit, now it is explicit in ISO 9001:2015 revision.

We are seeing something similar with ERM and ISO 31000:2018. ISO 31000:2018 is the risk reference to support ISO 9001:2015 and RBT. ISO 31000:2018 risk authorities now affirm that ISO 31000 is an ERM standard. So, if we follow this logic, ISO 9001:2015 having adopted RBT may be moving towards ERM.

Lesson Learned: The future of ISO management systems may be RBT, risk assessment, risk management, and finally ERM. So, purchase ISO 31000:2018 guidelines and see if risk management or Enterprise Risk Management may fit your organization and context. Remember, apply and tailor them to your RBT and QMS processes.

Resource: Read Decisions@Risk Articles At CERM Risk Insights: Http://Insights.CERMacademy.Com/Category/Decisionsrisk/

What are QMS challenges for managing in VUCA time?

We have written best-selling books on quality. We believed and practiced quality management, assurance, and control. We believed that a QMS approach and certification worked well in many circumstances, but it did not seem to work when there was external management volatility, disruption, or uncertainty or in other words VUCA.

This introduces a paradox in quality management. Quality management and Six Sigma entail the control of variation or specifically ensuring consistent variation around a target or business objective. Process controls are developed for critical and major product attributes or process control points. Upper and lower control limits are calculated based on process variation. Controls are imposed at the product or process levels. The focus is on the internal context of the organization.

The challenge is quality management and quality control may not work well in a dynamic external market that is constantly changing. External contextual changes can force internal management systems to become volatile. Lean, Six Sigma, and QMS controls may starve lean processes to the point where they induce more process risk. Let us look at lean, which advocates single source partnering and no buffer inventories (incoming, in process, and final). If a critical, single source supplier shuts down, then the supply chain breaks down. If this concept does not make sense now, hopefully it will become clearer as you move through the book.

We believe the volatility of the external world is a reason why ISO incorporated risk into ISO 9001:2015 and other families of management system standards. ISO decided to integrate the best of both worlds - quality and risk - and develop standards based on stable process controls, RBT, and sustainable management systems. While some readers would disagree with the above assertion, we have seen too many instances where management systems could not maintain stability in an inherently unstable business climate.

Lesson Learned: Learn and apply RBT into your management systems and processes. It may be tomorrow's new management paradigm.

Resource: Read 'Transform Now … Or Struggle To Survive' Http://Insights.CERMacademy.Com/2013/10/28-Transform-Now-Or-Struggle-To-Survive-Daniel-Burrus/

Will ISO companies adopt the RBT ideas in this book?

Companies and large organizations are adopting ERM as a result of contractual and statutory requirements.

The ISO adoption drivers for RBT adoption are largely contractual. In Chapter 8, Risk Based Thinking Journey, we discuss the Risk Capability and Maturity Model (RCMM). In that chapter, we see four possible scenarios of RBT and risk management adoption by ISO 9001:2015 and other certified companies:

- Companies may say the new ISO 9001:2015 revision does not offer sufficient value and drop their ISO certifications. We hope this is not the case because ISO 9001:2015 with its emphasis on RBT is a key competitive value differentiator. In this book, we call these Level 0 (adhoc) companies.

- Small companies, the majority of ISO certified companies, will adopt low level, risk assessment and RBT processes simply to comply and be certified. These organizations will not mature their risk processes. We call these Level 1 (RCMM) companies.

- Companies will go beyond ISO 9001:2015 requirements and adopt elements of a capable risk assessment system, such as elements of risk management. These companies will certify to ISO 9001:2015 as the basic QMS standard and adopt sector specific quality and risk requirements such as in aerospace, automotive, and telecommunications sectors. These companies will develop mature and capable risk processes. We call these Level 2 (RCMM) companies.

- Companies may already have a mature system that is effectively managing risks. These will be bigger organizations that must comply with regulatory statutes requiring higher levels of risk management and quality management. We call these mature risk organizations Level 3 (RCMM) companies.

Lesson Learned: 'Do what works for you' is the refrain throughout this book. What works entails determining the appropriate level of risk capability and maturity for your organization.

Resource: Read 'Context Matters When Discussing Risk'
Http://Insights.CERMacademy.Com/2013/06/15-Context-Matters-When-Discussing-Risk-Mark-Jones/

CHAPTER 3:

RBT CONTEXT, FRAMEWORKS, & DEFINITIONS

What is the key idea in this chapter?

The key idea in this chapter is operations and quality professionals need to know a new vocabulary involving risk, RBT, governance, and compliance.

Is there an international risk language that can be applied to ISO 9001:2015?

Guide 73 and ISO 31000:2018 define key ISO risk terms. ISO 31000:2018 risk management framework terms are defined in Chapter 5. COSO ERM risk management framework terms are defined in Chapter 6. Risk assurance concepts and terms derived from Yellow Book and Red Book standards are discussed in Chapter 12. Risk management and control terms are defined in Chapter 14. As well, a glossary of terms can be found in the appendix.

We introduce critical risk terms and concepts that have not been defined or are confusing in ISO standards. We define critical risk concepts and terms so you can understand risk context and can develop your own risk taxonomy or tailor a risk framework to your organization. These additional risk definitions will facilitate your application of RBT and certification to ISO 9001:2015.

Lesson Learned: A number of critical risk terms can be confusing in ISO 9001:2015 and ISO 31000:2018. Read the **Resource** articles mentioned in this book. The articles will help you develop your risk vocabulary and understand RBT. As well, you can find an extensive Glossary at the end of this book.

Resource: Read 'Risk Management Is About Context'
Http://Insights.CERMacademy.Com/2013/07/20-Risk-Is-All-About-Context-Mark-Jones/

What is 'context'?

Context is a critical concept introduced and used extensively in ISO 9001:2015. ISO 31000:2018 defines context as the environment in which the organization operates, competes, and achieves its business objectives.

In ISO 9001:2015, context may also include the following:

- Culture, tone at the top, Corporate Social Responsibility (CSR) and other critical competitive attributes.
- Governance, Risk, and Compliance (GRC) business environment and management systems.
- Business environment in which the organization operates and competes.
- Business strategies, plans, and tactics developed to achieve QMS objectives.
- Product standards, guidelines, and corporate business model.
- Type of value added and services produced.
- Resources assigned to achieve QMS objectives.
- External and internal stakeholder expectations and requirements.
- Suppliers critical to the development of a sustainable business

model.

Context is critical in ISO standard because it defines the nature, type, extent, and level of controls to be developed to mitigate risks. Context also ensures a tailored RBT framework is architected, designed, deployed, and assured.

Lesson Learned: Remember: if you master context, you can and will master RBT.

Resource: Read 'Context Matters When Discussing Risk (Event Risk)' Http://Insights.CERMacademy.Com/2013/09/22-Context-Matters-When-Discussing-Risk-Event-Risks-Mark-Jones/

Why is 'context' worth 20 IQ points?

A number of years ago, a friend told me understanding context is worth 20 IQ points. We did not get it at first. What did he mean? Every organization operates, competes and profits within a business context. Understanding the organizational and competitive context helps you understand the business environment and the system of risk-control to be architected, designed, deployed, and assured.

So as more VUCA disruption occurs, then understanding context helps you anticipate disruptive change. If you understand the vector (direction and magnitude) of the disruptive change, you will be able to architect, design, deploy, and assure suitable controls to mitigate disruptive risks. Think of this as the basis of risk assessment, RBT and risk management.

Lesson Learned: Understand how context is an important criterion of ISO 9001:2015 and all management systems.

Resource: Read 'Risk Context Is Everything' Http://Insights.CERMacademy.Com/2012/09/Context-Is-Everything/

What is the definition of 'risk' in ISO 9001:2015?

ISO 9001:2015 defined risk as the "effect of uncertainty on an expected result." Is this cryptic? Yes. Is this an usable definition? Maybe.

We define risk in this book as: "effect of uncertainty in achieving a business objective." Or expressed another way: "risk is the impediment or obstacle in the achievement of a business objective." We believe this definition of risk is more usable.

Interestingly, there were 4 clarifying Notes to the ISO 9001:2015 definition of risk:

- **Note 1.** Risk is a deviation from the expected result or outcome, which can either be positive or negative. Or expressed another way, risk is the variance or deviation from a business objective. For example in a project, risk could be the variation in project scope, cost, quality, or schedule. This brings up an interesting point. Risk has both an upside and a downside or what is called sometimes called positive risk and negative risk.

- **Note 2.** Risk can include various aspects or areas, such as financial, operations, or environmental obstacles to meet an objective.

- **Note 3.** Risk can be characterized in terms of consequences or a combination of events and consequences.

- **Note 4.** Risk can be expressed in terms of consequences of an event and its likelihood of occurring.

Lesson Learned: We find the notes and definitions of terms in ISO 9001:2015 cryptic and sometimes unusable. So, we added our interpretation to the above notes in this book.

Resource: Read 'What Is Risk'
Http://Insights.CERMacademy.Com/2013/05/15-What-Is-Risk-Linda-Westfall/

What is the definition of 'risk' in ISO 31000:2018?

Risk is identified in ISO standards in different ways. Risk is defined in ISO 31000:2018 as the "effect of uncertainty on objectives." Much in the same way, ISO 31000:2018 clarified its risk definition in the following Notes:

- **Note 1.** Risk can be a positive or negative deviation from the expected.
- **Note 2.** Objectives can be financial, health, safety, or environmental goals at the strategic, project, product, or process level.
- **Note 3.** Risk is characterized in terms of events and consequences.
- **Note 4.** Risk is characterized qualitatively in terms of likelihood and consequence.

As you can see, the ISO 31000 and ISO 9001:2015 are similar, but ISO 31000:2018 is clearer and actionable.

Lesson Learned: Much like quality can mean consistency, customer satisfaction, or fitness for use, there are multiple definitions of risk. Each is correct, valuable, and applicable depending on the context of the user, product, and its intended use. Understand the different definitions and nuances of risk.

Resource: Read 'Will The Real Users Of ISO 9001 Please Stand Up?' Http://Insights.CERMacademy.Com/2014/02/40-Will-Real-Users-Iso-9001-Please-Stand-T-Dan-Nelson/

What is 'upside risk'?

In today's global and highly competitive marketplace, every organization faces uncertainty and risk. This is the fundamental premise of the ISO 9001:2015 standard. It could be upside risk as to where a company is going to invest, how it will invest, and what type of business outcomes it expects to achieve based upon its investment risk profile. These are fundamental business model and market issues.

Upside risk focuses on opportunity where an investment can guarantee returns substantially above the firm's rate to borrow money. Executive management hopes the upside opportunity can also be replicated and scaled globally so there are multiple opportunities to recoup the investment.

Upside risk can be a strategic decision. Upside strategic risk can entail the evaluation of mergers, acquisitions, capital investments, and other upside risk areas. But, upside risk can also entail operational excellence or project management decisions involving how to allocate resources to ensure the successful completion of a project.

Upside risk is a new concept in ISO 9001:2015 with which quality professionals may not be familiar. Most companies have an upside risk evaluation process, such as for capital investment, cash flow, mergers, and acquisitions. But, the challenge is these upside capital decisions are often made in an isolated fashion by senior financial managers focusing on a particular project or opportunity. Senior financial managers and quality professionals usually are not exposed to each other.

Lesson Learned: The basis of good decision making and operational excellence will be the ability to make better choices under uncertainty and constraints. The hoped for result is organizations will become more competitive and make smarter decisions given the regulatory, competitive, economic, and other forces that impact the organization. This means managing upside risks as well as down side risks.

Resource: Read 'Risk/Opportunity Balance'
Http://Insights.CERMacademy.Com/2013/06/16-Riskopportunity-Balance-Linda-Westfall/

Figure 2: Upside and Downside Risk

What is 'downside risk'?

Every successful organization or person takes risks. ISO 9001:2015 and RBT do not ensure if an organization takes risks, there will be commensurate rewards. However, RBT emphasizes risks should be known and should be documented. RBT hopefully will ensure QMS and business objectives are met. The hoped for result is managers throughout the organization will gain confidence in their ability to read situations (context), identify the organization's (upside/downside) risks, understand the risk profile (risk appetite/acceptance/tolerance) of the organization, and make educated RBT and QMS decisions. See Figure 2. Much of this book discusses the previous points.

The organization may face downside risk where it needs to develop suitable risk-controls based upon its risk profile. The traditional approach of risk management has been on downside risk management or in other words loss prevention. The challenge is loss prevention does not grow the business in terms of innovation and new product development. Loss prevention also implies a command - and - control approach to business, which is anathema to today's focus on sustainability, partnering, and collaboration.

Lesson Learned: Focus on and assess downside risk first in your ISO 9001:2015 certification. We recommend certified companies focus on risks that may impede the attainment of QMS objectives.

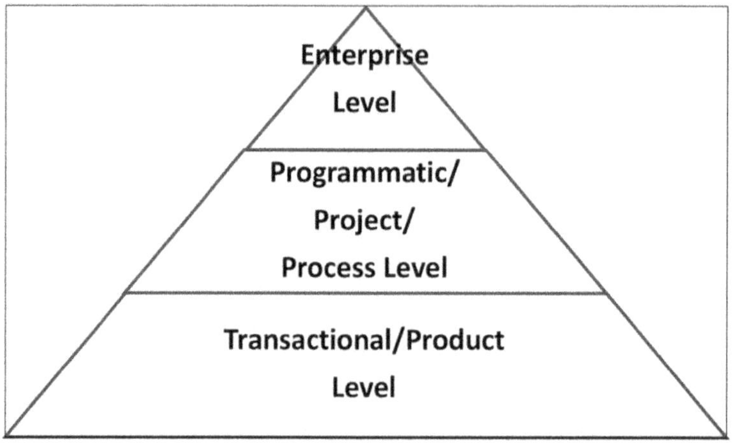

Figure 3: ***Organizational Hierarchy***

Resource: Read 'Geo-Political Instability & Consequences To The Supply Chain'
Http://Insights.CERMacademy.Com/2014/02/42-Geo-Political-Instability-Consequences-Supply-Chain-Stuart-Rosenbert/

What is a 'risk-control'?

Risk is an interesting and complex concept. One of the critical elements of risk is the concept of control. Risk and control go hand in hand. When you think of salt, pepper immediately comes to mind. When you think of black, the color white comes to mind. When you think of bad, good comes to mind. Some philosophers go so far to say, that one cannot have good without the opposing concept of bad. Much in the same way, if you have risk, then control comes to mind. Or, if control comes to mind, then it must be mitigating risk.

Risk and control are complementary concepts. Much like, salt and pepper, good and bad, conformance and nonconformance, you cannot have risk without a control. And vice versa, a control implies a risk that is mitigated. Risk-control is an important element and some would say the most critical element of risk management or treatment. Risk-control is the basis for an internal control system or the deployment of a risk management framework.

Risk-control is defined by ISO 31000:2018 as measures that can modify risk. Controls can be applied at the 1. Enterprise level; 2. Programmatic/Project/Process level; 3. Product/Transactional level of an organization. See Figure 3

Lesson Learned: Risk-control is the basis for RBT, risk assessment, risk management, and enterprise risk management.

Resource: Read 'Secret For Managing Risk - Internal Control' Http://Insights.CERMacademy.Com/2013/09/23-Value-Of-Internal-Control-Greg-Hutchins/

What is an 'objective'?

ISO 9001:2015 described an objective as a 'result to be achieved.' A little cryptic, so 4 Notes were appended for clarification. However, a consultant may still scratch his or her head about the consistency of critical terms. And, a CB may wonder about auditability based on these terms and ultimately wonder how to determine compliance and certification.

So, let us look at the 4 Notes:

- **Note 1.** Defines the type of objective by stating it can be strategic, tactical, operational, or by extension a supply chain objective.
- **Note 2.** States how and where the objective can be used. It can be a manufacturing, environmental, financial, or information security objective at the highest or lowest level of the organization.
- **Note 3.** States an objective can address a vision, mission, outcome, output, or target.
- **Note 4.** Focuses on QMS objectives dealing with quality standards, policies and procedures.

Lesson Learned: Notes seem to be critical in understanding ISO 9001:2015 concepts. So, try to focus on the achievement of critical QMS objectives. All management system standards will be structured in terms of meeting specific management standard objectives. For ISO 9001:2015, it will be the ability to meet critical QMS objectives.

Resource: Read 'Does Management By Objectives Stifle Excellence?' Http://Insights.CERMacademy.Com/2014/06/53-Management-Objectives-Stifle-Excellence-John-Dyer/

What is a 'risk inventory'?

Risk inventory is the output of a risk assessment. Risk inventory is a list of prioritized organizational risks, including those in the supply chain. Developing a risk inventory that can impede the attainment of QMS objectives is critical in ISO 9001:2015.

The following are benefits of developing a risk inventory:

- Use the inventory to determine ISO 9001:2015 compliance and start the RBT journey.
- Identity events, threats, and risks to the organization that can impede meeting QMS objectives.
- Prioritize the list of events, threats, and risks.
- Identify treatment or remediation to the above risks.

Lesson Learned: The risk inventory helps scope the ISO 9001:2015 or any certification. So, develop a risk inventory early in your ISO 9001:2015 and RBT journey.

Resource: Read 'Building A Risk Inventory To Prepare For Managing Project Risks Part 1'
Http://Insights.CERMacademy.Com/2013/06/16-Building-A-Risk-Inventory-To-Prepare-For-Managing-Project-Risks-Howard-Wiener/

What is a 'risk event'?

ISO 31000:2018 defines an event as "an occurrence or change in a particular set of circumstances." ISO 31000:2018 includes a number of explanatory Notes. An event can lead to a range of positive or negative consequences (think upside risk and/or downside risk), which can be described quantitatively or qualitatively.

An event risk consists of an unexpected or unforeseen event that can positively or negatively impact an organization. An event risk can be internal or external to an organization. Events can be unknown, unknowable, or uncontrollable. Unknown events are those that may be surmised but may not be anticipated. Unknowable events cannot be surmised and often cannot be anticipated. Uncontrollable events are those that cannot be predicted or prevented.

An event can be one or more occurrences that can have several causes. An event can consist of something not occurring. An event can also be an accident or incident. And, an event can be an occurrence such as a near miss or close call without any particular consequences.

An event is something that can impede a company from achieving a business or QMS objective and then becomes a risk. An event that results in a positive consequence is the upside risk and represents opportunity. Likewise an event that results in the negative consequence is a downside risk. An event can also be internal or external to an organization.

Lesson Learned: Identify risk events early in your ISO 9001:2015 compliance and RBT journey that can pose risks to your organization to meet its critical objectives. A 'black swan' is an event of high consequence and low likelihood, that should be identified. Visualize and brainstorm events that may result in risks to achieving QMS objectives.

Resource: Read 'Manage Supply Chain Risks Using ERM'
Http://Insights.CERMacademy.Com/2014/08/55-3-Political-Events-Putting-Supply-Chains-Risk-Kelly-Eisenstadt/

Who are 'interested parties'?

ISO 9001:2015 defines an 'interested party' as a person or organization that can be impacted by a decision or activity. Interested parties can be customers, owners, employees, suppliers, bankers, unions, partners, suppliers, competitors and pressure groups. Critical ISO stakeholders such as national standards organizations, accreditors, global CB's, and even stakeholders can be 'interested parties'.

Lesson Learned: Determine if interested parties are customers in terms of QMS compliance. This will impact the scope of your risk assessment, RBT, and certification.

Resource: Read 'ISO Stakeholders Adjust To Changes In ISO 9001:2015'
Http://Insights.CERMacademy.Com/2014/12/73-ISO-Stakeholders-Adjusting-Changes-ISO-90012015/

What is 'inherent risk'?

Inherent risk is not defined in ISO 9001:2015. However, this is a critical concept in RBT and should be addressed when companies certify to ISO 9001.

We define 'inherent risk' based upon the COSO ERM standard. COSO defines inherent risk as:

> "The risk to an entity in the absence of any actions management might take to alter either the risk's likelihood or impact."

Or expressed another way, inherent risk is the risk that exists in an organization before the application of additional risk-controls or controlled processes. An easy way to think of inherent risk is the steady state or baseline condition an organization has without any additional risk-controls or risk treatment. Inherent risks exist in the system or process before additional policies, procedures, or other types of controls have been defined and implemented.

Inherent risk should not be confused with residual risk. They are different concepts.

Lesson Learned: Some inherent risks may be unknown or unknowable. Attempt to identify as many inherent risks as you can in your organization. This is discussed later in the book.

Resource: Read 'Setting The Organization's Risk Management Context' Http://Insights.CERMacademy.Com/2014/11/69-Setting-Organizations-Risk-Management-Context-Rod-Farrar/

What is 'risk appetite'?

ISO 31000:2018 defines risk appetite in terms of the amount and the type of risk an organization wants to take or keep. ISO definitions are often written loosely and can be cryptic and difficult to apply. The definition of 'risk appetite' needs further elaboration.

COSO definition views risk appetite in terms of enterprise strategy, specifically its ability to achieve a business objective. Risk appetite is often a reflection of the organization's culture, business model, and operations model. For example, high tech startups and consulting companies are often risk taking, while power utilities are more conservative and risk averse.

The Board of Directors and executive management help to define the organization's risk appetite. Business unit leaders within their purview define the risk appetite of their units. Plant managers, program managers, project managers and process leads define risk appetite or acceptance based on their span of control. It is critical individual risk appetites throughout the organization are aligned with overall or overarching organizational risk appetite.

How is risk appetite determined? Risk appetite can be described in terms of high, medium or low. Or, risk appetite can be identified in terms of economic value in a project.

Who determines risk appetite? The Board of Directors and the executive officers determine what is the organizational or enterprise culture in terms of pursuing opportunities and living with downside risks. Each organizational level or process owner is responsible for defining the work unit's appetite.

Lesson Learned: Money is universally understood. Frame risk appetite in terms of the context and culture of the organization and then attempt to quantify risk appetite in terms of economic value. In our experience, it is difficult to define organizational risk appetite.

Resource: Read 'What You Need To Know About Risk Appetite And Risk Threshold'
Http://Insights.CERMacademy.Com/2013/06/18-What-You-Need-To-Know-About-Risk-Appetites-And-Risk-Thresholds-Mark-Moore/

What is 'risk tolerance'?

Risk appetite and risk tolerance are closely aligned concepts. Risk tolerance is the acceptable level of variation a company or an individual is willing to accept in the pursuit of a specific objective. Tolerance is sometimes described in terms of 'what can we afford' in case of a possible loss.

COSO ERM defines risk tolerance as: "perceptible variation relative to the achievement of an objective." This is a definition that can be used in ISO 9001:2015 in the pursuit of a QMS objective.

Let us look at some of the differences between risk appetite and risk tolerance. Risk appetite has a strategic and enterprise point of view. Risk tolerance is a tactical concept. This tolerance primarily relates to the achievement of a business objective, such as a product or process quality objective.

Risk tolerance can be illustrated in terms of process capability or project objectives. Quality professionals define process capabilities in terms of capability indices, which define acceptable process variation or tolerance. Project professionals define upper and lower tolerance limits for project cost, scope, schedule, or quality objectives.

Tolerance can be used to describe legal compliance, Corporate Social Responsibility (CSR), or financial considerations. Let us look at each. Legal compliance is the cost of not being compliant and the cost of applying suitable controls to be compliant. In terms of CSR, an organization may define tolerance in terms of reputation loss or acceptable methods of conducting business. Or, the organization may define acceptance for a maximum tolerable loss.

Lesson Learned: Understand and quantify your risk tolerance. It is one of the hardest things to do in risk management.

Resource: Read 'Is Your Safety Policy VUCA-Sized?' Http://Insights.CERMacademy.Com/2013/04/13-Is-Your-Safety-Policy-Vuca-Sized-Roman-Gurbanov/

What is 'risk management'?

ISO 31000:2018 defines risk management as:

> "coordinated activities to direct and control an organization with regard to risk."[iii]

The Risk and Insurance Management Society (RIMS) defines risk management as:

> "A decision - making discipline that reduces uncertainty and manages potential variations from expected outcomes in achieving company goals."[iv]

Most risk management definitions are similar. Common elements of most management definitions include:

- Risk management is the control or treatment of risk, adverse events or situations.

- Risk management is the upside opportunity from making calculated and smart decisions.

These straightforward definitions do not define or explain how to manage risk. This is a challenge for organizations that want to implement RBT or a risk assessment system.

Risk management is also called risk treatment or risk mitigation. Risk management may also involve:

- Accepting risk that is within the organization's risk appetite.
- Sharing risk with other parties such as through risk financing or multiple sourcing.
- Lowering the consequence of risk within the organization's risk appetite.
- Lowering the likelihood or probability of risk occurring within the organization's risk appetite.
- Eliminating the source of risk, which may mean finding a new supplier.
- Accepting risk and even increasing the risk if it is within the organization's risk appetite to pursue an upside opportunity.
- Avoiding risk by deciding not to pursue the opportunity such as by eliminating inputs to a process, finding an alternative method to produce a product, or proactively and preemptively doing something to eliminate the risk.

Lesson Learned: Risk management should be viewed as a fluid concept that is largely defined by the context, stability, capability, and maturity of your organization. Remember ISO 9001:2015 does not specifically require risk management, but implies it throughout the standard.

Resource: Read 'Risk Management: Today's Quality Management Paradigm'

Http://Insights.CERMacademy.Com/2013/04/12-Risk-Management-Todays-Quality-Management-Paradigm-Greg-Hutchins/

What is the purpose of RBT or risk management?

Risk concepts in this book are explained in terms of technical terms found in international or national standards. The definitions tend to be formal and often difficult to use. Linkedin had a spirited discussion on 'What is the purpose of risk management?' We found the discussion interesting as the concept of risk has moved into everyday vocabulary. So, here are some generic thoughts on the purpose and benefits of RBT and risk management:

- Inform management about the risks associated with business decisions.
- Understand and be prepared for the potential of risk treatment to fail, or residual risk to materialize in unexpected ways, or unexpected events to occur with dire consequences to stakeholders.
- Make appropriate tradeoffs between risk and reward decisions.
- Influence the shapes of the distributions (densities) of company earnings, capital, ROE, etc. in an 'optimal' way while conforming to legal, compliance, and regulatory constraints.
- Assist the organization and people to take more risks within acceptable limits.
- Provide different lenses on risk based, problem solving and risk based, decision making.
- Make and take calculated risks.
- Anticipate threats before they materialize.
- Protect a company's financial bottom line.
- Ensure or guarantee the organization's longevity.

- Protect and support business decisions and add continuing strategic value.
- Safeguard the asset base of the enterprise's owners against decisions and behavior's that could impair them.
- Improve an organization's capability to operate successfully and achieve its goals.
- Allow people to think in a structured manner.
- Is the science of common sense?
- Address the future of present decisions, not future decisions.
- Ensure a safe future built on pragmatic decisions.[v]

Lesson Learned: RBT and risk management are today's competitive differentiators.

Resource: Read 'Bad Risk Management Decisions Made By Executives' Http://Insights.CERMacademy.Com/2013/03/Call-For-Examples-Bad-Risk-Management-Decisions-Made-By-Executives/

What is 'Enterprise Risk Management (ERM)'?

ERM is a relatively new concept. There is a robust discussion among experts what it really means. Common ERM elements in most definitions include:

- Follows a Governance, Risk, and Compliance (GRC) approach to business.
- Is applied in strategy and tactical settings.
- Is a top down approach to business system management and execution?
- Is designed to identify potential events and risks that can impact the organization.

- Is a management system that can be architected, designed, deployed, managed, and assured?
- Is a management system that can be applied at various organizational levels including: 1. Enterprise level; 2. Programmatic/Project/Process level; and 3. Product/Transactional level. Please see figure on the right.
- Is based on the risk appetite and tolerance of the organization.
- Is focused on the achievement of business objectives.
- Provides reasonable assurance on the achievement of business objectives.
- Is a risk management process that has inputs, involves a consistent process and has outputs?
- Is managed by people at every level of an organization and including the supply chain.

Lesson Learned: ERM is the end state of the RBT journey.

Resource: Read 'How To Manage A Successful Enterprise Risk Management Program'
Http://Insights.CERMacademy.Com/2013/09/25-How-To-Manage-A-Successful-Enterprise-Risk-Management-Program-Troy-Hackett/

Does ISO 9001:2015 imply risk management?

Maybe. ISO 9001:2015 explicitly states that risk management is not required. However, there is still confusion on this topic. ISO 9001:2015 has specific risk requirements to ensure QMS objectives can be achieved. This is where the confusion occurs. ISO 9001:2015 implies risk management through its language of controls and objectives. What do we mean? ISO 9001:2015 states that risks are assessed. OK. But if there are critical risks, would you expect these risks to be mitigated or managed. Yes! The mitigation or treatment of risk is the same as the management of risk. So in other words, ISO 9001:2015 implies risk management.

ISO 9001:2015 uses the expression 'address risks.' However in a footnote, various options for addressing risks are identified, such as risk avoidance, risk mitigation, and risk acceptance, which are elements of a risk management process. Is this an ISO mistake or not fully understanding the unintended consequences of the new standard? We do not know!

Also, ISO 31000:2018 can be used as an Enterprise Risk Management system. So more often, ISO management system experts are calling ISO 31000:2018 an ERM standard. Sound far-fetched? Maybe. However, most large companies are already implementing ERM processes often as a form of advanced risk assessment or risk management. Why? ERM provides the organization with a higher level of confidence and assurance that QMS objectives are met and critical processes are stable, capable, and improving.

Lesson Learned: ERM implies stable and capable risk management processes. Define RBT, RM or ERM based on your business requirements and QMS context. ERM is a maturing definition that can be sector based. ERM may be defined differently in different sectors. Some sectors may focus on a compliance definition and others focus on a governance approach. Or, each sector may develop its own approach to RBT and risk management.

Resource: Read 'ISO 9001:2015 DIS Concerns'
Http://Insights.CERMacademy.Com/2014/06/51-ISO-9001-Dis-Concerns-Umberto-Tunesi/

What are ERM and TQM similarities?

Enterprise Risk Management (ERM) and Total Quality Management (TQM) share similarities:

- Both grew to prominence as a result of competitive challenges and policy circumstances - quality as a result of Japanese competitiveness and risk as a result of financial excesses in corporate America and threats to homeland security.

- Both share common concepts and techniques, but use different words for them.
- Both follow a Capability Maturity Model (CMM) curve.
- Both rely on the Board of Directors and executive management to set the example to lead the initiatives.
- Both focus on variance from targets or objectives.
- Both emphasize responsibility for quality and risk rest with process owners.
- Both emphasize ultimate responsibility rests with top management.
- Both are enterprise wide initiatives.
- Both focus on achieving business objectives.
- Both are process based.
- Both have a hard technical side and soft people side.
- Both follow a similar deployment methodology.

Lesson Learned: Understand how the following are analogous:

- Enterprise risk management **< = >** Quality management
- Risk assurance **< = >** Quality assurance
- Risk-control **< = >** Quality control

Resource: Read TQM & ERM Similarities And Differences' Http://Insights.CERMacademy.Com/2014/06/51-Tqm-ERM-Similarities-Differences-Greg-Hutchins/

What are ERM and TQM differences?

The differences between the two are also revealing:

- Risk management is relatively in its infancy, while quality is a mature technology.
- Quality and Six Sigma seem to have a tactical focus, largely emphasizing execution and metrics.
- Risk management is currently more compelling to Boards of Directors, CEO's, and CFO's.
- Risk management was largely driven by financial regulatory and statutory compliance concerns but now focuses on operational and supply chain risks as well.

The similarities between ERM and TQM are more pronounced than the differences, which is why we believe that ERM is the natural evolution of TQM.

Lesson Learned: Integrate RBT into ISO 9001:2015 and other families of ISO standards based on how ERM and TQM are similar management systems. It will enhance the acceptance of RBT and ISO 9001:2015 in your organization.

Resource: Read 'Risk And Quality: Similarities And Differences' Http://Insights.CERMacademy.Com/2013/12/32-Risk-Quality-Similarities-Differences-T-Dan-Nelson/

What are differentiating questions between a quality focus and risk focus?

Clive Robertson, Leading Advisor for Quality Management for Statoil, believes risk and quality share two sides of the same coin. He shared the following from Statoil, which was adapted from quality authority, David Hoyle:

Quality Focus:

- What are you trying to do?

- How are we going to make it happen?
- How do we know it is right?
- How do we know we are doing it the best way?
- How do we know it is the right thing to do?
- What can we learn from this?

Risk Focus:

- What could go wrong?
- What opportunities are there?
- How might this affect performance?
- How is the risk being handled?
- How do we know our actions are effective?
- Will the barriers prevent a recurrence?
- What can we learn from this?

Lesson Learned: Risk and quality are complementary concepts. We recommend you understand how quality management and risk management are related, then make them work together in your ISO management systems. Do not treat them separately. Life will be easier for you.

Resource: Read 'Risk Management Or Quality Management: Which Is On Top?' Http://Insights.CERMacademy.Com/2013/12/31-Risk-Management-Quality-Management-Top-Greg-Hutchins/

Are RBT and risk management processes?

Yes. RBT and risk management are processes. If we look at the COSO

ERM framework, it consists of the following process components: 1. Internal environment; 2. Objective setting; 3. Event identification; 4. Risk assessment; 5. Risk response; 6. Control activities; 7 Information and communication; and 8. Monitoring. This is explained further in Chapter 6: COSO ERM.

Lesson Learned: Process thinking and application are inherent in all risk management and assessment frameworks. So, develop a risk assessment process in your organization that is repeatable and scalable.

Resource: Read 'The Process Approach Of ISO 9001'
Http://Insights.CERMacademy.Com/2014/02/Process-Approach-Iso-9001-T-Dan-Nelson/

What is a 'risk taxonomy' and 'risk syntax'?

One of first things organizations should do in their RBT journey is to develop a risk taxonomy to make sure that everyone speaks a similar risk language. Wikipedia defines taxonomy as: "the practice and science of classification of things or concepts plus the principles that underlie the classification." The risk taxonomy is based on the competitive marketplace, context of organization, culture, and operating style of the enterprise.

Syntax is the way risk concepts and words are put together to form phrases in the risk taxonomy. While taxonomy may form risk strategy, syntax is the common operating or tactical language of RBT within the enterprise.

Why are these critical for RBT and QMS? RBT is new to ISO 9001:2015. It is very critical the enterprise including quality and other operational units understand, form, and use a common language for RBT and risk assessment. A common RBT language facilitates communicating risk concepts across the organization and into the supply chain. If the enterprise is effectively communicating risk information then it will be in a better position to adopt ISO 9001:2015. COSO and ISO 31000:2018 are commonly used risk frameworks for establishing a risk taxonomy, process classification, and risk syntax. Both are explained in the following chapters.

Lesson Learned: Learn and use a risk vocabulary that can be used to understand all elements of risk including RBT, risk assessment, and risk management.

Resource: Read 'Exposing The Uncertainty About Risk In ISO DIS 9001:2015 (Part 1)'
Http://Insights.CERMacademy.Com/2014/09/59-Exposing-Uncertainty-Risk-ISO-Dis-90012015-Part-1-David-Hoyle/

What should the user do when confronted with confusing ISO terms?

The writers and developers of the ISO 9001:2015 standard have spent much time clarifying and simplifying terms so they are universally understandable and usable. However, ISO 9001:2015 has terms that may be new to the reader. As well, ISO 9001:2015 does not map or is consistent with ISO 31000:2018. These will challenge many certified organizations.

Lesson Learned: In the index of this book, the 'Risk Glossary' defines critical risk concepts. So, develop a risk vocabulary for your organization when starting the RBT journey.

Resource: Read 'The More The Communication Method, The Easier It Is To Remain Unreachable'
Http://Insights.CERMacademy.Com/2014/03/43-Communications-Choices-Mark-Moore/

Is the U.S. Federal government requiring ERM?

Yes. The Office of Management and Budget A-123 circular that defines the management responsibilities for internal controls in Federal agencies. In 2016, OMB adopted new ERM requirements for all U.S. Federal departments. OMB stated:

> "OMB is updating this Circular to ensure Federal managers are effectively managing risks an Agency faces toward achieving its strategic objectives and arising from its activities and operations. ...

> Over the years, government operations have changed dramatically, becoming increasingly complex and driven by changes in technology. At the same time, resources are constrained and stakeholders expect greater program integrity, efficiency and transparency into government operations. … requiring agencies to implement an Enterprise Risk Management (ERM) capability coordinated with the strategic planning and strategic review process…"[vi]

ERM in the U.S. government, states, and municipalities is growing exponentially. We believe that 17 sectors will require some type of risk management.

Lesson Learned. The government issued **Playbook: Enterprise Risk Management for the U.S. Federal Government**. You can google and download it for free.

This is an essential document for everyone working in or for the Federal government. According to the Federal Government, the document can be:

Resource: Playbook: ERM for the U.S. Federal Government
https://cfo.gov/2016/07/28/enterprise-risk-management-erm-playbook-released/

Why did the Baldrige Excellence framework add ERM to their Criteria for Performance Excellence?

The Baldrige since 1987 focused on leadership driven, customer focused, quality management systems. Over the last ten years, the Baldrige has focused on operational and performance excellence.

As part of the 2015-2016 revision, the framework added the following areas to the framework: 1. Enterprise Risk Management (ERM) and 2. Cyber security.

Baldrige provided the following rationale for adding ERM:

> "No organization is risk free. Intelligent risk management requires an enterprise to decide when and how risks should be taken and

managed. Such management can mean the difference between extinction, survival, or role-model performance. Through a systems perspective of organizational performance management, the Baldrige framework has long addressed ERM, defined by ISO 31000: Risk Management - Principles and Guidelines as an organization's coordinated activities to direct and control the effect of uncertainty on achieving its objectives.

The future competitive advantage that will flow from good ERM is based on the holistic addressing of risk and the actions taken - including the pursuit of intelligent risks - as part of an overall strategic approach to managing organizational performance. In this revision, some Health Care Criteria requirements and notes have been revised to highlight (1) that risk is inherent in everything organizations do and (2) that the challenge is to balance the level of risk taken with the sustainability of the organization and the opportunity for innovation."[vii]

Lesson Learned: Baldrige added ERM using ISO 31000:2018 preferred standard. We will be seeing many more organizations adopting ERM as part of their operational and performance excellence initiatives.

Resource: Baldrige Criteria Poses Challenges to the Quality Profession
http://insights.cermacademy.com/2017/03/166-baldrige-criteria/

CHAPTER 4:

ISO 9001:2015 STANDARD

What is the key idea in this chapter?

The key idea in this chapter is ISO 9001:2015 risk ideas and processes are new and may be challenging until all ISO management systems are consistent under Annex SL.

Who develops and writes ISO 9001:2015?

ISO developed the following description of its standards development process:

> "ISO develops high quality, voluntary International Standards which facilitate international exchange of goods and services, support sustainable and equitable economic growth, promote innovation, and protect health, safety and the environment."[viii]

Technical Committee (TC) 176 for Quality Management and Quality Assurance develops quality standards. TC 176/SC 2 is the subcommittee responsible for writing ISO 9001:2015 and ISO 9004. See the figure on the next page. The committee is composed of experts nominated by their national standards bodies. See Figure 4.

The mission is the ISO 9001:2015 SC 2 subcommittee is to:

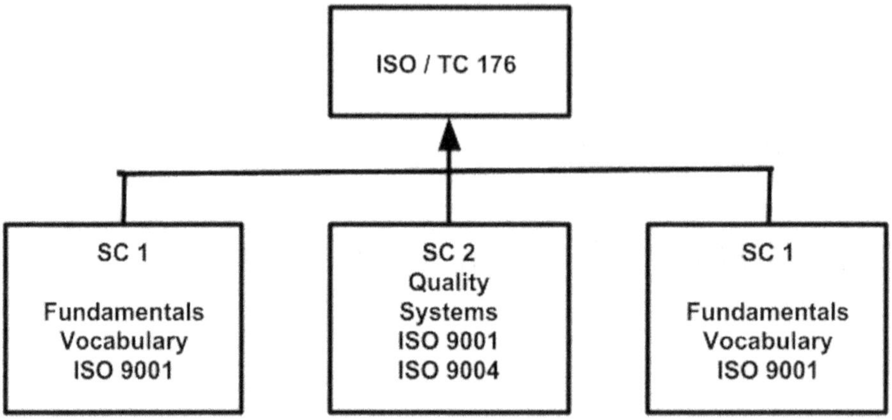

Figure 4: ***ISO Standards Structure***

- Provide support and guidance to ensure credibility of the standards.
- Establish generic QMS requirements.
- Develop, maintain, and support a portfolio of products that enable organizations to improve performance.

Lesson Learned: Many ISO committees intend to add risk and RBT concepts into their families of standards.

Resource: Read 'Quality Futures: Management Systems Integration' Http://Insights.CERMacademy.Com/2013/04/1192/

What is an 'ISO management system'?

The concept of a 'management system' is fundamental to all ISO standards. ISO defines a 'management system' as a:

> "Set of interrelated elements of an organization to establish policies and objectives, and processes to achieve these objectives."

Lesson Learned: ISO management systems may evolve into business management systems over the next five years.

Resource: Read 'ISO 9001 System Challenges' Http://Insights.CERMacademy.Com/2014/08/55-ISO-9001-System-T-Dan-Nelson/

What standards or other documents should you purchase?

In each chapter, we recommend obtaining documents or purchasing standards. ISO offers the following ISO 9001 documents:

- **ISO 9000:2005.** This covers the fundamentals and vocabulary used in ISO 9000 standards.
- **ISO 9004:2009.** This provides guidance on how to achieve sustained QMS success.
- **ISO 9001:2015.** This is the latest iteration of ISO's most popular management system standard. ISO Technical Committee (ISO/TC 176), Quality Management and Quality Assurance, Subcommittee SC2, is writes the standard.
- **TS 9002.** This is a guidance document on how to certify to ISO 9001:2015. It will be developed some time in 2016.

Lesson Learned: Purchase the above standards to understand RBT and to secure compliance to ISO 9001:2015 and other standards.

Resource: Read 'Going To Version 2.0' Http://Insights.CERMacademy.Com/2014/04/45-Going-Version-2-0-Mark-Moore/

What is ISO TS 9002?

Technical specification (TS) 9002 was written to provide guidance and insights on how to certify to ISO 9001:2015. ISO TS 9002 was available in 2016.

Why was the technical specification developed? It was proposed almost a year and half before the introduction of ISO 9001:2015 because there were international concerns about how companies will certify to ISO 9001:2015 especially to its new RBT and risk requirements.

Lesson Learned: Purchase TS 9002 and other ISO guidance documents. It will shed light on how ISO expects companies to certify.

Resource: Read 'A Poem: ISO 9001 Is Changing' http://insights.cermacademy.com/2013/12/31-poem-iso-9001-changed-sandy-liebesman/

What are the major changes in ISO 9001:2015?

ISO 9001:2015 incorporates the following changes:

- Made the standard more generic and easier to use by service industries.
- Added 'context of the organization' to determine requirements that can impact planning and development of the QMS.
- Re-emphasized the process approach when developing and improving the effectiveness of the QMS. While ISO 9001:2008 offered the process approach, certified companies did not adopt it as much as ISO expected.
- Emphasized a risk driven approach to preventive action in the development and implementation of the QMS. As well, ISO introduced the RBT concept.
- Added the term 'documented information'. Previous iterations of

ISO 9001 used the terms 'document' and 'record.' 'Documented information' will allow the certified company more latitude for demonstrating compliance.

- Added a clause on the control of external provision of 'goods and services.' This expression addresses the lifecycle from provisioning of products from purchasing through outsourcing processes.
- Imposed new responsibilities on top management such as planning for change, requiring knowledge of standard, and ensuring responsibility for compliance.
- Emphasized top management engagement with RBT and QMS. Management representative is no longer required. Top management must be involved in deploying a process approach.
- Changed critical words and concepts, such as 'development of goods and services' which was previously 'design and development' and 'external provision of goods and services', which was previously 'purchasing'.

Lesson Learned: The development of ISO 9001:2015 through CD, DIS, and FDIS resulted in more disagreements than previous revisions. So, understand the changes in the standard and how they will impact your organization after transition to the new standard.

Resource: Read 'Ambiguities In ISO 9001:2015 Initial Observations Part Ii'
Http://Insights.CERMacademy.Com/2013/09/24-ISO-9001-2015-Initial-Observations-Part-Ii-David-Hoyle/

Why does ISO 9001:2015 not require a quality manual and ISO 9001:2008 did?

Since 1987, each ISO 9001 certified organization was required to have a quality manual with specific procedures. In the ISO 9001:2008 version, the manual had to address 6 specific procedures. ISO 9001:2015 does not require a quality manual and does not require specific documentation to demonstrate compliance. This could be a challenge for companies and CB auditors.

So, what is happening? Several things: the importance of the quality manual has diminished as some organizations simply copied an ISO quality manual from a book or off the web. These quality manuals were not generated or tailored to the organization. And, the company still received its ISO 9001 certification. This is a recurring problem with ISO certification.

ISO certification is not going away. Early drafts of the standard stated: "the organization shall establish, implement and maintain a QMS." This will continue.

The new iteration of ISO 9001 did not eliminate the need for QMS evidence but adopted a discretionary approach to the extent, nature, and type of evidence. So, what other forms of documentation can a company offer to demonstrate compliance? The new ISO 9001 standard did not eliminate the need for evidence. Quality activities may be documented through process flowcharts, risk maps, project plans, edocs, and other forms of documentation to indicate quality activities are prescribed and followed.

The decision to architect, design, deploy, and audit a QMS quality manual was originally a strategic decision to focus on quality and customer satisfaction. Many quality manuals are valuable documents. So, should this documentation be tossed out just because there is a new revision of ISO 9001? No. The new standard uses the following KISS principle, which is an acronym for Keep It Simple and Sustainable.

Lesson Learned: If you are using a quality manual as your form of evidence, retain and update it for ISO 9001:2015 certification.

Resource: Read 'Quality Manual Seen Through The Manual'
Http://Insights.CERMacademy.Com/2014/03/43-Quality-Management-Seen-Manual-T-Dan-Nelson/

What are ISO 9001:2015 risk requirements?

ISO 9001:2015 has a number of risk requirements. The following sections in ISO 9001 2015 reference and/or require risk and controls:

Section 4.4.1 Quality Management System and Its Processes
The enterprise will design and deploy a Quality Management System. When planning the QMS, the enterprise will determine the upside and downside risks that can impact the determination of conformance to QMS requirements for customer satisfaction, intended output, and process effectiveness.

Section: 5.1.1 Leadership and Commitment
Executive management will support the QMS by promoting RBT and a process based approach to QMS.

Section 5.1.2. Customer Focus
Executive management will support the QMS to identify upside and downside risks that may impede conformance to requirements and impact customer satisfaction.

Section 6.1.1 Actions to Address Risks and Opportunities
When planning and designing the QMS, the organization will review upside and downside risks to:

1. Assure the QMS can achieve its intended outcomes and objectives.
2. Ensure the enterprise can achieve customer satisfaction and consistently produce goods and services that conform to requirements and specifications.
3. Treat downside risks, specifically by reducing the impacts of negative consequences and preventing risks from occurring.
4. Achieve improvement, which would be determined by meeting business objectives or achieving customer satisfaction.

Section 6.1.2 Planning
The enterprise will plan how to treat upside and downside risks in the

QMS. Treatment may include: avoiding, accepting, sharing, or reducing risks. The risk treatment must be cost effective to ensure customer satisfaction and assure conformance to requirements.

6.3 Planning of Changes

The enterprise will review and plan for QMS changes as well as find opportunities to improve QMS performance. The enterprise must consider the value of the proposed changes as well as potential upside and downside consequences.

7.1.2 People

The enterprise will have adequately trained personnel to implement the QMS and control its processes.

8.1 Operational Planning and Control

Enterprise will plan, design, and control its critical processes to ensure product conformance and customer satisfaction. Operational planning includes:

- Identifying product requirements.
- Determining process control criteria.
- Deploying resources to ensure product conformity.
- Controlling processes based on the criteria.
- Documenting controls.

Changes to the above are also controlled and unintended consequences are reviewed and mitigated. Enterprise will also ensure that outsourced processes are controlled.

8.2.1 Customer Communication

Enterprise will establish communication protocols with customers including contingency plans in the event of a risk event.

8.3.2 Design and Development Planning

Enterprise will determine its design gates and develop controls based on the nature and complexity of the design, control design interfaces, and consider customer input.

The level of control is based on the context and customer requirements.

8.3.3 Design and Development Inputs
Enterprise will identify product requirements and identify possible modes of failure.

8.3.4 Design and Development Controls
Enterprise will deploy controls and will conduct reviews of the design and development process. Reviews include verification, validation, monitoring, and other checks to ensure design requirements are met.

8.3.6 Design and Development Changes
Enterprise will review and control design and development changes to the extent that conformance and customer satisfaction are impacted.

8.4 Control of Externally Provided Processes, Products, and Services
Enterprise will ensure that supplier provided products and services are controlled.

8.4.2 Type and Extent of Control
Enterprise will design and deploy the appropriate level of controls as required by the QMS. Control effectiveness will be monitored periodically verified.

9.2. Internal Audit
The enterprise will conduct internal audits to assure the QMS conforms to ISO 9001:2015 requirements. Internal reviews will focus on the ability of the organization to meet quality objectives, focus on critical processes, review related risks, and review results of prior audits.

Lesson Learned: RBT will be implemented into additional management system standards. Conflicts in interpretation will arise. Your CB may not understand and even agree with the changes, so keep on top of the ISO management systems that apply to you. Also, read the above ISO 9001:2015 clauses very carefully and understand what they mean within the context and scope of your QMS certification. There could be some zingers that you may not expect. Understand the changes in ISO 9001:2015 and evolving ISO risk guidelines as ISO 9001:2015 goes through it revisions. As well, follow the supporting standards are being developed such as ISO 9002.

Resource: Read 'ISO Shares Its Risk Vision For ISO 9001:2015' Http://Insights.CERMacademy.Com/2014/01/37-Iso-Shares-Risk-Iso-9001-2015-Greg-Hutchins/

How does risk relate to ISO 9001:2015 objectives?

The concept of risk relates to the uncertainty in achieving QMS objectives and more generally the uncertainty in achieving business objectives. The main QMS objectives are to:

- Provide confidence in the organization's ability to consistently provide customers with conforming goods and services.
- Enhance customer satisfaction.
- Satisfy 'interested party' requirements. This is a little broad so we recommend the certified organization defines and scopes 'interested parties.'

We believe the ability of meeting business objectives is very critical which are related to quality objectives. If you take the broader point of view of meeting business objectives, then quality and QMS would become integrated into the organization's business model, core competencies, and capabilities.

Lesson Learned: ISO should provide guidance on how to satisfy RBT and risk requirements in ISO 9001:2015. Otherwise, QMS and risk consultants will provide best practices that may be beyond the scope of ISO 9001:2015. So, one of the first things we recommend is to develop a business case for how key QMS and RBT processes can be integrated into the business's core processes.

Resource: Read 'ISO Risk In Bob's Machine Shop (ISO Risk Case Study)'
Http://Insights.CERMacademy.Com/2013/10/26-ISO-Risk-In-Bobs-Machne-Shop-T-Dan-Nelson/

Why does ISO 9001:2015 focus on establishing QMS objectives?

ISO 9001:2008 describes the importance of quality objectives to meet the requirements of the product or service. ISO 9001:2015 emphasizes the analysis of risk that can impede achieving conformity, customer satisfaction, and other objectives.

Business objectives are important to RBT, risk assessment and risk management. Business objectives are an expression of what the organization wants to achieve in terms of goals or targets. Risks can be thought as roadblocks or obstacles to achieving QMS objectives. Also, business objectives ensure the risk assessment and RBT are focused on strategic QMS targets critical to the organization.

Lesson Learned: Use the 'objectives' approach with ISO 9001:2015, ISO 14001:2015, and ISO 27001 as a common risk strategy. Then in the future, the CB will be able to conduct one integrated audit, which should reduce audit time and save you money.

Resource: Read 'Consequences Of Misapplying A Quality Standard'
Http://Insights.CERMacademy.Com/2013/09/25-Consequences-Of-Misapplying-A-Quality-Standard-T-Dan-Nelson/

Are ISO risk and management systems standards consistent?

No. The purpose of Annex SL is to create consistency in the approach to ISO standards development, frameworks, definitions, and application. The challenge is this will take about 5 or more years to be universally applied to all ISO standards. Why? The standards development cycle takes 5 to 7 years to update an ISO family of standards. All new ISO management system standards will reflect Annex SL. However, existing management system standards will have to wait for the next revision cycle when they will be updated to incorporate Annex SL requirements.

Lesson Learned: ISO is still years away from developing consistent risk processes within and across its families of management system standards. So, start to develop your own RBT taxonomy, processes, and vocabulary for your ISO management system standards.

Resource: Read 'Is ISO 9001 Working?'
Http://Insights.CERMacademy.Com/2013/10/29-Is-ISO-9001-Working-T-Dan-Nelson/

Why is an external focus emphasized in ISO 9001:2015?

ISO 9001:2008 and prior iterations seemed to be internally focused. The current revision of the standard requires an understanding of internal and external contextual issues, understanding the needs and expectations of interested parties, and defining the scope of the QMS application. Once these are understood, they can be analyzed to assess the risks (upside opportunities and downside consequences) they represent.

Also, 'outside factors' must be understood in terms of how QMS objectives are met. The organization must understand how QMS interested parties relate to each other and how their satisfaction can be achieved.

RBT has a wide scope in ISO 9001:2015. It is important to understand the context and the scope of the risk issues in ISO 9001:2015 as applied to the certified organization. A narrow focus misses the big picture and the broad focus loses important details. So, there has to be an understanding of both the overarching issues as well as the detailed risks in developing RBT. Both are very critical.

A story may help. If one focuses on the knothole in a twig of a tree, the person will not understand and not see the twig, branch, trunk, tree, and forest. This also applies with a top down view of the forest; much of the tree detail will be lost.

Lesson Learned: ISO 9001:2015 seems to be confusing accreditors, CB's, certified companies, and quality/QMS experts because of RBT, risk requirements, and new language in the standard. A simple issue as who are 'interested parties' is confusing. So, we recommend, that you identify all critical customers. This will impact the scope of the ISO 9001:2015 certification. If your scope is too broad, then the cost of your QMS will increase rapidly. Develop and scope your QMS while developing your business case for your ISO 9001:2015 certification.

Resource: Read 'FDA Discouraging Third-party MDSAP'
Http://Insights.CERMacademy.Com/2014/06/52-Fda-Discouraging-Third-Party-Mdsap-Grant-Ramaley/

What happened to preventive action in ISO 9001:2015?

'Preventive action' was deleted from the standard. The current thinking is risk mitigation or also called risk treatment provides the same results as preventive action.

Lesson Learned: Migrate your preventive action to risk assessment and even risk mitigation. Your Corrective Action/Preventive Action (CAPA) program will also change.

Resource: Read 'The Reality Of Risk'
Http://Insights.CERMacademy.Com/2013/05/14-Reality-Of-Risk-Malcolm-Peart/

Does ISO offer guidance regarding RBT and risk?

Yes. ISO/TC 176 developed a slide deck called 'ISO 9001: 2015 Risk Based Thinking' in December 2013.[ix] It offers guidance on RBT and risk, specifically:

- Identify risk and opportunities in your organization.
- Analyze and prioritize risks and opportunities in your organization.
- Plan actions to address the risks.
- Implement the plan to mitigate the risks.
- Check effectiveness of your actions.
- Learn from the experience through continual improvement.

A few early takeaways from the deck include:

- ISO TC 176 is serious about risk and RBT.
- Above steps follow a process and cycle.
- Risk criteria are integrated in ISO 9001:2015. ISO 31000:2018 is the preferred guidance document to ISO 9001:2015.
- Formal risk management is not required in ISO 9001:2015.
- Guidance is confusing in what is in scope and not in scope for risk.

Lesson Learned: Google 'ISO 9001: 2015 Risk Based Thinking' and you can obtain the deck. Also, join ISO LinkedIn communities and contribute to the discussions on the changes in ISO standards.

Resource: Read 'Context Matters When Discussing Risk' Http://Insights.CERMacademy.Com/2013/06/15-Context-Matters-When-Discussing-Risk-Mark-Jones/

What is the difference between business objectives and outcomes?

Objectives and outcomes are key concepts in ISO 9001:2015 and they are sometimes confused. The achievement of a business objective is a critical element of the QMS. The achievement of a business or QMS objective can be measured. Obstacles or risks that impede the attainment of business objectives can be eliminated, controlled, and/or risk managed.

Outcomes are the results of a process. Outcomes are closely related to process management and can also be risk-controlled and measured. Statistical Process Control (SPC) is an example of controlling and measuring a process and ensuring the outcome is within process capability and specification limits. We would measure process outcomes in terms of capability indices.

Lesson Learned: Use RBT for defining business and QMS objectives and measuring outcomes.

Resource: Read 'ISO Risk In Bob's Machine Shop (ISO Risk Case Study)'
Http://Insights.CERMacademy.Com/2013/10/26-ISO-Risk-In-Bobs-Machne-Shop-T-Dan-Nelson/

Will other sectors with QMS requirements adopt risk like ISO 9001:2015?

This question is being debated in sectors that have adopted ISO 9001 as their baseline QMS standard. Why is this question contentious? The bottom line is too many changes in too short a time have erupted in push back in some sectors.

This will be an ongoing challenge with the adoption of ISO 9001:2015 with sectoral ISO 9001 equivalent standards. In the past, ISO sectoral technical specifications such as aerospace (AS 9100) and auto (TS 16949) were harmonized with ISO 9001.

ISO 9001:2015 adoption will be a sector by sector decision. Many sectors have adopted QMS as the basis for their quality architecture, process, and language. In these sectors, they will probably adopt RBT and ISO 9001:2015 - maybe later than sooner.

We believe some sectors will not harmonize their sectoral standards or technical specifications with ISO 9001:2015. What will the sectors do?

They will develop their own risk specifications, and standards.

Lesson Learned: Understand how sectoral standards based on ISO management systems will adopt RBT, risk management, and even ERM requirements that are broader and more specific than ISO 9001:2015 QMS requirements. Why does this occur in some sectors? RM and ERM are moving into statute and specific sectors may adopt statutory risk requirements on top of ISO 9001:2015.

Resource: Read 'Quality Futures: Management Systems Integration' Http://Insights.CERMacademy.Com/2013/04/1192/

What are 'exclusions' of specific requirements?

'Exclusion of specific requirements' refers to scoping the standard to determine compliance to the QMS. Depending upon the context in the organization, the term exclusions can be confusing. In previous ISO 9001 iterations, the term exclusion usually referred to a company that claimed conformity to the ISO 9001 requirements but would exclude certain areas that did not apply to their business.

ISO 9001:2008 allowed an organization to exclude the QMS requirements under the following conditions:

- Exclusions were allowed for the requirements, which could not be applied due to the nature of the business.
- Exclusions were limited to the standard's Clause 7 'Product Realization.'
- Exclusions could not and did not impact the organization's ability to provide products, which met customer requirements and applicable legal requirements.

This will change with ISO 9001:2015. The new standard does not allow exclusions of an area if the certification falls within the scope of QMS and if its non - applicability could lead to a failure of conformity to meet statutory requirements or lead to a lack of customer satisfaction.

Lesson Learned: Understand how the new language on exclusions will impact your ISO 9001:2015 certification.

Why did ISO replace 'product' with 'goods and services'?

ISO 9001:1987 used the term 'product' and this worked since ISO 9001 in its early days had a manufacturing emphasis. For years, ISO 9001 standard writers still retained the manufacturing bias of tangible products.

The ISO 9001:2015 standard writers wanted to make the standard more generic and applicable. They believed the term 'product' may imply services but were not sufficiently explicit. Since many ISO certified companies offered services, ISO wanted to be more inclusive and expanded the reference to 'goods and services.'

This is a heartburn issue with many ISO consultants who are used to the 'product' reference. They maintain 'product' includes services by inference. They may be right. However, TC 176, the ISO 9001:2015 standards writing group, thought the term 'product' to describe a service output was too limiting. 'Goods and services' is a better descriptor of tangible (products) and intangible (services) outputs.

The bottom line is ISO 9001 methodology, terms, processes, and outcomes can be applied to delivering a service just as well as manufacturing a product. The hallmark of quality is consistency whether its consistency in fast food delivery, software development, or consistency in manufacturing a product.

Lesson Learned: ISO is creating a more generic standard. It expands the application of the standard and requires the certified company to be more precise in its certification language.

Does ISO 9001:2015 emphasize and even mandate a process approach?

Yes. ISO 9001:2015 reemphasizes the process approach that was first introduced in ISO 9001:2000. We are now seeing it mandated.

ISO 9001:2008, the last revision of ISO 9001, emphasized the process approach when designing, developing, deploying, improving, and assuring the efficiency and effectiveness of a QMS. We saw many certified companies adopt the process approach

ISO 9001:2015 is more explicit in clause 4.4 requiring an organization to adopt or deploy a process approach to each requirement in the standard. The critical elements of 4.4.2 are:

- Identify QMS processes and their applications.
- Identify the inputs and outputs of these processes.
- Identify the sequence and interaction of these processes.
- Identify the risks to determining the conformity of goods and services and to customer satisfaction due to 1. Unintended outputs or 2. Process interrelationships are not effective.
- Identify performance indicators that process operations and controls are effective.
- Identify appropriate resources to ensure process effectiveness.
- Ensure process accountabilities and responsibilities are assigned.
- Deploy controls to achieve planned results.
- Monitor, change, and assure processes are delivering required outputs.
- Assure process improvement.

Lesson Learned: Process management is the future of QMS. So, learn how to architect, design, deploy, and assure a process management system. This will be used in each of your management system standards.

Is ISO 9001:2015 maturing from a Quality Management System to a business management system or to a RBT system?

Maybe. This will be a highly debated and even contentious question over the next 5 years. Quality purists want to keep quality at its foundation roots, which were articulated by W. Edwards Deming and other quality gurus. Others will advocate quality has moved to operational excellence and ERM. We are in the latter camp. We have been advocating the integration of QMS and ERM concepts for over a dozen years.

Lesson Learned: Understand how risk is becoming more critical in each management system standard.

Resource: Read 'Risk Management: Today's Quality Management Paradigm'
Http://Insights.CERMacademy.Com/2013/04/12-Risk-Management-Todays-Quality-Management-Paradigm-Greg-Hutchins/

Will ISO derivative management system standards such as AS 9100 in aerospace and TS 16949 in automotive be harmonized to ISO 9001:2015?

Several sector specific, quality standards incorporate ISO 9001. Over the last few ISO 9001 iterations, there have been discussions of decoupling sector specific, quality and operational standards from ISO 9001 and other ISO management system standards. Sector specific requirements are usually added to the basic ISO 9001 QMS. This has worked in industries such as aerospace, auto, telecommunications, and other sectors. But, things are now changing.

We may see more sector specific RBT or risk management frameworks being developed. ISO would prefer management system initiatives such as the automotive, aerospace, pharmaceutical, medical device, food, and other sectors develop their specific requirements on top of the base ISO management system standards.

There are a number of reasons why some sectors may decouple from ISO management system standards:

- ISO 9001:2015 introduces new numbering and risk requirements.
- ISO 9001:2015 especially is becoming more generic and interpretive.
- Sector specific requirements are becoming more technical and specific just when ISO 9001:2015 is becoming more generic.
- Aerospace and automotive industries address safety, regulatory, and statutory issues. These cannot be adequately addressed by a generic quality standard.
- Quality advocates and industry professionals want ISO 9001:2015 to be more definitive and prescriptive. Let us face it: it is much easier to audit 'shall' ISO requirements, than interpretive and discretionary requirements.
- Current ISO CB auditing can be discretionary. In other words, CB's want to conduct consistent QMS audits. Audit requirements should be uniform and easily interpretable. There are audit variances among CB auditors. Variances are conformity assessment risks that are waiting to be realized.

With the above said, industry standard organizations may not be moving fast enough. Let us take a look at AS 9100. The standard is based on the ISO 9001 platform. Additional requirements are added for suppliers to comply. Some aerospace experts say that AS 9100 should diverge from ISO 9001:2015. But…

So, there is going to be a lot of discussion over the next few years as many quality standards become harmonized to ISO 9001:2015.

Lesson Learned: Be flexible. Some QMS sectors, initiatives, and programs will go their own way. That is OK! They may be tightly or loosely integrated with the new ISO 9001:2015 management system standard.

Resource: Read 'Consequences Of Misapplying A Quality Standard'
Http://Insights.CERMacademy.Com/2013/09/25-Consequences-Of-Misapplying-A-Quality

Is ISO 9001:2015 still a compliance standard?

Yes. But with a few major caveats!

RBT has introduced a number of questions in terms of controls. What types of controls? What is the extent of the controls? Where will they be applied and what is the scope? And, what will the ISO audit determine?

ISO 9001:2015 has performance requirements. The concept of 'effectiveness' is integrated into the standard. This is a messy concept. What is 'effectiveness'? How is 'effectiveness' determined? Who determined 'effectiveness'? Is effectiveness determined at one point in time or throughout the certification? What type of evidence is required?

Lesson Learned: ISO 9001:2015 is moving beyond simply a compliance, yes/no standard. We do not know where ISO management system standards will go. However, we know there are more changes coming other families of standards are harmonized to Annex SL. And, it is too early to speculate. Hopefully, this book can shine some light on the future.

Resource: Read 'Must Know Risk Facts For Quality And All Professionals'
Http://Insights.CERMacademy.Com/2013/05/13-Variation-And-The-Quality-Professional-Greg-Hutchins/

Is RBT in ISO 9001: 2015 the first step in a risk management journey?

As discussed, ISO 9001:2015 amended the concept of continual improvement to simply improvement. This has resulted in a lot of discussion and even anger among quality professionals. For too many years, the concepts of continual improvement and continuous improvement (kaizen) have been integral to quality management.

It now seems that improvement and RBT are integral to ISO 9001:2015. So, how does the improvement concept address risk? Risk management, much like quality management can be defined in terms of a risk capability and maturity model (RCMM) as a company moves up the RCMM curve from ad hoc risk, to RBT, risk assessment, risk management to enterprise risk management.

Higher maturity and capability also imply extensive RBT application and more risk management processes are architected, designed, deployed, and assured throughout the enterprise and into the supply chain. As this occurs, risk management systems and QMS are integrated. They will use the same processes to demonstrate improvement in the enterprise.

It is interesting to understand that implementing Six Sigma processes so that an organization can move from inspection to increased process capability to Six Sigma process capability implies lower risk of nonconformances and higher customer satisfaction. RBT follows a similar journey.

Lesson Learned: Expect RBT to be a journey with ever higher requirements. This is covered in depth in Chapter 8: Risk Based Thinking Journey.

Resource: Read 'Poor Reliability: A Risk To Production'
Http://Insights.CERMacademy.Com/2013/10/26-Poor-Reliability-A-Risk-To-Production-John-Ayers-2/

What is the source of the resistance against the new ISO 9001:2015 standard?

This is a hard question to answer because there are many points of view. Hopefully, we can provide some context.

First, there has been push back on the standard. A number of national ISO 176 bodies voted against passing the CD, DIS, and FDIS to the next stage of the standard development process.

One big reason for the lack of enthusiasm is too many changes in the standard. We even read the following in social media: "ISO 9001:2015 is all about eliminating risk at every clause." But, but perceptions and fears of the new standard continue to circulate.

Some think the changes will cost too much to implement and still maintain certification. Some believe the changes are driven by money mongering consultants who want to move QMS to risk. Some believe quality is being diluted by new risk and process requirements.

Lesson Learned: Understand the changes occurring in the quality profession and ISO standards development. The changes will result in good discussions, more transparency, and better understanding.

Resource: Read 'Is ISO 9001 Working?'
Http://Insights.CERMacademy.Com/2013/10/29-Is-ISO-9001-Working-T-Dan-Nelson/

How many companies transitioned to the new standard?

The ISO 9001:2015 standard was released in September 2015. There was a three - year transition period for certified companies to adopt the new standard. ISO currently does not keep an exact count of certified companies. It defers to Certification Bodies to self - report certifications, which have been inaccurate. We believe that in some developed countries, 50% or fewer companies will transition to ISO 9001:2015. In developing countries, 80% to 90% of the companies will transition.

Lesson Learned: ISO 9001:2015 and other ISO standards with RBT and risk requirements offer obstacles that prevented companies from transitioning. As well, the ISO 9001:2015 and other new ISO standards do not offer an explicit value proposition for many companies.

Resource: Read 'Quality Futures: Management Systems Integration' Http://Insights.CERMacademy.Com/2013/04/1192/

Where do you obtain a copy of ISO 9001:2015 and other ISO standards?

You can purchase a copy from your standard developers, such as ANSI in the U.S., BSI in the UK. Or, you can purchase a copy from your CB.

A number of people obtain development copies of the standard such as the CD, DIS, or FDIS, and assume that they can obtain certification from one of these documents. We believe it is good management practice to purchase the final standard from your CB, ANSI, or ASQ.

Lesson Learned: Purchase the final standard so you really know the specific requirements

Resource: Read 'ISO Shares Its Risk Vision For ISO 9001:2015' Http://Insights.CERMacademy.Com/2014/01/37-Iso-Shares-Risk-Iso-9001-2015-Greg-Hutchins/

CHAPTER 5:

ISO 31000:2018 GUIDELINE

What is the key idea in this chapter?

The key idea in this chapter is ISO 31000:2018 is the risk guidance document for ISO 9001:2015. ISO 31000:2018 is more often considered an ERM standard. In this chapter, we cover ISO 31000:2018 and in the next chapter we cover COSO enterprise risk frameworks. We refer to ISO 31000:2018 as 'ERM light' and COSO as 'ERM heavy.'

What are commonly used ERM frameworks?

The number of risk frameworks seems to increase. The following is only a partial list of risk frameworks:

- **ISO 31000:2018 Risk Management - Principles and Guidelines on Implementation.**
  Available from:
  http://www.iso.org/iso/catalogue_detail?csnumber=51073
- **COSO Enterprise Risk Management - Integrated Framework.**
  Available from:
  http://www.coso.org/ERM-IntegratedFramework.htm.
- **U.S. Department of Energy: Electricity Sector Cybersecurity Risk Management Process Guideline.**
  Available from:

http://energy.gov/sites/prod/files/Cybersecurity%20Risk%20Management%20Process%20Guideline%20-%20Final%20-%20May%202012.pdf

- **BS 31100 Risk Management Code of Practice for Risk Management.**
  Available from:
  http://shop.bsigroup.com/en/ProductDetail/?pid=000000000030191339

- **FERMA Risk Management Standard.**
  Available from:
  http://www.ferma.eu/wp-content/uploads/2011/11/a-risk-management-standard-english-version.pdf

- **OCEG Red Book 2.0 (GRC Capability Model).**
  Available from:
  http://www.oceg.org/store/books/grc-capability-model-oceg-red-book/

Lesson Learned: Risk management frameworks are similar. They all incorporate RBT as a fundamental premise. Review several risk frameworks. Adopt and adapt the risk framework that works best for you.

Resource: Read 'Basics: Develop A Risk Management Framework' Http://Insights.CERMacademy.Com/2014/12/70-Basics-Develop-Risk-Management-Framework-Rod-Farrar/

What is the ISO 31000 series of standards?

The ISO 31000 series consists of core guidance documents that can be applied with most families of ISO standards. The series consists of the following documents:

- **ANSI/ASSE/ISO 31000:2018.** Risk Management - Principle and Guidelines.

- **Guide 73.** Vocabulary for Risk Management.

- **ISO 31004.** Technical Report for implementing ISO 31000:2018.
- **ANSI/ASSE/ISO 31010.** Risk Assessment Techniques.

We discuss each in this book.

Lesson Learned: It is really critical that CB's, consultants, and certified companies speak the same risk language. Again, we strongly recommend you purchase the above documents. Also as a tip, shop around the web for standards. The pricing of ISO standards varies greatly from country to country. Also, you can get the same standard offshore at a lower price than in many developed countries.

Resource: Read 'Cyber Risk Frameworks'
Http://Insights.CERMacademy.Com/2013/09/25-Cyber-Risk-Framework-Update-Ed-Perkins/

What is ISO Guide 73:2009?

ISO Guide 73 consists of common risk management definitions that will be incorporated into each management system using RBT. The purpose of the guide is to provide consistent definitions of risk frameworks, principles, terms, processes, and activities across management systems. ISO 31000 risk definitions are derived from Guide 73.

ISO Guide 73 can be used by:

- Companies intending to become certified to ISO 9001:2015.
- Consultants providing management system advisory services and products.
- Developers of national or sector specific standards such as AS 9100.

Lesson Learned: Guide 73 offers risk definitions found in ISO 9001:2015. We recommend you start with Guide 73 risk definitions for your risk taxonomy. While it was written before RBT, it offers risk definitions that you can use. However be aware, Guide 73 risk definitions are not consistent with non ISO risk frameworks and many risk concepts and definitions are not addressed in the Guide. For a comprehensive list of definitions, visit the Glossary in this book.

Resource: Read 'Proactive Vs. Reactive Risk Management With ISO 31000'
Http://Insights.CERMacademy.Com/2014/05/48-Proactive-Vs-Reactive-Risk-Management-ISO-31000-Greg-Carroll/

What is ISO/TR 31004:2013?

ISO 31004 is titled: Risk Management - Guidance for the Implementation of ISO 31000. ISO 31004 is a technical report (TR) that provides guidance, examples, and illustrations on how to assess and manage risk using ISO 31000. It follows the PDCA cycle as well.

More families of ISO standards will be adopting some form of risk. The critical issue in terms of standards development is to ensure uniformity for harmonizing risk definitions, systems, and processes around ISO 31000:2018.

ISO 31004 consists of the following sections:

Introduction

1. Scope

2. Normative references

3. Implementing ISO 31000

   3.1 General

   3.2 How to implement 31000

   3.3 Integration of ISO 31000 into the organization's management processes

Annex E. Integrating risk management within a management system

E.1 General

E.2 What is a management system?

E.3 Integrated management system and risk management

E.4 Implementing risk management into a quality management system framework

E.4.1 General

E.4.2 Identification and awareness of decisions

E.4.3 Risk assessment

E.4.4 Implications for the risk management framework

Lesson Learned: RBT has its own language and processes that are new to most certified companies. Again, consistency of interpretation and implementation of risk is key to a successful certification. So, purchase ISO 31004 to understand how to implement ISO 31000:2018. ISO 31004 is also a helpful guidance document to conduct risk assessments required by ISO 9001:2015. Be aware, ISO will be providing additional risk guidance in 2016.

Resource: Read 'Quality And Risk Management Global Standards' Http://Insights.CERMacademy.Com/2014/10/64-Quality-Risk-Management-Global-Standards-Denis-Leonard/

What is ISO 31010:2009 standard?

ISO 31010 presents and explains risk assessment techniques. ISO 31010 should be used with ISO 31000:2018, ISO/TR 31004 and ISO 9001:2015.

ISO 31010 risk assessment consists of risk tools, which decision makers and process owners can use to identify risks (both positive and negative) that inhibit the achievement of quality and business objectives. Once risks are identified, then the adequacy of controls can be evaluated. ISO 31010 risk assessment tools are covered in Chapter 13, Risk Assessment Tools.

Remember that ISO 31000 was first developed in 2009, six years before ISO 9001:2015. ISO 31000 was updated in 2018. However, RBT is not explicitly part of either ISO 31000 standards.

Lesson Learned: Purchase ISO 31010. It provides examples of risk assessment tools that you can use in ISO 9001:2015 compliance and RBT.

Resource: Read 'ISO 31000: Requisite Risk Standard For ISO 9001:2015'
Http://Insights.CERMacademy.Com/2014/11/67-ISO-31000-Requisite-Risk-Standard-ISO-90012015/

What is ISO 31000:2018?

The title of ISO 31000:2018 is 'Risk Management Guidelines.' ISO 31000:2018 standard is a guideline to be used as a reference with ISO standards. Companies cannot be certified to ISO 31000:2018. ISO 31000:2018 states: Managing risk is part of all activities of an organization and includes interaction with stakeholders. ISO 31000 has three key elements: 1. Risk management process, 2. Risk management principles, and 3. Risk management framework.

ISO 31000:2018 is intended to promote consistency within and across an enterprise especially if it will be used with ISO 9001:2015 or other ISO standards.

ISO 31000:2018 is a descriptive and not a prescriptive guidance document. The standard is 16 pages long. Most risk management guidelines or ERM standards mentioned earlier are much longer and often prescriptive. ISO 31000:2009 can be used by public, commercial, and community enterprises in any industry or sector.

ISO 31000:2009 is first designed around a Plan, Do, Check, and Act cycle. ISO 31000:2018 is the preferred reference document for ISO RBT and risk management system development. ISO 31000:2018 can be applied throughout the lifecycle of a project or process. It can be used in operations, supply management processes, internal functions, projects, product development, and service deployment.

ISO 31000:2018 provides risk principles and generic guidelines on the design, development and deployment of risk management systems. ISO 31000:2018 can also be used as part of a risk capability and maturity model. It can be the basis for an ad hoc to an intermediate maturity level risk management system. Some gurus believe that ISO 31000:2018 is the basis for an ERM system.

Caveat: ISO 31000:2018 is a guideline and is not intended for certification. However, we are seeing this may change as global certification bodies expand their portfolio of risk and assurance services.

Lesson Learned: The design and deployment of a RBT or risk management system will have to be tailored to the needs, context, stakeholders, interested parties, products, and requirements of the organization. ISO 31000:2018 does not have to used verbatim or even in its entirety. Get a risk professional to help you in your ISO certification. As a standalone guideline, ISO 31000:2018 is relatively difficult to implement without risk expertise or consultation.

Resource: Purchase **ISO 31000:2018: ERM Standard**
http://cermacademy.com/iso-31000-enterprise-risk-management/

What are elements of the ISO 31000:2018 risk management framework?

The structure of ISO 31000:2018 is shown in the figure (© ISO) on the next page. ISO 31000:2018 risk management framework consists of 8 elements (see Figure 5):

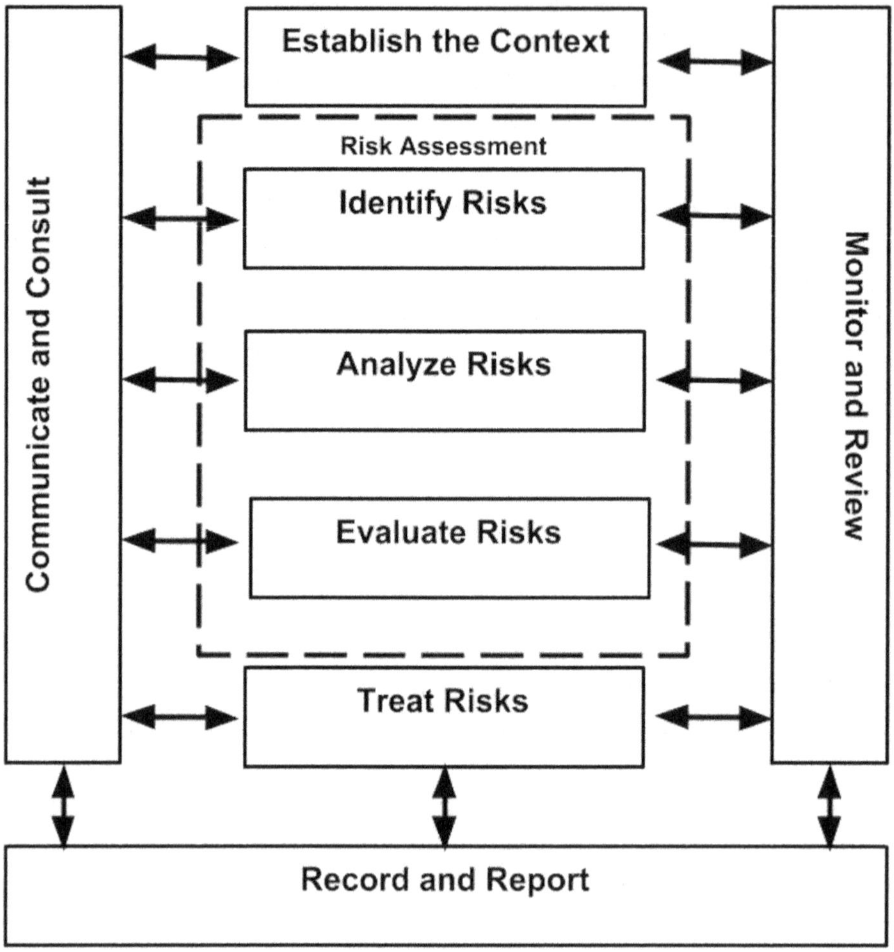

Figure 5: ISO 31000:2018

- **Establish the context**. Sets the scope and risk criteria, defines the internal and external parameters, and sets the objectives of the risk management system.
- **Identify risks.** Identifies the sources of risk, areas of impact, possible risk events, their causes, and probable consequences. In this step, the organization develops a list or register of risks.

- **Analyze risks.** Involves developing an understanding of the nature, extent, sources, and causes of the risks. Consequences and likelihood of the risks are also analyzed.
- **Evaluate risks.** Involves comparing the risk with the appetite and tolerance of the organization to determine if risk treatment is required.
- **Treat risks.** Involves selecting high or unacceptable risks to mitigate or reduce.
- **Monitor and review.** Involves reviewing the efficiency, effectiveness, and economics of the risk treatment controls.
- **Communication and consult.** Tracks effectiveness and communicates results of the risk management framework to ensure continuous improvement, learning, and compliance.
- **Record and Report.** Risk stakeholders are identified as well as their information requirements. Critical risk management activities are mapped to these information requirements and risk reports are generated satisfy these requirements.

Lesson Learned: ISO 31000:2018 is a must know document for all quality and operations professionals.

Resource: Read 'ISO 31000 & ISO 9001:2015: Thoughts On The Future'
Http://Insights.CERMacademy.Com/2014/05/49-ISO-31000-ISO-90012015-Integration-Alex-Dali/

What are the risk principles in ISO 31000:2018?

Risk management frameworks have similar principles. ISO 31000:2018 are structured around the following risk principles:

1. **Integrated.** Risk management is an integral part of all decision making and organizational processes.

2. **Structured and comprehensive.** Risk management is systematic, structured, and timely.
3. **Customized.** Risk management must be tailored to the organizational context.
4. **Inclusive.** Risk management is transparent and inclusive.
5. **Dynamic.** Risk management is dynamic, iterative, and response to change. Risk management is becoming the basis for all decision making.
6. **Best available information.** Risk management is based on the best available information. Accurate, reliable, sufficient, and suitable information about context, events, risks, and sources of risk must be available for Risk Based Decision Making.
7. **Human and cultural factors.** Risk management takes human and cultural factors into account. Risk management traditional takes into account organizational risk capabilities, maturity, and stakeholder capabilities to ensure that organizational objectives can be met.
8. **Continual improvement.** Risk management facilitates continual improvement of the organization.[x]

We could spend more time explaining each principle. However, you will notice these principles are integrated into this book.

Lesson Learned: Most 'Lesson Learned' recommendations in this book emphasize the above risk management principles that are sometimes reworded to apply to the specific question. Understand what the principles mean and integrate them into your RBT and risk management system vocabulary and deploy RBT around the above principles in your RBT journey.

Resource: Read '7 Examples Linking CSR Risk Management To ISO 31000'
Http://Insights.CERMacademy.Com/2014/08/56-7-Examples-Linking-Csr-Risk-Management-ISO-31000-Kelly-Eisenhardt/

Why do you advocate ISO 31000:2018 use with ISO 9001:2015?

Risk management is explicitly not required for ISO 9001:2015 certification. However, as you design, deploy, and assure your risk-controls, you will seek the guidance of ISO 31000:2018 to establish your RBT. ISO 31000:2018 risk management principles and guidelines are the preferred standard to use with ISO 9001:2015. ISO 31000:2018 is 'ERM light'. We advocate the use of ISO 31000:2018 principles with ISO 9001:2015 for smaller organizations because it:

- Is a RBT and risk assessment/management framework. ISO 31000:2018 has the critical elements of a risk framework, including a focus on context, culture, risk philosophy, risk definitions, common risk approach, common risk processes, defined roles and responsibilities, importance of accountability, risk competencies, and risk appetite of the organization.

- Is harmonized with other ERM standards and frameworks. While the standard does not map 1 to 1 with more comprehensive ERM frameworks, it offers many of the critical elements to start the RBT journey.

- Follows a risk framework that can be applied to any ISO management system standard.

- Offers the option of simple risk management (ERM light) or enterprise risk management program (ERM heavier). Both options can be used in the RBT journey for certified organizations to mature and make risk processes more capable.

- Follows an enterprise wide approach to risk management considering the potential impact of risks on critical management systems, processes, stakeholders, interested parties, product development, stakeholders, outcomes, products, and services.

- Addresses the upside (opportunity risk) as well as the downside (consequence risk).

- Follows the achievement of business objectives approach based upon the risk appetite of the organization.

- Focuses on risk-controls as well as other risk treatment options and mitigations.
- Allows an organization to identify, prioritize, and control significant risks.
- Is a process that is based on a set of unified risk management principles.
- Is supported by a structure that is appropriate to the context of the organization, external environment, and internal environment.
- Is supported by a risk taxonomy and risk vocabulary that is appropriate to the organization.
- Explains risk management and its application proportionate to the level of acceptable risk for any type of organization.
- Emphasizes the objective of risk management is to ensure stakeholder and customer satisfaction.

Lesson Learned: Use ISO 31000:2018 as the primary risk management framework for ISO 9001:2015 certification, RBT, and ISO management systems deployment for a small company.

Resource: Read Using ISO 31000 With ISO 9001:2015'
Http://Insights.CERMacademy.Com/2014/09/57-Using-ISO-31000-ISO-90012015-Greg-Hutchins/

Should an ISO 9001:2015 certified company implement ISO 31000:2018 or some other standard?

There is confusion surrounding ISO 9001:2015. No formal risk management or risk treatment system is required in ISO 9001:2015. But, the standard suggests risks are identified and acted upon. So, 'acted upon' risks implies that risks are assessed, controlled, and mitigated, which is the equivalent of a low level, risk management system.

It is unnecessary to architect, design, and deploy mature risk management techniques to comply with ISO 9001. However, ISO 9001:2015 has a number of requirements that address risk. And, the maturity and capability of the RBT and risk management processes should be tailored to the company.

We recommend if a company is publicly listed, has global operations, sells regulated products, has multiple certifications (EMS, QMS, etc.), then it should consider the value of adopting a risk management or an ERM system. The challenge is few organizations can justify the resources to design and deploy a risk management or ERM system, unless there is a compelling business driver such as a statute or customer requirement.

For most ISO 9001 certified companies, we recommend ISO 31000:2018. However, there are other choices. COSO is another option of a more mature risk management framework, which we describe in the next chapter.

ISO 31000 may be the preferred choice for a smaller organization that seeks ISO certification or wants to improve their operations. Again, this depends on whether the product or service provided by the organization is regulated. As well, the process risk maturity of the organization may also be a critical factor. We discuss the technical definition and attributes of a Risk Capability and Maturity Model (RCMM) in Chapter 8, Risk Based Thinking Journey.

The choice of which framework to use is not an easy answer. ERM heavy guideline, such as COSO discussed in the next chapter, would probably work best in a large, complex, and global organization listed in public exchanges such as NYSE, London Exchange, or NASDAQ. Large organizations already have some form of ERM as part of their GRC systems. As well, most if not all product regulated organizations have some form of risk management as a public safety or statutory requirement.

Lesson Learned: Risk assessment in less mature organizations will be different than in companies with ERM systems. Again, do what works best for you.

Resource: Read 'Integrated ERM And Cybersecurity' Http://Insights.CERMacademy.Com/2012/11/306/

What are benefits of implementing ISO 31000 with ISO management system standards?

As discussed in Chapter 2, take a look at any magazine or listen to any news broadcast. Most news broadcasts seem to focus on uncertainty and risk. Why? We live in VUCA time. In other words, we like in risky times.

Critical benefits for implementing ISO 31000:2018 in support of ISO 9001:2015 or any other certification include:

- Improve operational reporting to executive management.
- Improve the identification of opportunities and threats.
- Comply with relevant legal and regulatory requirements and international norms.
- Ensure conformity to requirements.
- Achieve customer, stakeholder, and interested party satisfaction.
- Improve quality and operational governance.
- Improve stakeholder confidence and trust.
- Improve the probability that business and quality objectives are met.
- Ensure project, process, and operational controls are stable and capable.
- Minimize project and process variation.
- Define QMS objectives used to develop plans and methods to mitigate these risks.
- Evaluate strategic alternatives and objectives.

- Facilitate 1. Risk based, problem solving and 2. Risk based, decision making.
- Introduce a step by step process for managing risks.
- Create awareness of the need to identify and treat risk throughout the organization.
- Manage portfolio risks across the organization and into the supply chain.
- Manage opportunity (upside) risk.
- Encourage proactive management.
- Establish a reliable basis for risk based planning.
- Improve supplier risk-controls.
- Effectively allocate and use resources for risk treatment.
- Treat risks, specifically through risk avoidance, reduction (control), sharing, and/or acceptance.
- Improve operational effectiveness and efficiency.
- Enhance health and safety performance, as well as environmental protection.
- Improve loss prevention and incident management.
- Minimize losses.
- Improve organizational learning.
- Improve organizational resilience.[xi]

Lesson Learned: Remember RM and ERM are processes that follow a maturing journey, much like quality, lean or Six Sigma.

Resource: Read 'Risk Management Is On Risky Ground' Http://Insights.CERMacademy.Com/2014/07/54-Risk-Management-Is-On-Risky-Ground-Tony-Bendell/

What are the challenges in implementing ISO 31000:2018 with ISO management system standards?

Challenges to implementing ISO 31000:2018 include:

- Language and terminology used in ISO 31000:2018 are not consistent in ISO 9001:2015 and among other risk management frameworks.
- ISO 31000:2018 does not include the concept of RBT.
- ISO 9001 and ISO 31000:2018 are not mapped and are not entirely consistent.
- ISO 31000:2018 is descriptive not prescriptive.
- Step by step procedures for implementing RBT or risk management are not in ISO 31000:2018.
- Users, consultants, and auditors must interpret and use discretion in applying the standard.
- ISO 31000:2018 critical risk definitions are missing. Additional standards have to be purchased.
- Risk management standards require a risk assessment. Risk assessments are detailed in ISO 31010, which has to be purchased.
- ISO does not provide guidance on using ISO 31000:2018 with ISO 9001:2015.
- ISO 31000:2018 does not recommend a specific risk assessment system and leaves it up to the organization to design one based upon its context, business model and the challenges it faces.

- Organizations will need to define and implement their own risk definition and measures of likelihood of occurrence and severity and/or consequence.
- Organizations implementing ISO 31000:2018 will have to develop their own risk scheme to conduct enterprise and process risk assessments.
- Companies will also have to develop their own risk taxonomy and classification. They will be different for each company. Risk classification can include scope of risk, nature of risk, timing of risk, risk stakeholders, risk assessment process, sectoral requirements, risk tolerance, risk appetite, risk management controls, and organizational culture.
- Risk classification systems are based on the complexity, nature, and size of the enterprise and may be different for each organization. Many QMS consultants do not understand RBT and risk management.
- Many CB auditors are not trained in RBT and risk based auditing.
- ISO consultants must be sensitive to these bullets and make appropriate adjustments in assessing conformance to ISO 9001:2015.
- CB auditors will have to learn a company's risk taxonomy and RBT implementation.
- ISO 31000:2018 does not address enterprise GRC issues satisfactorily.

Lesson Learned: Standardize your risk management framework, risk vocabulary, approaches, processes, and taxonomy. Again, consistency is the hallmark of quality management as well as risk management.

Resource: Read 'Three Underlying Risks Of Documented Quality Systems'
Http://Insights.CERMacademy.Com/2014/10/61-Three-Underlying-Risks-Documented-Quality-Systems-Ed-Grounds/

Does ISO 9001:2015 require a 31000 risk management framework?

ISO 9001:2015 does not require any specific risk framework, risk process, risk management system, or risk approach. However, ISO 9001:2015 does reference ISO 31000:2018 in the bibliography, which means it may become the risk management reference document.

ISO 9001:2015 states the level of risk-control should be proportionate to the potential consequences of low customer satisfaction and nonconformity of good and services. This implies the RBT or risk management system should be cost effective. RBT processes should be scoped because they can be expensive and time consuming to implement. As a certain point, there will be a point of diminishing return on the risk investment for a mature RBT or risk management system.

An ISO 9001:2015 certified organization can take a limited and practical approach to implementing and integrating RBT into its QMS. However, we believe RBT, risk management, and ISO 31000:2018 Enterprise Risk Management will be integrated into more international standards over the next five years.

Lesson Learned: Understand ISO 9001:2015 stakeholder requirements. Scan the risk environment, interested parties, and stakeholders to determine risk needs and risk requirements. This is a simple statement with potential layers of meaning. What do we mean? What may work for you and the quality organization may be different for the business unit you are in, internal audit, the enterprise, Board of Directors Audit Committee, and other interested parties. So, stay flexible.

Resource: Read 'One Short Of Infinity'
Http://Insights.CERMacademy.Com/2014/04/45-One-Short-Infinity-T-Dan-Nelson/

Will all ISO families of standards defer to ISO 31000:2018?

Yes. There are a lot of implications in this statement. ISO wants to provide an identical structure, common terms, common text, and definitions for all management system standards. This means ISO 9001, ISO 14001, and ISO 27001 will use a common structure. Again, consistency between standards is the hallmark of quality.

If risk is integrated into all families of ISO standards, ISO 31000:2018 may become a reference to all ISO management systems standards. This implies that risk and risk management will provide the framework in all management systems, which is the next step in the integration of risk into all ISO standards.

Lesson Learned: RBT is a new ISO concept that needs to be defined and tailored for each ISO family of standards.

Resource: Read 'Going With The Flow: Experiences In Micromanagement'
Http://Insights.CERMacademy.Com/2014/08/56-Going-Flow-Experiences-Micromanagement-Malcolm-Peart/

How do you obtain ISO 31000:2018?

You can purchase ISO management system standard through your national standards organization or CB.

Lesson Learned: Shop around for ISO standards. Google the standard you want to purchase. You will find the cost of the same management system standard can be purchased from Bangladesh at 1/5 the cost than from a developed nation.

Resource: Read 'Transform Now … Or Struggle To Survive'
Http://Insights.CERMacademy.Com/2013/10/28-Transform-Now-Or-Struggle-To-Survive-Daniel-Burrus/

Why are ISO standards expensive?

We went to the ANSI Standards Store (U.S.) to purchase IEC/ISO 31010:2009. The standard is titled: 'Risk Management - Risk Assessment Techniques.' This is an essential document for all companies and consultants assisting companies to move to ISO 9001:2015. The non-member price for the ISO 31010 standard is $285.00. The standard is 90 plus pages.

Every country prices its ISO and national standards. And, they differ widely. This story from the web ('Best Prices for ISO 26000) illustrates the differences for ISO 26000:2010.

> "Rather than paying up to €171 to ANSI (USA) or €157 to ISO, you can buy the English version as the South African national standard SANS 26000, which is identical to ISO 26000:2010, from the South African Bureau of Standards (SABS) for only €30. INTECO in Costa Rica offers the official Spanish version at the bargain price of only €31. The 'cheapest' French version is available as NF ISO 26000 at AFNOR for €121."

So, why are ISO standards so expensive? First of all, most national and international standards are expensive. Standards development follows a rigorous process, which includes bringing together international standards developers, peer reviews, and multiple iterations to ensure international consensus.

There is also a market process that increases price. If the standard is required for certification or is required by statute, then it becomes a matter of supply and demand. Statutory requirements, high demand, and specialized requirements imply that the market decides the price.

Lesson Learned: Shop around for the ISO standards you need. They are pretty much the same standard all around the world. If you follow this tip, you may save thousands.

Resource: Read 'Yes Virginia, A Process Approach Really Is Required' Http://Insights.CERMacademy.Com/2014/01/34-Yes-Virginia-Process-Approach-Really-Required-T-Dan-Nelson/

CHAPTER 6:

COSO ERM GUIDELINE

What is the key idea in this chapter?

The key idea in this chapter is if you are going to install risk-controls in your organization to comply with Governance, Risk, or Compliance (GRC) requirements, then consider COSO ERM as the framework for your system of internal risk-control.

What is COSO?

COSO is an acronym for 'Committee of Sponsoring Organizations.' COSO consists of the following organizations: the Institute of Internal Auditors (IIA), Financial Executives International (FEI), Institute of Management Accountants (IMA), American Accounting Association (AAA), and the American Institute of Certified Public Accountants (AICPA). The common element of these associations is they focus on accounting and financial reporting.

COSO's purpose is to develop a comprehensive framework and provide guidance on how to improve the quality of Internal Control over Financial Reporting (ICFR) or financial reporting. The goal starting in 2015 has been to improve organizational performance, control, and oversight.

Many companies, usually larger organizations, adopted COSO for financial reporting and are currently using the guidelines for controlling operational and supply chain risks. We call this internal control over operational reporting. This is a critical point in this book. ISO 31000:2018 and ISO 9001:2015 are control systems that may not be relied upon by the financial auditors or statutory authorities. Why? Financial auditors are not familiar with the risk language and processes of ISO 31000:2018.

Lesson Learned: Purchase COSO ERM guidelines from www.COSO.org because they are an important resource for ISO 9001:2015 certification of publicly listed companies that want to develop an internal control system to manage operational and supply chain risks.

Resource: Read 'COSO Or ISO 31k: Which Is The ERM Standard?' Http://Insights.CERMacademy.Com/2013/03/COSO-Or-ISO-31k-Which-Is-The-ERM-Standard/

How does COSO define ERM?

COSO defines ERM as:

> "A process, affected by an entity's Board of Directors, management and other personnel, applied in a strategy setting and across the enterprise, designed to identify potential events that may affect the entity, and manage risk to be within its risk appetite, to provide reasonable assurance regarding the achievement of entity objectives"[xii]

This definition of ERM has a number of notable components:

- ERM is a process.
- Board of Director's directs, shapes, and oversees the ERM program including organizational risk appetite.
- Executive management owns the ERM program.
- ERM is applied in a strategic setting across the enterprise into the supply chain.
- ERM is designed to identify potential events that can impact the

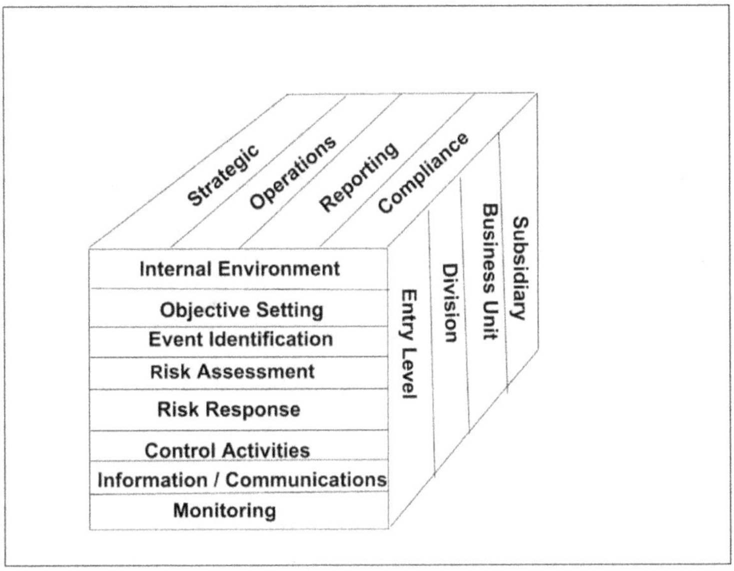

Figure 6: ***COSO Cube***

enterprise both positively and negatively.

- Enterprise manages risk within its risk appetite.
- ERM provides reasonable assurance, not absolute assurance, that risks are managed suitably and effectively.
- ERM focuses on achieving business objectives.

Lesson Learned: Understand the elements and nuances of the COSO definition of ERM because it is often the de facto risk definition in large, publicly listed organizations and government organizations. While the COSO Cube was updated in 2018, it is still largely in use.

Resource: Read "ERM Systems That Aren't" Http://Insights.CERMacademy.Com/2013/10/28-ERM-Systems-That-Arent-Greg-Carroll/

What is the COSO Enterprise Risk Management - integrated framework?

The COSO ERM cube is designed as a three-dimensional cube or matrix. The cube consists of 8 elements as can be seen in Figure 6, specifically:

- **Internal environment.** Reflects the organization's ERM philosophy culture, risk appetite, oversight, people development, and ethical values. 'Tone at the Top' is often heard as a short cut reference to the state of the internal environment.

- **Objective setting.** Consists of strategic and tactical objectives, which provide the context for operational risk reporting and compliance. Objectives should be aligned with the enterprise risk appetite of the organization.

- **Event identification.** Identifies potential risks that may positively or negatively impact the organization's ability to design and implement a risk strategy so it can meet its strategic and tactical business objectives. Positive risk is considered upside risk or opportunity. Negative risk is considered downside risk or threat or hazard.

- **Risk assessment.** Consists of the quantitative and qualitative methods, processes, and tools to evaluate the likelihood and consequence of potential events. Common qualitative risk methods include risk maps, turtle diagrams, and FMEA. Common quantitative research methods include SPC charts and statistical analysis.

- **Risk response.** Consists of evaluating various risk response options and their impact on risk likelihood and consequence. Risk response is the equivalent of risk management. Items to consider in terms of an appropriate risk response can include cost-benefit analysis, evaluation of variation in cost, schedule, scope, quality; and analysis of risk against risk tolerance.

- **Control activities.** Consists of a system of policies, procedures, and work instructions that are integrated throughout the organization and into the supply chain. Control activities can also consist of process flow charts and project tools dealing with scope, quality, cost, and schedule variances. Control activities ensure business objectives can be met.

- **Information communication.** Consists of the notification and dissemination of critical information from internal and external sources so responsible parties are aware of risks and can mitigate them appropriately. Effective communication flows vertically and horizontally in the organization and into the supply chain.

- **Monitoring.** Consists of ongoing activities to ensure the appropriate level of risk assurance and monitoring is appropriate to the organization. If there is unusual variation within the organization, the variation is monitored and root-cause corrected so the problem variation does not recur.

The top face of the cube consists of types of objectives specifically strategic, operations, reporting, and compliance. The right face of the cube consists of entity or enterprise components, specifically entity, division, business unit, and subsidiary levels.

Lesson Learned: Notice that COSO is a similar risk management framework to ISO 31000:2018. COSO specifically focuses on a system of internal controls.

Resource: Read 'From ERM To Extended ERM'
Http://Insights.CERMacademy.Com/2014/10/64-ERM-Extended-ERM-Institute-Risk-Management/

Why do you propose COSO for ISO 9001:2015 RBT?

Interestingly in a survey conducted 3 years ago, executives were asked: "Who is responsible for risk in your organization?" Guess who? Most executives surveyed said it was the Chief Executive Officer (CEO). Since Sarbanes Oxley (U.S. governance and reporting statute developed in 2002), many companies now have a Chief Risk Officer who is an Executive Vice President (EVP) or Senior Vice President (SVP).

We endorse the COSO ERM framework because it emphasizes ERM at the senior levels of the organization. Senior managers understand the COSO ERM framework, taxonomy, and its purpose. ERM is incorporated into the enterprise DNA and decision making processes. As more managers become responsible for risk, more employees will be implementing COSO controls in their areas of responsibility including in operations and in the supply chain.

The COSO framework since its inception emphasized the CEO is ultimately responsible and assumes ownership for risk implementation. The CEO sets the 'Tone at the Top' and asks the critical questions about the management of risks and effectiveness of controls. The Board of Directors provides the requisite oversight and governance.

Lesson Learned: We believe every operations manager will become a risk manager. Therefore, COSO is a must know risk management framework for all operations and quality managers and consultants.

Resource: Read 'Seven Guiding Principles To Successful ERM' Http://Insights.CERMacademy.Com/2014/06/53-Seven-Guiding-Principles-Successful-ERM-Greg-Carroll/

Why was the COSO ERM Integrated Framework revised?

The COSO Framework was revised to include expanded reporting, such as non-financial reporting, specifically internal reporting of operational control effectiveness because business has changed significantly since its last update. We are going to see COSO being used as an operational and even supply chain risk management framework.

As well, since the last revision of COSO, the following changes have occurred:

- Increasing Volatility, Uncertainty, Complexity, and Ambiguity (VUCA).
- Increased disruptive technologies and 'black swan' events.

- Globalization of markets, supply chains, and operations.
- Increased risk requirements for governance oversight by the Boards of Directors.
- Increased complexities in Governance, Risk, and Compliance (GRC).
- New laws, rules, regulations, and standards on financial reporting.
- New business, cyber security, and operating models.
- Increased expectations for organizational competencies and individual accountabilities.
- Increased susceptibility of loss of intellectual property due to cyber penetration.
- Increased expectations related to detecting and preventing fraud and other abuses.
- Increased expectations of operational and supply management controls.

Lesson Learned: COSO is the risk management and ERM framework of executive management. It is also the language of executive management.

Resource: Read 'Risk As A 'Historic' Or 'Experiential Measure' Http://Insights.CERMacademy.Com/2014/06/51-Risk-Historic-Experiential-Measure-Bill-Barto/

Why is COSO 'ERM heavy' and ISO 31000:2018 'ERM light'?

COSO ERM and ISO 31000:2018 are both reliable risk management frameworks. So why is COSO 'ERM heavy?' COSO ERM addresses GRC, ERM, and other organizational issues. COSO has been used by companies to design, deploy, and assure internal control systems. COSO has developed non-financial control systems that integrate well with financial control systems. COSO emphasizes a system of control.

COSO risk taxonomy is also more mature than ISO 31000:2018. Let us look at the difference in the definition of 'risk appetite.' ISO 31000:2018 defines 'risk appetite' as:

> "The amount and type of risk that an organization is prepared to pursue, retain, or take."[xiii]

COSO defines risk appetite as the:

> "... Amount of risk, on a broad level, an organization is willing to accept in pursuit of value. Each organization pursues various objectives to add value and should broadly understand the risk it is willing to undertake in doing so. "[xiv]

COSO has a Board level, strategic, and more nuanced definition of risk appetite. This is one of the reasons why we consider COSO to be more comprehensive, mature, and authoritative ERM guideline than ISO 31000:2018. ISO 31000:2018 is 16 pages, while the original COSO ERM is more than 150 pages of narrative and guidelines.

Lesson Learned: Follow these guidelines if you are in doubt about where to start your RBT journey and what risk management framework to choose. If you are a small company and are pursuing ISO 9001:2015 certification, adopt and adapt ISO 31000:2018 for your RBT. If you are a medium to large company pursuing ISO 9001:2015 certification, adopt and adapt COSO. COSO has a financial orientation, is mature, is broader, and chances are your organization is already using it for Sarbanes Oxley compliance.

Resource: Read 'ERM At Paychex Inc.' Http://Insights.CERMacademy.Com/2014/08/55-ERM-Paychex-Inc-Frank-Fiorille/

Is COSO ERM a risk management system?

ISO 9001 is a Quality Management System. ISO 14001 is an Environmental Management System. ISO 31000:2018 is a Risk Management System. COSO is an Enterprise Risk Management System.

So, if ISO 31000:2018 is a Risk Management System, expect the RBT journey will start with RBT and mature to some form of ERM.

Lesson Learned: Expect confusion, positioning, and posturing among QMS consultancies over the next few years as RBT or some form of risk assessment is integrated into more ISO management systems. Expect the RMS (Risk Management System) may become as prevalent as a QMS or EMS within the next five years. You are also going to hear more of COSO ERM.

Resource: Read 'Enterprise Architecture And Business Risk Management'
Http://Insights.CERMacademy.Com/2014/09/58-Enterprise-Architecture-Business-Risk-Management-Howard-Wiener/

Can ISO 31000:2018 and COSO ERM work together?

Yes. The COSO definition of control supports and reinforces ISO 9001:2015 control requirements. Specifically, both ISO 31000:2018 and COSO ERM frameworks are:

- **Process based.** COSO is a process consisting of ongoing tasks and activities. ISO 31000 emphasizes the process approach throughout the standard.
- **Affected by people.** Both frameworks are affected by people.
- **Guideline documents.** Both are risk management guideline documents. Both allow an organization to architect, design, deploy, and assure risk management systems based on the company's context.

- **Interpretive.** Both are discretionary and interpretive documents. This is critical since ISO 9001:2015 has eliminated the need for a quality manual in QMS documentation. Management system owners have more latitude in the design and deployment of management systems.

- **Provide reasonable assurance, not absolute assurance.** COSO emphasizes reasonable assurance, which is implied in ISO 31000:2018.

- **Provide for internal auditing.** Both COSO and ISO 31000:2018 rely on internal auditing to provide the requisite monitoring of control effectiveness.

- **Focus on the achievement of business objectives in operations and compliance.** Both focus on meeting business objectives. ISO 31000:2018 focuses on the achievement of objectives, which can be scoped to specific management system objectives.

- **Adaptable to different enterprises.** Both can be used in different types of organizations in different sectors.

Lesson Learned: COSO and ISO 31000:2018 are mutually compatible. They can be melded into a RBT or risk management system that is adaptable and meets varying requirements.

Resource: Read 'How To Build A Reliable And Repeatable ERM Process' Http://Insights.CERMacademy.Com/2014/10/63-Build-Reliable-Repeatable-ERM-Process-Apqc/

Why are Boards of Directors interested in COSO ERM?

Most publicly held companies such as those listed in international financial exchanges such as New York Stock Exchange (NYSE), NASDAQ, and London Exchange have listing requirements that require Boards of Directors to have an Audit Committee addressing Governance, Risk, and Compliance (GRC) issues. For publicly listed companies, COSO is the preferred ERM standard.

The Board of Directors Audit Committee and the CEO are concerned about these risk questions:

1. Are there any known, unknown, or unknown exposures that can create material risks to the organization?
2. If risk exposures exist then what type of cost effective controls can mitigate these risks?
3. If there are unknown or unknowable events, what can the organization do to prepare for these?

Lesson Learned: Check if your organization is publicly listed and has operational risk reporting requirements. If it is, we recommend integrating ISO 31000:2018 with COSO ERM.

Resource: Read 'How Not To Make Bad Decisions'
Http://Insights.CERMacademy.Com/2013/11/30-How-Not-To-Make-Bad-Risk-Decisions-Ed-Perkins/

What does an ISO certified company do if COSO is the de facto risk framework?

What do we mean? If the organization uses COSO, how does ISO 31000 fit in? This can be a tough issue for an ISO certified company. Here are some preliminary thoughts:

A critical idea throughout this book is quality should *harmonize up* the organization by designing risk management systems and deploying risk processes that support the enterprise Governance, Risk, and Compliance reporting requirements. If the enterprise is already implementing COSO risk systems, then it would make sense for the ISO RBT and ISO 9001:2015 certification to support COSO ERM.

Another option is for the certified company to integrate ISO 31000:2018 and COSO guidelines. We do not usually recommend this because of resulting variability and uncertainty.

Lesson Learned: Adapt your RBT and QMS approach to your organization's existing internal control framework. Most frameworks follow a similar process, use a similar vocabulary, and have similar mitigation/control approaches.

Resource: Read 'Why ERM Fails?'
Http://Insights.CERMacademy.Com/2014/05/47-ERM-Fails-Mary-Driscollkristina-Narvaez/

What are the benefits to quality professionals for learning COSO ERM framework?

The COSO framework was developed and deployed largely by the financial and public accounting organizations. COSO designed its framework around ERM principles, practices, and tools. Most Boards of Directors are very familiar with COSO. Unfortunately, they are not familiar with ISO 31000:2018.

The biggest benefit to the quality professional for learning COSO ERM is the COSO risk framework is adopted by Boards of Directors and executive management in most global organizations. Boards of Directors and executive management use the COSO framework as a means to identify internal controls and assess risks. Most importantly, the framework can be used to develop risk treatment, remediation, and management processes in operations and supply management based upon acceptable levels of risk to the organization.

The COSO ERM framework is being updated and we believe expanded beyond financial reporting to support a universal framework of internal control covering operations, design development, cyber security, and supply management. The new framework will be updated to apply the internal control concept to any type of enterprise regardless of industry, location, culture, product or service. As well, the COSO ERM framework will integrate a principles based approach that allows it to be applied in operations. We discuss this in Chapter 14: Risk Management and Control.

The benefits to operations professionals for learning COSO include:

- Learn and speak the language of the Board of Directors and executive management.
- Understand GRC and how to align ISO 31000:2018 and ISO 9001:2016 with enterprise GRC requirements.
- Learn the language of internal control systems.
- Develop an understanding of risk assurance beyond quality assurance.
- Develop an understanding of risk-controls beyond quality control.
- Develop a greater understanding of the criteria used to architect, design, deploy, and assure a system of internal control that is compatible with ISO 9001:2015.
- Develop greater confidence in the ability to respond to risk events and improve operational processes.
- Enhance personal knowledge, skills, and abilities in risk based, problem solving and risk based, decision making.
- Improve personal judgment and abilities to stabilize processes, reduce variation, eliminate redundancies, and improve internal controls.
- Align internal controls in operational and supplier processes.

Lesson Learned: The opportunity to integrate QMS controls with COSO controls is critical to ensure that key operational and supply chain risks are identified, controlled, assured, and reported to executive management.

Resource: Read 'History Lessons And The Musty Smell Of Regret' Http://Insights.CERMacademy.Com/2013/09/25-History-Lessons-And-The-Musty-Smell-Of-Regret-Mark-Moore/

What do you do if your organization uses two or more risk frameworks?

Finance may use the COSO risk management framework. Operations may use ISO 31000:2018. IT may use NIST 800 - 37 or ISO 27001 risk frameworks. Other areas may even use different risk management frameworks. If finance, internal audit, compliance, executive management, and the Board want integrated risk reporting, risk management frameworks should be harmonized using a common risk vocabulary.

Lesson Learned: Multiple risk management frameworks can be challenging because of differing taxonomies, definitions, and approaches. Ensure the organization speaks one risk language.

Resource: Read 'Airline Short Term Tactics Add Passenger Pain' Http://Insights.CERMacademy.Com/2013/04/13-Airline-Short-TERM-Tactics-Add-Passenger-Pain-Carolyn-Turbyfill/

Why do you need to pay attention to RBT and risk management, when you work for a small company?

OK, you work for a small company. You are certified to ISO 9001:2008. You may think that much of this book has nothing to do with you. Or, so you think?

Are you supplying products or services that are ultimately secured by a global corporation or governmental agency? A large customer may impose ISO 9001:2015 requirements as well as additional sectoral supplier requirements upon you that will be risk based. And, complying with risk requirements may be a condition of business.

And, we are seeing that risk management and ERM are being put into national statutes and rules in more than 20 sectors. As well, the United Nations and Non-Governmental Organizations are adopting RM and ERM. Bottom Line: this is not going away!

Lesson Learned: Develop a list of possible customers or government agencies that may add risk requirements beyond ISO 9001:2015 as a condition of business and note this in your business case as risk drivers.

Resource: Read 'Quality Inputs To The 2013 Revision Of COSO Guidance'
Http://Insights.CERMacademy.Com/2013/06/16-Quality-Inputs-To-The-2013-Revision-Of-COSO-Guidance-Sandford-Liebesman/

How many ISO 9001 certified companies have implemented COSO ERM processes or a risk management system?

Sarbanes Oxley was promulgated in 2002. Compliance with financial reporting was a primary driver of Sarbanes Oxley legislation. Publicly held companies had to implement improved disclosure practices and develop Internal Control over Financial Reporting (ICFR) practices.

COSO ERM integrated framework became the preferred model to assist management in designing and deploying controls to comply with Sarbanes Oxley legislation. COSO was used by companies to architect, design, deploy, and assure effective internal controls. It is safe to say that publicly held companies with ISO 9001 certification have implemented COSO ERM. If companies have adopted COSO ERM controls, then COSO will be the de facto ERM or RM framework and RBT should be harmonized up.

Lesson Learned: Learn about Sarbanes Oxley if you work for a publicly held company in North America. If you are ISO certified, learn about your public listing requirements in your country. Your country's regulatory authorities may require risk management or ERM as a governance requirement.

Resource: Read 'Risks Of The Unicorn Hunt'
Http://Insights.CERMacademy.Com/2013/07/20-Risks-Of-The-Unicorn-Hunt-Mark-Moore/

How do you obtain the COSO ERM documents?

The COSO ERM framework can be purchased at www.coso.org.

Purchase the new 2017 revision of COSO ERM. Google and search 'COSO ppt', which will show power points that have been delivered on the new guideline.

Lesson Learned: Once you have viewed the Power Point presentations, you can get a good idea of what is in the new COSO guideline and then decide if you want to purchase it.

Resource: Read 'MBO, ISO, And Deming'
Http://Insights.CERMacademy.Com/2014/11/69-Mbo-ISO-Deming-T-Dan-Nelson/

CHAPTER 7:

BUSINESS CASE FOR RISK

What is the key idea in this chapter?

The key idea in this chapter is ISO 9001:2015 and RBT may be sufficiently different than traditional certification that it may require additional investment in resources. The business case is the vehicle to communicate the value and need for additional resources.

What do you expect from ISO 9001:2015?

Executive management in many companies views ISO 9001 certification as a contractual requirement and a cost of doing business with certain customers.

Quality is simply not as important as it was when Ford's marketing tagline shouted: 'Quality is Job # 1.' Quality was then the value added differentiator for business success.

What happened? Organizations took a checklist approach to conformity assessment and ISO management system certification. This is when ISO 9001 became commoditized since ISO 9001 was not linked to the organization's business model, core processes, and profitability.

So, what is your reason for pursuing ISO 9001:2015? So, ask yourself: 'Are you implementing risk for the sole purpose of demonstrating ISO 9001:2015 compliance.' If yes, this is acceptable. This is a tactical and operational ISO risk perspective. Or, are you implementing risk for the sake of improving organizational controls, improving profitability, and satisfying customers. This is a strategic, specifically Governance, Risk, and Compliance (GRC) emphasis. The answer to these questions will determine the need for and the elements of a business case.

Lesson Learned: In the first through fourth revisions of ISO 9001, the emphasis was on customer satisfaction and demonstrating conformance to a QMS. The emphasis in ISO 9001:2015 is broader with a business and strategic perspective as well as traditional customer satisfaction and conformity assessment.

Resource: Read 'Risk Driven Business Model '
Http://Insights.CERMacademy.Com/2014/10/65-Risk-Driven-Business-Model-Greg-Hutchins/

Why do you need a business case for ISO 9001 when you are already certified?

Too often, we have seen the rationale for ISO certification based on weak reasoning, such as 'we have been certified for 15 years,' 'we have always done it this way,' 'customers require certification,' and so on. Annex SL and new management system standards adopting RBT and risk may require a higher level of rationale and due diligence.

ISO 9001:2015 has RBT, risk assessment, and top management requirements. We believe ISO 9001:2015 may be the best thing that has happened to the quality profession in 20 years.

RBT is a game changer in the ISO standards development world. RBT may impact each family of management system standards. It may also impact operational professions as well as others involved with ISO standards such as supply management (ISO 28000), information security (ISO 27001), etc.

ISO standard developers clearly want quality to be part of a company's core business mission by expanding the boundaries of required controls, including:

- Conformance to the QMS.
- Strategic and overarching view of the organization's competitive environment.
- Needs and expectations of interested parties who can impact product specifications and other requirements.
- Organizational mission and risk-control approach based on an analysis of opportunities (upside risks).
- Prioritizing risks in strategic planning, specifically providing leadership and commitment planning as well as a review of intended outcomes.

If ISO 9001:2015 is evolving into a strategic planning and risk-control standard, executive management will be engaged in the QMS and quality reports should achieve higher visibility.

Lesson Learned: ISO 9001:2015 focuses on developing QMS objectives. If you can develop QMS financial targets such as profitability, return on investment, return on equity, these will secure executive management support.

Resource: Read 'C-Level Risk Management'
Http://Insights.CERMacademy.Com/2013/03/C-Level-Risk-Management/

What are elements of a business case?

There are no standard elements of a business case. However, the following is a general outline that can be modified for your organization:

Executive summary:

- Identify stakeholders, interested parties, and customers requiring certification.

- Discuss how certification can add specific value to the strategic direction of the organization.
- List generic benefits of ISO 9001:2015 certification, RBT, and quality.
- Recommend decision for ISO 9001:2015 investment based on tangible business benefits.

Introduction:

- Define ISO 9001:2015, ISO 31000:2018, etc. context.
- Identify business, quality, and risk drivers.
- List statutes and customers requiring certification.
- Define purpose of RBT and ISO 9001:2015 certification.
- Scope ISO 9001:2015 certification and RBT.
- List hard, GRC, and other financial benefits of ISO 9001:2015.
- Define enterprise risk and financial impacts of ISO 9001 compliance, RBT and risk management.

Analysis:

- List assumptions OF ISO 9001:2015 certification and RBT.
- Segment ISO markets and products/services requiring and/or benefiting from certification.
- Discuss direction of other management system certifications (Annex SL).
- Analyze Product, Place, Promotion, and Price benefits for certification in the different markets.
- List Strengths - Weakness - Opportunities - Threats (SWOT) analysis of certification and RBT.
- Identify Costs/Benefits of RBT and certification.

- Develop plan for certification and RBT.

Conclusions:

- List options for proceeding with implementing RBT and ISO 9001:2015 certification.

Lesson Learned: Most ISO management systems will integrate some form of risk within five years. Use the business case for ISO 9001:2015 as the template for future certification of ISO management systems.

Resource: 'Taking A SWOT At Risks' Http://Insights.CERMacademy.Com/2013/08/22-Taking-A-Swot-At-Risks-Mark-Moore/

What is the business case for a complex organization?

For a global company, target the business case to the geographies, markets, and segments in which the firm operates. Philip Kottler's 4P marketing model seems to work well in framing the business case: Product, Promotion, Place, and Price.

ISO compatibility in different cultures, geographies, and markets is a major benefit in implementing ISO 9001:2015 because the standard has become generic and is easier to adapt globally as well as locally.

Focus on specific services and products being provided in these markets and address how ISO 9001:2015 RBT and certification can impact the 4P's of marketing.

Quite often, ISO 9001 is used to access certain markets where ISO 9001 certification is required to sell products. Also many markets require ISO 9001 certification to demonstrate to the customer or regulatory authority that requirements are being satisfied. And in other markets, ISO 9001 is used to differentiate products and services from competitors.

Lesson Learned: Understand the global value proposition of ISO 9001:2015 RBT and certification, then develop hard business numbers to verify and validate its value. Monetize the benefits.

Resource: Read 'Redefining The Business Impact Assessment' Http://Insights.CERMacademy.Com/2014/02/39-Redefining-Business-Impact-Assessment-Geary-Sikich/

What are critical board and executive level questions to address in the business case?

Additional questions, you may want to ask are:

- Which stakeholders have the most to gain from successful adoption of ISO 9001:2015, RBT, and risk-controls?
- Who is the most important sponsor of the RBT journey?
- What is in it for the sponsor to support ISO 9001:2015 certification?
- What are the specific business objectives for ISO 9001:2015 deployment and certification?
- What would be the value adding difference to the organization if ISO 9001:2015 certification and RBT were successful?
- How would stakeholders be better served by RBT, risk-controls, and ISO 9001:2015 certification?
- What is the demonstrable impact on return on the organization's investment/equity/sales?
- Can any impact be demonstrated on shareholder value?
- What is the market share/profitability/productivity/ improvement expected?
- How will Governance, Risk, and Compliance be improved?
- Will regulators be satisfied and if so, how?

- How is Board of Director's operational and materiality reporting improved?

We address these questions throughout this book.

Lesson Learned: Risk management and RBT are vehicles to mainstream your ISO management system process into the organization's core processes.

Resource: Read '#1 Reason To Transition To ISO 9001:2015' Http://Insights.CERMacademy.Com/2014/05/47-1-Reason-Transition-ISO-90012015-Greg-Hutchins/

Who are the readers and customers of the business case?

Unlike developing a business case for previous ISO 9001 revisions, frame the business case to executive management. In previous ISO 9001 revisions, we focused on the benefits to a plant level manager or similar level certification stakeholders.

Executive management is the primary customer of the business case for ISO 9001:2015. These are corporate officers with Vice President (VP), Senior Vice President (SVP), and Executive Vice President (EVP) titles. The business case should emphasize how the organization will benefit from supporting ISO 9001:2015 and RBT. Why? Operational and supply risk reporting are now critical Board and executive concerns.

Executive management is concerned about identifying and managing operational risks. Executive management and the Board of Directors want to assure investors and other stakeholders that they are focused on profitability, know how to achieve profitability, understand how to remove impediments (risks) to profitability, and develop appropriate risk-controls to sustain profitability. Secondly, the organization wants its stakeholders and interested parties to know that it embraces good governance, RBT, ERM, and compliance with applicable statutes.

Lesson Learned: An organization has many working components and stakeholders with differing requirements. Know who will benefit from certification and RBT and align the business case to these requirements. As well, understand concepts such as GRC and ERM. The business case should provide the rationale in terms of costs, monetary benefits, success factors, and key risk indicators. The business case provides the financial justification to proceed and implement RBT in ISO 9001:2015.

Resource: Read 'Are The Feds Mandating ERM? Yes.'
Http://Insights.CERMacademy.Com/2014/10/64-Feds-Mandating-ERM-Yes-Greg-Hutchins/

What are the benefits of developing a business case?

The benefits of a business case include:

- Provide appropriate GRC guidance on reporting operational and supply chain risks.
- Improve regulatory compliance, transparency, and reporting.
- Instill confidence in the investor community that material, chronic, systemic, and operational risks are controlled within the organizational risk appetite.
- Align enterprise quality and RBT appetite with the business strategy.
- Enhance organization's brand equity and protect its reputation through RBT design, deployment, and assurance.
- Define materiality throughout the organization so it can focus on critical QMS objectives.
- Focus on developing a shared vision of the value proposition of RBT deployment and risk-controls.
- Define the QMS value proposition for architecting, designing, deploying, and assuring RBT. The value proposition of RBT can be

defined at the.

- **Enterprise level.** RBT and ERM assist the Board of Directors Audit Committee and CEOs by providing a framework for operational oversight, control, and assurance.
- **Programmatic level.** RBT and ERM help project managers mitigate scope, quality, cost, and schedule variances.
- **Product level.** RBT and ERM help quality professionals meet quality of service and product conformance requirements.

- Describe compelling costs and benefits of implementing ISO 9001:2015.
- Clarify why ISO 9001 is needed for operational and supply chain risk management.
- Distill the organization's gaps for managing risks and the rationale for developing an infrastructure to close the significant gaps.
- Focus on developing a compelling mission on the future state of operations, QMS, and supply management risk-controls.
- Establish realistic QMS risk plans and goals for action.
- Identify risks throughout the organization and supply chain (at least for first-tier suppliers).
- Treat QMS risks at the appropriate organizational level.
- Compare residual risk against the risk appetite of the organization at the 1. Enterprise level; 2. Programmatic/Project/Process level; and 3. Product/Transactional levels.
- Limit QMS redundancies and unnecessary controls throughout the organization and supply chain.
- Improve risk based, problem solving and risk based, decision making throughout the organization.

- Reduce QMS operational uncertainty losses through change management processes.
- Is systematic, logical, structured, and timely by focusing on the achievement of business goals and QMS objectives.
- Can be monitored, assured, and improved.

Lesson Learned: When developing the business case, frame the benefits around QMS benefits, which apply to your organization. If you work for a small company, target the business case to the scope of the ISO 9001 certification. For example if the certification is at a plant level, develop the business case and identify benefits in the context of the scope of the certification to the plant. If the certification is at the enterprise level, develop a business case that addresses enterprise benefits.

Resource: Read 'What Is Lending And Investment Risk For Innovation?' Http://Insights.CERMacademy.Com/2015/01/76-Lending-Investment-Risk-Innovation-Iam-Rosam/

What are hard benefits of ISO 9001:2015 certification?

We have discussed this question already, but it bears repeating. ISO 9001:2015 and RBT should be seen as an investment. The organization wants to know its return on investment (ROI). You want to convey to management the value proposition for aligning ISO 9001:2015 quality and risk with the strategic direction of the organization.

Also, frame the benefits of ISO 9001:2015 in terms of the hot buttons of your organization. Some organizations focus on Corporate Social Responsibility (CSR) while others focus on Return on Investment (ROI), and others focus on stakeholder satisfaction. Your organization should develop a business case around its hot button, which in many cases may address some form of RBT and risk management.

Executive management will focus on ROI; opportunities and rewards; risks; competitive/comparative advantage; value added differentiation; or unique selling proposition.

BSI, the global Certification Body, recently listed the following hard benefits of ISO 9001 certification:

- **Finance.** Companies (55%) using ISO 9001 achieved bottom line cost savings.
- **Management.** Certified companies increased their share price and outperformed the market by more than 100%.
- **Sales/Marketing.** Companies (71%) using ISO 9001 differentiated themselves, secured new customers, and retained existing clients.
- **Services.** Companies (75%) improved their levels of customer satisfaction and loyalty.
- **Product Development.** Companies increased their speed to market with higher quality products, and reduced their manufacturing cycles by 48%.
- **Operations.** Companies improved their operational performance by 75% including improved process efficiency, reduced errors, and reduced costs.[xv]

Lesson Learned: Who is the sponsor of the ISO 9001:2015 certification? Then answer the question: "What is in it for me and for my organization?" This is the basic question of executive management. We would like to think that executives have higher motives dealing with CSR, ethics, global warming, and other high-level goals, but personal benefits still matter.

Resource: Read 'Key Risk Questions For All ISO Registered Companies- ISO 9001'
Http://Insights.CERMacademy.Com/2013/05/14-ISO-Risk-Greg-Hutchins/

What are critical success factors for implementing RBT and risk into ISO 9001:2015?

The critical success factors for ISO 9001:2015 RBT are much like Six

Sigma and lean. Our hard lessons learned over the last dozen years migrating organizations from quality to ERM include:

- **Obtain executive support, resources, and commitment.** Whether the organization is just starting the RBT journey or has mature ERM processes, executive management and even the Board should support the initiative. This is the #1 criterion for success. No executive management support leads to a failed ISO 9001:2015 initiative. It is that simple. Senior executives should also understand the monetized benefits to ISO 9001 certification and to implement RBT processes.

- **Develop a strong business case.** The business case should provide a strong business rationale for RBT and ISO 9001:2015 certification. The business case should be structured to reflect the context, culture, and business model of the organization.

- **Focus on strategic and business model alignment.** Executive management will endorse, sponsor, and resource ISO 9001 certification if it provides demonstrable value to the organization. So whether implementing a very tactical and limited risk assessment or aligning with an ERM initiative, executive management must understand its strategic and monetary benefits. The business case should detail costs and hard benefits of pursuing certification. This should eventually be articulated in a compelling vision for RBT and certification.

- **Establish attainable goals for ISO 9001:2015 certification.** Do not develop organizational objectives you cannot attain because this will become a prescription for failure.

- **Develop a realistic plan of action to implement ISO 9001:2015 systems and processes.** The plan should support the business case. The plan can be a work breakdown roadmap with concrete steps for achieving compliance to ISO 9001:2015 and implementing RBT.

Lesson Learned: Deliver on your promises and do not over promise in the first six months or even first year. Remember, RBT is an ethos or attitude that takes time to adopt.

Who owns ISO risk in ISO 9001:2015?

The quality organization should own the ISO 9001 QMS and RBT. Since ISO 9001:2015 is the latest revision of the QMS, it makes sense that quality should own the new QMS.

The challenge for quality is other organizational areas may claim RBT including legal, compliance, operations, internal auditing, and supply management.

Lesson Learned: Clarify ownership of RBT in your business case. Does quality want to own RBT and the QMS? Or, does the enterprise own COSO ERM and hence RBT and QMS. The organization may maintain that risk is an executive function and should own ISO 9001:2015. Answering this question will facilitate adoption and adaptation of risk based, ISO management system standards

Resource: Read 'Rolling Risk Downhill'
Http://Insights.CERMacademy.Com/2012/12/6-Rolling-Risk-Down-Hill-Paul-Kostek-Suppliersrisk/

Why should the business case be tailored to the organization's business model?

We have been working with ISO 9001 since 1987, when the standard was first developed. The biggest challenge we have seen is ISO 9001 has not been aligned with the company's business model, strategic plans, or profitability. The result is QMS lost some of its importance and became marginalized.

We have asked the following simple question in many presentations, "how many of the attendees know their company's business model?" A few hands go up. So, we drill down and ask what is their business model? Operations professionals will say they make this product or provide that service. The problem is these are not business models. They are product or transactional responses to a deeper question.

A business model "describes the rationale of how an organization creates, delivers, and captures value, in economic, social, cultural or other contexts."[xvi] The point is many professionals and even managers do not know their employer's business model. So, how can you communicate the value of ISO 9001:2015 certification or RBT if you cannot articulate your company's business model?

The organization's business model provides the important context for implementing ISO 9001:2015 and RBT. Most QMS's seem to be generic. If a company has to deal with regulatory product quality requirements then the QMS has some specific language and controls to meet regulatory requirements.

If the business case justification or economic rationale can be targeted to the organization's business model then it has a higher probability it will be accepted and economic resources can be justified and approved to implement ISO 9001:2015.

Lesson Learned: Use RBT as the vehicle to integrate your ISO management systems into your core business model. This will enhance the credibility and acceptance of your management systems including QMS, EMS, ISMS, etc.

Resource: Read 'Doing Well In An Increasingly Poor Market' Http://Insights.CERMacademy.Com/2014/11/67-Well-Increasingly-Poor-Market-Umberto-Tunesi/

Do you know what is critical to your organization?

Great question. We hope so.

ISO 9001 certification took off because it became a contractual requirement and companies certified as a condition of continuing business. Will this be sufficient and necessary in the future? We do not know. We believe ISO management systems will need to be coupled with the organization's business model and core processes so it can be demonstrated that ISO 9001:2015 certification enhances profitability.

Quality to a large extent is defined by the ability of an organization to create consistent processes that satisfy customer requirements. ISO 9001:2015 and many of the ISO management system standards have focused on customer satisfaction, sustainability, compliance, and meeting regulatory requirements. While these are important, ISO 9001 would have more acceptance if there was a direct link from QMS compliance to profitability.

ISO 9001 has always emphasized meeting requirements and ensuring customer satisfaction. The prevalent thinking is customer satisfaction and quality ensure organizational profitability and sustainability. Is this a correct assumption? Maybe. Let us discuss this further.

There seems to be a price and quality threshold that customers now want that is acceptable to them. Too much customer satisfaction may be cost prohibitive. Also in a world where good is good enough, customers may want the lowest price for the product or service. If this is acceptable to the customer, then great products or services are not required.

Or, companies may perceive customers as users. This is a significant change where technology, software, and other products are sold for high margins with relatively low customer satisfaction. Why? Users not customers may not have options for products or services they want. Think Apple products or even specialized healthcare.

The truth is customer satisfaction does not imply profitability. Any customer would be satisfied with a high quality product or service that may not generate sufficient margin or profitability to the company.

Companies want profitability and competitiveness as well as customer satisfaction. Also, companies are sometimes willing to accept a lower level of customer satisfaction to obtain market share, lower costs, or improve margins. Or their business model is to sell at high volume, low margin, and lower customer satisfaction.

Lesson Learned: Understand what drives your organization and focus on what is important in framing your business case.

Resource: Read 'How To Manage Quality Risks' Http://Insights.CERMacademy.Com/2014/08/56-Manage-Quality-Risks-Afaq-Ahmed/

Why do you emphasize risk based, problem solving and risk based, decision making in the business case?

Harvard Business Review (HBR) magazine two years ago had a number of issues focused on how to manage in VUCA (Volatility, Uncertainty, Complexity, Ambiguity) time. The risk articles emphasized that uncertainty and risk are increasing.

We discussed in Chapter 2, that uncertainty is the new normal. There seem to be few well defined and well accepted rules for managing in today's new normal. Management needs a new set of management principles and practices to address the new normal and for the organization to be sustainable.

In other words, all organizations and managers need to know:

- Risk based, problem solving.
- Risk based, decision making.™

Lesson Learned: Learn risk based, problem solving and risk based, decision making. These are critical element in the new management paradigm.

Resource: Read 'Can Innovation Really Overcome Tradition?' Http://Insights.CERMacademy.Com/2015/01/75-Can-Innovation-Rally-Overcome-Tradition-Umberto-Tunesi/

What level and breadth of RBT or risk assessment does an organization need in ISO 9001:2015?

At a minimum, ISO 9001:2015 requires RBT and risk assessment, which are integral to risk management. However, the language is vague and may even seem contradictory if one reads for intent or letter to the standard. We have had many conversations with QMS consultants who read for intent or letter. Each came away with different interpretations of how to use ISO 31000:2018 with ISO 9001:2015.

So, there is no easy answer to this question. Lots of important RBT questions have not been addressed by ISO and Certification Bodies. And, answers will depend on organizational risk context, maturity, and capability. Is the company going to become certified? Does it want to improve operations? What are the costs and benefits of RBT, risk assessment, risk management, and ERM? Lots of questions that are based on the important question of context.

As well, the need for additional risk assessment or management may be influenced by the CB, internal audits (first-party), customer audits (second-party), customer complaints, cost, and many other factors.

Lesson Learned: The business case will be a living document that will need to be updated as the organization certifies to additional ISO management system standards that incorporate RBT or risk.

Resource: Read 'Three Potent Secrets To Innovation'
Http://Insights.CERMacademy.Com/2015/01/74-Three-Potent-Secrets-Innovation-Daniel-Burras/

What do you see as the challenges for implementing ISO 9001:2015?

Challenges or risks to implementing ISO 9001:2015 should also be addressed in the business case. While we applaud the changes in ISO

9001:2015, we see a number of challenges after companies have transitioned. The challenges of implementing ISO 9001:2015 overwhelmed smaller to medium sized companies to the point where the pain of certification was higher than the value gained. As this this occurs, a number of certified companies may self-certify or drop certification.

The following are challenges to implementing ISO 9001:2015:

- Executive management is skeptical of the value of ISO 9001:2015 certification.
- Executive management does not understand RBT and its benefits.
- ISO 9001:2015 certification may take too much time, resources, and effort resulting in executive management walking away from ISO certification.
- Operational management and quality management do not buy into the new standard.
- RBT is not well understood by the quality organization and other operational departments, which result in internal resistance or confusion.
- Tone at the top, culture, context, social responsibility, and stakeholders are not considered in the design and deployment of ISO 9001:2015 RBT.
- Consultants sell a ‘one size fits all’ RBT solution resulting in false starts and unnecessary activities.
- Quality management does not integrate risk into quality management and other management systems.
- ISO 9001:2015 RBT is not aligned with the Board’s ERM direction and results in conflicting goals and objectives.
- ISO 9001:2015 implementation requires new risk roles and responsibilities. If these are not defined and clarified, they may conflict with other risk management and process management initiatives.

- ISO 9001:2015 and RBT may become a change and culture management process. Failure to communicate risk goals and objectives and manage change may result in problems.
- QMS and EMS consultants suddenly become risk experts. They provide conflicting messages to the certified organization.
- CB's are new to risk based auditing and conduct certification audits differently.

Lesson Learned: Address as many of the above issues in your business case.

Resource: Read 'How to See the Future with Science: Part #2 of Predicting Process Behavior'
http://insights.cermacademy.com/2013/10/26-how-to-see-the-future-with-science-part-2-on-predicting-process-behavior-giovanni-siepe/

CHAPTER 8:

RISK BASED THINKING JOURNEY

What is the key idea in this chapter?

RBT is a journey much like quality improvement is a journey. The RBT journey is based on a Risk Capability Maturity Model (RCMM), which should be incorporated into your business case. In this journey, there really is no destination, just enhanced organizational value through RBT, risk management, and enterprise risk management.

Is there a road map for the ISO 9001:2015 RBT journey?

While there is no roadmap, the following are lessons learned from organizations that have implemented risk assessment, risk management, and ERM successfully.

In this chapter, we describe steps and milestones for starting the RBT journey. There is no roadmap for the journey. However, there are two methodologies that are essential in identifying the steps and milestones in the RBT journey: 1. Risk Capability and Maturity Model (RCMM) and 2. ISO 31000:2018 risk management framework. Both are described in this chapter. COSO controls are another method and are described in Chapter 14, Risk Management and Control.

Lesson Learned: Risk may be part of each ISO family of standards. The RBT journey is a story that may be core to all ISO management system standards.

Resource: Read 'Innovation And The Quality Process' Http://Insights.CERMacademy.Com/2014/05/50-Innovation-Quality-Process-Ken-Peterson/

What is a Capability and Maturity Model (CMM)?

Risk Based Thinking is the start of a journey that can be mapped to a Capability Maturity Model (CMM). The RBT journey involves architecting, designing, deploying, and assuring management system capabilities.

A number of years ago, organizations would mature their quality systems from inspection (Acceptable Quality Level based) to statistical process control (SPC) to quality assurance (QA) to quality management (QM). During the quality journey, organizations would also adopt lean, Six Sigma, project management, and other operational excellence processes. This process was sometimes referred to as increasing the capability and maturity of the organization.

An organization would mature its quality processes from an 'ad hoc' state to one that was repeatable, defined, managed, and optimized at the highest level. At the lowest CMM level, organizations were starting the quality journey and usually had ad hoc inspection processes dependent on individuals and often people heroics. As processes matured, they became highly repeatable processes that were defined in terms of standardized policies, procedures, and work instructions. This was defined as a Level 3 process, that usually had qualitative and quantitative metrics. Managed processes were considered a Level 4 quality system, which was measured and managed quantitatively throughout the enterprise.

At the highest level, quality was institutionalized and optimized throughout the organization, which involved Six Sigma quality or best in class processes deployed throughout the organization. And it was common for organizations to apply for the Malcolm Baldrige National Quality Award.

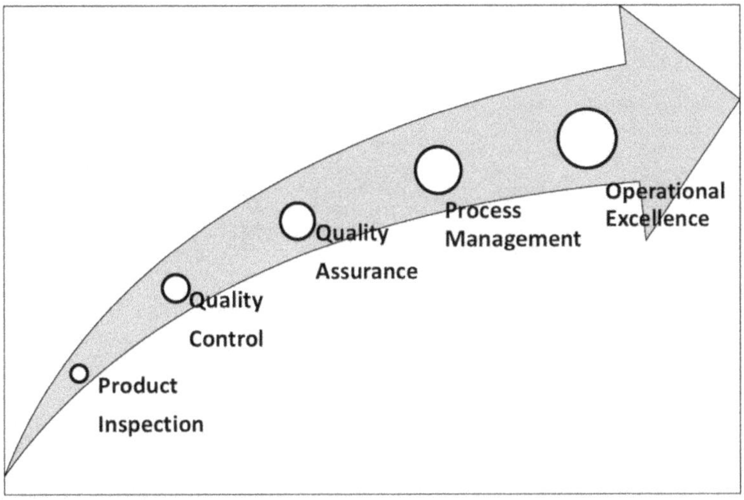

Figure 7: Quality Maturity Curve

Lesson Learned: Conduct a gap analysis of your risk maturity especially if you are certified to a number of ISO management system standards. This will establish a common baseline level of risk across your enterprise and into your supply chain.

Resource: Read 'Basics: Describing Your Risks' Http://Insights.CERMacademy.Com/2014/11/68-Basics-Describing-Risks-Rod-Farrar/

What is a Risk Capability and Maturity Model (RCMM)?

The generic Risk Capability and Maturity Model (RCMM) is a process and procedural model that is used to determine the repeatability, control, and maturity of a risk management framework.

The term risk 'maturity' describes the extent, depth, and improvement of an organization's standardization and control of its critical processes. Capability refers to the ability of the organization to effectively meet risk and customer requirements.

The RCMM can be viewed in terms of a ladder of five structured levels. Each level from the lowest 'ad hoc' or also referred to 'initial' or 'chaotic"

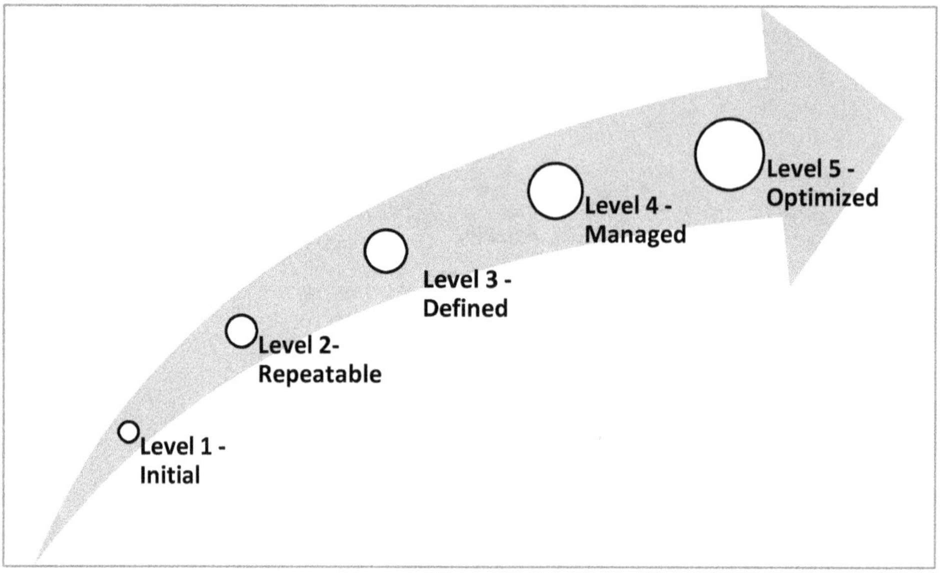

Figure 8: Risk Capability and Maturity Model (RCMM) Curve

level to the highest level called 'optimized.' This is shown in the above figure.

Lesson Learned: Use the RCMM as the basis for your step by step plan in your business case to mature your RBT processes, specifically through architecting, designing, deploying, and assuring risk-controls.

Resource: Read 'When Risks Attack' Http://Insights.CERMacademy.Com/2013/06/16-Five-Stages-Of-Engagement-John-Blakinger-Greg-Ranstrom/

What are the five levels in the RCMM journey?

QMS refers to 'continual improvement' or simply as 'improvement' in ISO 9001:2015. Much as QMS is a quality improvement journey, RBT is a risk enhancement journey.

The Risk Capability Maturity Model (RCMM) journey involves five destinations:

- **Level 1: Initial/ad hoc.** RBT is largely ad hoc with limited transactional/product level controls. RBT is not understood. See figure on the previous page.

- **Level 2: Repeatable.** Risk assessment is applied in limited areas across the organization at the process and transactional/product levels with repeatable controls. Risk taxonomy is developed which becomes the basis for the system of internal control. RBT has evolved into a formal risk assessment process.

- **Level 3: Defined.** At this level, risk management basics are implemented into the organization. Risks are identified and controlled throughout the organization and into the supply chain. RBT has evolved into a risk based, decision making process which forms the basis for a low level, ERM system.

- **Level 4: Managed.** Risk management has evolved into ERM. Risks are managed extensively and preemptively throughout the organization. Risk based, problem solving and risk based, decision making are the foundation of good management and is in the DNA of the organization.

- **Level 5: Optimized.** RBT has evolved into a mature ERM system that is optimized throughout the organization and into the supply chain.

Lesson Learned: Google 'Software Engineering Institute CMM.' You will be able to download many free CMM resources.

Resource: Read 'Evidence Of RBT And Process Approach'
Http://Insights.CERMacademy.Com/2015/01/74-Evidence-RBT-Process-Approach/

What are the attributes of Level 1 RCMM organization?

At the 0 to 1 level, the organization may be aware of the need for RBT as a result of ISO 9001:2015 requirements. Risks are addressed in a reactive and corrective action manner at the product and transactional level. Few or no QMS business objectives have been identified and risk assessed. Quality tools may be rebranded into risk tools.

Additional attributes at this level include:

- Ah hoc, chaotic, fire-fighting, or heroics are commonly used terms to describe the approach to risk and RBT at this level.
- Executive level and enterprise interest is lacking in RBT and formal risk assessment.
- Risk-controls are often reactive meaning that an event occurs then symptomatic fixes are applied.
- Key people with institutional memory and tribal knowledge are the key organizational controls.
- Organization has a Corrective Action - Preventive Action (CAPA) program focused on quality, but not risk management.
- Organization may have quality metrics, but no or few risk metrics.
- Quality tasks and objectives are defined at the product and transactional level.
- Process controls are largely quality and production focused
- Failure Mode and Effects Analysis, Six Sigma, and Statistical Process Control are commonly used quality control methodologies and tools.
- ISO 9001 QMS focus is on clause-by-clause compliance.
- RBT and risk assessment are not understood.
- No one has been trained in RBT.

Lesson Learned: Move from ad hoc to the next RCMM level is a cultural issue more than a technical issue. The move to the next RCMM level is often the biggest challenge for an organization because it involves behavioral changes. This does not come easy to an organization. The organization needs to be ready to adopt RBT. Executive support is critical to move to the next stage.

Resource: Read 'When To Incorporate A Risk Into The Baseline Schedule Or Risk Register'
Http://Insights.CERMacademy.Com/2013/09/22-When-To-Incorporate-A-Risk-Into-The-Baseline-Schedule-Or-Risk-Register-John-Ayers/

What are the attributes of Level 2 RCMM organization?

At this level, the organization is starting its RBT journey using ISO 31000, COSO, or some other risk management framework as a guide. The organization conducts risk assessments and has applied basic risk-controls in various areas, projects, and processes.

Additional attributes at this level include:

- Executive management supports risk assessment and RBT.
- Quality is aware of GRC requirements and discusses its operational system of control with Internal Audit, risk management, and executives.
- Enterprise understands RBT and the importance of risk-controls as part of ISO 9001:2015.
- Organization has a few QMS risk and RBT controls that may ensure compliance to ISO 9001:2015.
- Risk assessments are conducted as part of ISO 9001:2015 compliance.
- QMS risk-control objectives are developed in limited areas focused on QMS compliance.
- Risk procedures and work instructions are defined in critical few areas.

- Organization starts to define risk ownership and responsibilities in limited areas.
- Organization will use ISO 31000:2018 as its guidance document if it is a small company.
- Organization is still largely dependent on people to manage risks. If a key person leaves, then controls become unstable.
- Organization identifies subject matter experts for RBT and risk assessment.
- Organization starts to tailor a RBT or risk management framework based on its context and needs.
- Organization focuses on managing downside risk (consequence), but develops processes for reviewing upside risk (opportunities).
- Common risk taxonomy and language are developed and used.
- Quality and risk objectives required by ISO 9001:2015 are defined.
- Organization has developed critical risk procedures and processes.
- Risk training is offered to key process owners.
- RBT and risk management results and status reports are developed.
- Standardized risk assessment tools are deployed.
- SMART business objectives are established at several organizational levels.
- Organization starts to develop risk treatment capabilities.
- Organization starts asking 'what if' questions about business continuity and business impacts.
- Organization is more risk sensitive if not a risk aware organization.

Lesson Learned: Start the RBT process ensuring critical people are trained in risk and a common risk language is developed. RBT journey evolves into risk assessment at this level.

Resources: Read 'Understanding The Top Drivers For Reducing Quality Risk'
Http://Insights.CERMacademy.Com/2013/09/23-Understanding-The-Top-Drivers-For-Reducing-Quality-Risk-Lns-Reserach/

What are the attributes of Level 3 RCMM organization?

At this level, the organization has designed, deployed, managed, and assured risk-controls and treatment throughout the organization and into the first-tier of the supplier base.

Additional attributes at this level include:

- RBT and risk management are part of the organization's strategy, business management system, business model, and core processes.
- RBT is starting to be integrated into the organization's financial, GRC, and quality audit processes.
- Organization has integrated RBT into its IT and cyber processes.
- RBT performance is managed and risk assured.
- Executive management supports RBT, risk management and even ERM.
- Smaller organization may use ISO 31000:2018 as its guide for Enterprise Risk Management.
- Risk processes are stable and capable throughout organization.
- Risk is integrated with operational excellence methodologies, such as Six Sigma, Lean, etc.

- Risk analysis of opportunities (upside risk) has become institutionalized within the organization.
- Risk processes are integrated with financial internal control processes.
- Risk assessment moves from a qualitative to quantitative assessment.
- RM is proceduralized throughout organization.
- Organization develops limited risk profiles for assessment and treatment.
- RBT, risk management, and ERM effectiveness and efficiency are measured.
- Risk sponsors and risk owners collaborate on appropriate risk-control and treatment for the organization.
- Larger organizations may use COSO as their guide for ERM.
- Risk owners are identified and assigned risk responsibilities at the 1. Enterprise level, 2. Programmatic/Project/Process level, and 3. Product/Transactional level.
- Organization has a compliance based, GRC program.
- Organization has RBT, risk assessment, risk management and even ERM policies and procedures depending on its context.
- Organization complies with ISO 9001:2015 and other ISO management system requirements.
- Organization has a rigorous risk methodology and framework, which is consistently applied.
- Organization manages downside risk (consequence), but also reviews upside risk (opportunities).
- Organization understands interrelationships, dependencies, and white space risks within the enterprise and into the supply chain.

- Organization applies risk based, problem solving and risk based, decision making to every business decision.
- Organization conducts stress tests and scenario tests.

Lesson Learned: Pursue RCMM to the appropriate level of your organization based on context, which may be Level 2 or Level 3 for most organizations pursuing ISO 9001:2015 certification.

Resource: Read 'Sorting Out The Different Information On Risk' Http://Insights.CERMacademy.Com/2013/10/29-Sorting-Out-The-Different-Information-On-Risk-Tim-Landerville/

What are the attributes of Level 4 RCMM organization?

Most organizations seeking ISO 9001:2015 certification will stop their RBT journey at a Level 2 or Level 3 RCMM. Why? Organizations may view this RCMM level as the point of diminishing return for ISO certification. In other words, additional risk investment does not return any additional value. If the organization wants Enterprise Risk Management, then it will make additional investments and mature its risk processes.

At this level, the organization has a robust ERM system having moved from RBT to applying risk based, problem solving and risk based, decision making into the organizational DNA.

Additional attributes at this level include:

- ISO 31000:2018 Enterprise Risk Management or COSO ERM is implemented in the organization and supply base.
- Risk assessment can be integrated in more areas beyond the QMS into other management systems such as into the supply chain and business management systems.
- Risk likelihood and consequence are measured qualitatively and quantitatively.

- Risk-controls and treatment are assessed for efficiency, effectiveness, and economics.
- First and second-tier suppliers are part of the risk management system.

Lesson Learned: Develop a cost benefit analysis for pursuing higher levels of RCMM. Monetize the value of pursuing higher levels of risk CMM. Most ISO organizations will not go to this level of ERM.

Resource: Read 'Systemic Risk Based Thinking Part 1' Http://Insights.CERMacademy.Com/2014/12/72-Systemic-Risk-Based-Thinking-T-Dan-Nelson/

What are the attributes of Level 5 RCMM organization?

At this level, the organization has an extensive, effective, and mature ERM system based on ISO 31000:2018 or COSO. ERM is applied in most or all areas of the organization. Continuous improvement and innovation are ingrained in the organization. Systemic and emergent risks are anticipated and mitigated. All or most areas of risk are addressed and controlled.

Lesson Learned: Expect few certified companies to be at this RCMM level. Develop a plan for your organization to first become risk aware, risk sensitive, risk stable, risk compliant (ISO 9001:2015), risk capable, and risk maturing. Remember, this should not and cannot be done instantaneously, it takes patience and time.

Resource: Read 'Basics: Risk Culture Myth' Http://Insights.CERMacademy.Com/2014/12/72-Basics-Risk-Culture-Myth-Rod-Farrar/

Is there a preferred CMM level for ISO 9001:2015 risk deployment?

The vast majority of ISO 9001 certified companies will start their RBT journey at a relative low level such as Level 1 ad hoc. This means they do not have RBT processes or they are at a relatively low level. CB's understand this and will probably adjust their audits accordingly.

Lesson Learned: Learn how to identify and assess risk and then apply appropriate risk-controls to treat risks within the organization's risk appetite and RCMM level. Move to a suitable maturity in your RBT journey. Organizations depending on their context will have different levels of risk maturity, process management, and risk-controls.

Resource: Read '#1 Secret To Managing Project Risk'
Http://Insights.CERMacademy.Com/2013/06/19-1-Secret-To-Managing-Project-Risk-Daniel-Everhart/

How can ISO 9001:2015 certified companies start their RBT journey?

Most companies starting their RBT journey will start at the ad hoc RCMM level. ISO certified companies will tweak their quality controls and assurance such as SPC, FMEA, lean, and Six Sigma to meet ISO 9001:2015 risk requirements.

There are no firm rules. So practically what does this mean for the quality organization? We recommend that quality organization:

- Develop a business case similar to what is described in this book.
- Articulate the organizational RBT vision, mission, plans, goals and objectives.
- Develop QMS and RBT business objectives.
- Develop a plan for the next 6 months and year for what will be done where and by whom for architecting, designing, deploying, and assuring a RBT system.
- Adopt a common risk taxonomy, language, and risk framework.
- Determine risk appetite at the enterprise level and be as precise as

possible.

- Develop a plan for achieving visible and notable early successes.
- Adopt a plan to integrate RBT into each management system such as Environmental Management System (ISO 14001), Information Security Management System (ISO 27001), Quality Management System (ISO 9001), etc.
- Develop a common process for 1. Risk based, problem solving and 2. Risk based, decision making. These are the bases for demonstrating RBT.
- Understand what risk assurance means for your organization.
- Determine if you want to mature your RBT system to RCMM Level 1, 2, or 3
- Identify potential risks based on meeting QMS objectives and prioritize them within the organization and supply chain.
- Conduct a RBT gap analysis of current processes against 'to be' processes for ISO 9001:2015 certification.
- Develop RBT, risk assessment, and even risk management processes that are mapped to ISO 9001:2015 requirements to close the gaps.

A major challenge may be that ISO 9001 certified companies view risk as a non-value adder and requirement for ISO 9001:2015 certification. This form of RBT will be reactive, ad hoc, firefighting, and transactional.

Lesson Learned: Understand the concept of a Risk Capability Maturity Model and incorporate its ideas into your business case. This will be the basis of your RBT journey. This is very critical for your organization as you pursue ISO 9001:2015 certification and you mature your management system processes to risk.

Resource: Read 'Risk And Organizational Mindset: Learn To Think Like A Commodities Trader'

Http://Insights.CERMacademy.Com/2014/10/64-Risk-Organizational-Mindset-Learn-Think-Like-Commodities-Trader-Geary-W-Sikich/

What is a gap analysis of risk capabilities?

ISO 9001:2015 has basic risk requirements that are described in the ISO 9001:2015 chapter. There will also be other requirements that can impact a company's ability to meet customer and statutory requirements. A gap analysis is a method that determines what needs to be done from the 'as is' to the new 'to be' state.

A risk gap analysis involves the following steps:

- Identify the organization's risks in terms of its ability to meet QMS requirements or quality business objectives.
- Define the level of risk that is acceptable to the organization. This may involve identifying risk appetite and tolerance.
- Determine RCMM level that is appropriate (future or 'to be' state) to the organization and develop appropriate RCMM attributes, processes, and risk metrics for the desired level.
- Define the desired future state of the organization's RBT and risk capabilities, which may entail moving from Level 1 to Level 2 or even Level 3.
- Identify the current level of risks that can impede the achievement of QMS and business objectives.
- Identify the gaps between desired (future or 'to be') RCMM level and the present state.
- Analyze the size of the gap between the desired state and the present state and determine if the gaps require treatment or are acceptable to the organization in terms of risk appetite.
- Develop a business case for addressing the gaps and economic justification for closing the gaps.

- Develop a plan to develop the appropriate capabilities to close the gaps and identify the change issues in terms of technology, process, people, and system resources required to close the gaps.
- Provide program and project oversight and facilitation to ensure the effective integration of risk and QMS.
- Repeat for each ISO management system.

Lesson Learned: Conduct a gap analysis if you already have a risk management or RBT system in place. A gap analysis can be thought of as a 'Risk Capability and Maturity Analysis.'

Resource: Read 'ISO 9001 Risk Challenges'
Http://Insights.CERMacademy.Com/2013/02/8-Risk-Management-A-Must-In-Todays-Global-Economy-Sandford-Liebesman/

What are reasonable expectations for the first year?

If you are a small company, you can successfully launch a RBT and risk assessment initiative and complete many RBT tasks within the first year. You will develop Level 1 and some Level 2 controls.

If you are a larger company, then it will take longer. The biggest challenge will be getting buy in from executive management and employees for a new way to manage based on RBT and risk based, problem solving and risk based, decision making.

Some companies will bolt risk processes onto existing ISO 9001 QMS processes. This may work with some CB's. The larger CB's will conduct a process based, risk audit, which will require new types of risk-controls. The bolt on risk processes may or may not work. This will depend on the CB's interpretation of ISO 9001:2015 requirements.

Lesson Learned: Develop the business case for RBT and ISO 9001:2015. Then, develop reasonable expectations on what you can accomplish in the first year. RBT is a cultural and behavioral shift for some organizations. Culture shifts take time.

Resource: Read 'Your Risk Based Thinking (RBT) Journey' Http://Insights.CERMacademy.Com/2014/11/69-Risk-Based-Thinking-Journey-Greg-Hutchins/

How long will it take to implement RBT?

This depends on a number of factors such as the context of the organization. The length of time it takes to implement RBT will depend on culture, GRC, business environment, sector, products, etc.

From our experience of architecting, designing, deploying, and assuring risk systems, it takes X length of time to set up the risk assessment framework. But, it takes 3X to 5X length of time to implement the culture change from moving a clause-by-clause to a process based to a RBT approach of management.

Lesson Learned: Why does it take so long? RBT requires behavioral changes. People and organizations are resistant to change. It is what it is!

Resource: Read 'Learn From The Mistakes Of Others' Http://Insights.CERMacademy.Com/2015/01/74-Learn-Mistakes-Others-Rod-Farrar/

What are the critical steps for implementing ISO 31000:2018 with ISO 9001:2015?

If the organization is small to medium sized, then you will probably defer to ISO 31000:2018 as the preferred risk management framework. As we have discussed, ISO 31000:2018 is 'ERM light' and is applicable to most certified organizations starting their RBT journey.

We suggest that you purchase and follow the basic steps in ISO 31000:2018. The challenges of ISO 31000:2018 are discussed Chapter 5. The biggest challenge is the standard is not prescriptive and a certified organization has to develop its own tailored roadmap for its RBT journey, which we detail in the RCMM.

ISO 31000:2018 describes the following five steps, which can be used to start a RBT journey:

- Leadership and Commitment.
- Integration.
- Design.
- Implementation.
- Evaluation.
- Improvement.

The above steps follow a general Deming Plan - Do - Check - Act cycle. Each of the above steps is described in following questions. We suggest that you may integrate the above steps into the business case as part of the ISO 31000 plan to implement a risk assessment and management methodology.

Lesson Learned: If you are going to start with ISO 31000:2018, then the above steps will work for you. Remember; a 1000-mile journey starts with the first step. Use ISO 31000:2018 as your guide in the RBT journey.

Resource: Read 'Process Management Requirements In ISO 9001:2015' Http://Insights.CERMacademy.Com/2013/09/25-Process-Management-In-ISO-9001-2015-Lennart-Brandt/

What are the critical questions to address in 'Leadership and Commitment'?

Let us assume that most readers will defer to ISO 31000:2018 as their RBT risk reference guide for their RBT journey. It makes a lot of sense.

This section focuses on the importance of executive management support. You will notice several questions go beyond the scope of ISO 31000. Based on our experience, a larger organization may have adopted COSO and already has a mature and capable risk management system.

Critical questions to consider include:

- Are the Board and executive management committed to the RBT journey?
- Is the organization using a 'light' risk management or 'heavy' ERM framework?
- Is RBT or risk management policy defined?
- Are 'Tone at the Top', organizational culture, and RBT policy aligned?
- Is the RBT journey focusing on ad hoc risk, risk assessment, risk management, or ERM?
- Are Key Risk Indicators (KRI's) developed and are they aligned with QMS conformance, customer satisfaction, and strategic business objectives?
- Are ISO 9001 QMS objectives aligned with the enterprise risk objectives?
- Is conformity assessment of legal and regulatory compliance requirements effectively addressed?
- Are RBT and risk authorities and responsibilities properly assigned in the QMS and to the appropriate organizational level?
- Are appropriate and sufficient resources allocated to the design, deployment, and assurance of the RBT and risk management system?
- Are the costs and benefits of RBT and risk management properly communicated?

- Is the organization using the appropriate risk framework for assessing and treating risk?
- Does the organization know the RCMM level it wants to achieve?
- Does the organization know and define its risk appetite and tolerance?

Lesson Learned: Use the above checklist and those on the following pages as a guideline for your RBT journey. Remember: do what works for your organizational context.

Resource: Read 'The Reality Of Risk'
Http://Insights.CERMacademy.Com/2013/05/14-Reality-Of-Risk-Malcolm-Peart/

What are the critical questions to address in 'Integration?

This focuses on integrating the risk management framework, risk process, and risk classification scheme in your RBT journey.

Critical questions include:

- Is the organization's external context and internal context understood in designing or adopting a risk framework?
- Does the organization have an appropriate structure for risk management?
- Will the certified organization adopt an existing risk framework used by the organization such as COSO and adapt it for the RBT journey?
- Will the certified organization adopt ISO 31000:2018 as its risk framework since there is no preexisting risk framework?
- Is the external and internal context considered in the design and tailoring of the framework?

- In terms of external context, are the following factors considered in designing the framework such as culture, legal, financial, economic, technological, sustainability, standards, business model, competition, etc.?
- Are trends and key drivers considered that could impact the achievement of QMS and other management system objectives?
- Are interested parties and stakeholders identified as well as their requirements and expectations?
- Will interested parties and stakeholder requirements be risk assessed?
- Are suppliers and contractual relationships considered in developing the risk plan as part of the business case?

What are the critical questions to address in 'Design'?

This focuses on understanding the organization's context, articulating management's risk management commitment, assigning risk responsibilities, and allocating resources.

Critical questions include:

- In terms of internal context, are the following considered in designing and tailoring the framework:
    - Organization's risk vision and mission are defined.
    - Organization's QMS objectives are aligned with RBT policies.
    - Risk accountabilities and responsibilities are defined.
    - Management is committed to the necessary resources to manage risks in the achievement of QMS objectives.
    - RBT performance is measured.

  - Risk reporting and escalation of issues is appropriate to the level of controlling and mitigating the specific risk.
- Is RBT integrated into the organization's management system policies, procedures, and practices including:
  - RBT plan is developed.
  - RBT policy is implemented.
- Are sufficient resources provided to manage risks, including:
  - People with the requisite knowledge, skills, and abilities.
  - Resources to implement items identified in the risk framework.
  - Risk policies, procedures, standards, and work instructions are developed.
  - Appropriate risk tools and resources including IT capability.
  - Risk training is appropriate to the organization.
- Do internal communication, reporting, escalation, and correction protocols in the organization ensure the following:
  - Risk framework is understood and if changes occur to the framework they are communicated adequately.
  - Framework objectives are communicated effectively, efficiently, and economically.
  - Risk information is available throughout the organization.
  - Systems, processes, and protocols are appropriately designed for the treatment of risks.
- Do external communication, reporting, escalation, and correction protocols in the organization ensure the following:
  - Critical risk information is communicated with stakeholders and interested parties.

- Supplier reporting and other external reporting comply with governance, risk, and compliance requirements.
- Feedback, escalation, and resolution protocols are available and implemented effectively.
- Risk communication protocols promote management system consistency in terms of framework design, deployment, and assurance.
- External stakeholders understand the nature of the risk and contingency plans are in place in the event of an emergency.

Lesson Learned: Remember it is all about context. If you understand and can define your context, then you can start the RBT journey and become certified.

Resource: Read 'Risk Based Thinking + Process Approach' Http://Insights.CERMacademy.Com/2014/10/64-Risk-Based-Thinking-Process-Approach-Keeping-Real-T-Dan-Nelson/

What are the critical questions to address in 'Implementation'?

This focuses on deploying the risk management framework and risk classification scheme in your RBT journey.

Critical questions include:

- Has a risk management strategy, business plan, or business case been developed for deploying the RBT and risk management framework?
- Have risk management strategies and policies been integrated with the organization's core processes?
- Does the risk management program comply with GRC statutory requirements?
- Does the organization's decision making and business objectives

align with the outcomes of the risk management framework and procedures?

- Is the level of training aligned with the organization's risk capability and maturity level (RCMM)?
- Are interested parties and stakeholders consulted regarding the suitability, capability, and maturity adequate to the organization's needs?
- Does the risk management plan address implementation at appropriate organizational levels, functions, and areas?

Lesson Learned: Ensure consistency in the design and deployment of the risk management system. Lack of consistency is a critical risk in the RBT journey and meeting QMS objectives.

Resource: Read 'Risk Management In Successful Small Companies' Http://Insights.CERMacademy.Com/2013/09/24-Risk-In-Successful-Small-Companies-Adina-Suciu/

What are the critical questions to address in 'Evaluation'?

This focuses on deploying the risk management framework and evaluating effectiveness in your RBT journey.

Critical questions include:

- Is risk management performance and treatment measured?
- Are Key Risk Indicators (KRI's) periodically reviewed for suitability?
- Is risk management corrected if performance deviates from the business case, risk plan, or risk measures (KRI's)?
- Are risk treatment and controls periodically audited for effectiveness?

- Is risk management framework reviewed for effectiveness, efficiency, and economy?

Lesson Learned: Develop a plan to meet each requirement and add this to your business plan.

Resource: Read 'Magic Words And Enchanted Beans' Http://Insights.CERMacademy.Com/2013/09/23-Magic-Words-And-Enchanted-Beans-Mark-Moore/

What are critical questions to address in 'Continual Improvement'?

This focuses on improving the implementation of the risk management framework in your RBT journey.

Traditionally, quality focused on QMS processes. This was doable. The scope of the QMS was defined in a quality manual and other documentation.

The ISO 9001:2015 defines the limits or boundaries of the QMS as the quality component of the business processes. The challenge is to identify the critical quality components of business processes, which can incorporate many or almost all business processes.

The certified company needs to define the scope, limits, or boundaries of its QMS. Otherwise, the company will find itself boiling the ocean with extensive risk assessments that are not required in ISO 9001:2015.

Critical questions include:

- Are risk-controls evaluated and adjusted to changes in context or requirements?
- Are risk-controls adequate to the organization's risk assurance and risk appetite?
- Can the risk management framework and controls be improved?

- Are significant differences or gaps between actual and planned results evaluated?
- Is RBT adequately supported and applied in the organization?
- Is the risk management framework appropriate in terms of the context, capability and maturity of the organization?

Lesson Learned: Integrate your QMS, EMS, and other management systems into the organization's core business processes. Use RBT as the vehicle to move QMS into your organization's core processes.

Resource: Read 'Beyond PDCA - Continuous Improvement Best Practice'
Http://Insights.CERMacademy.Com/2014/11/69-Beyond-Pdca-Continuous-Improvement-Best-Practice-Greg-Carroll/

Who owns risk within the organization?

A quality adage is: "everyone is responsible for the quality of their work." This means that process owners are responsible for the quality of their work, including process inputs, process steps, and outputs.

Much in the same way, process owners are also responsible for the risk-controls of their processes, projects, and programs. This means all employees are risk owners or risk managers.

The understanding of risk ownership is a critical issue for ISO 9001 certified organizations. This has been an ongoing discussion in quality for the last half century. Most quality gurus and experts maintained everyone is responsible for quality. So, this begs the question, 'What is the role of the quality professional?' We are going to hear the same refrain regarding operational and supply chain risk management.

Lesson Learned: ISO 9001:2015 specifically focuses on the risk that inhibits achievement of QMS objectives. However, every organization seems to have quality objectives. In your business case, make it clear who is the owner of what ISO 9001:2015 QMS requirements.

Resource: Read 'The Moment Of Oh' Http://Insights.CERMacademy.Com/2013/04/13-The-Moment-Of-Oh-John-Blakinger-Greg-Ranstrom/

Who should lead the risk integration of ISO 31000:2018 with ISO 9001:2015?

This is one of the toughest questions in the book and is the reason we bring it up again. The common sense and obvious answer is the quality and operational organization. There are a lot of logical reasons for quality to take the lead. The quality organization knows ISO management systems, quality tools, and compliance requirements. The quality organization knows design, production, supply chain, and operational management. Many quality organizations have been working with ISO 9001 and have been certified since 1987. But?

The quality organization is getting into areas that it may not know well such as RBT, risk assessment, risk-controls, risk management, risk assurance, and ERM. Large organizations may already have extensive risk-controls probably using the COSO risk framework. They already have gone through the risk management battles within the organization and the supply base. They know what works and what does not. They know how to develop the business case for operational risk.

Then, the quality department comes along with ISO 9001:2015 and RBT. The quality organization may be fighting an uphill battle to own RBT because the organization already has a risk management or ERM system.

So in a larger organization, the political option may be to set up an ISO governance committee with influential stakeholders to guide the ISO 9001:2015 certification and RBT journey. Stakeholders would be engaged, resources would be approved, and there would be a higher probability of success.

Lesson Learned: Lean forward and raise your hand to lead the ISO 9001:2015 RBT journey. If you (quality) do not take the lead on RBT in operations, we guarantee Internal Audit, Engineering, or some other function will.

Resource: Read 'Tribal Knowledge - The Intentional Kind'
Http://Insights.CERMacademy.Com/2014/02/39-Tribal-Knowledge-Intentional-Kind-Mark-Moore/

How do you get support across the organization for ISO 9001:2015 risk deployment?

Quality function operates across the enterprise and into the supply chain. Many quality functions have been highly successful in obtaining support for ISO 9001 certification.

The value of implementing the new ISO 9001:2015 standard may be as simple as developing new RBT processes and passing a certification audit. Or, the value proposition may have to be explained to the Board of Directors, executive team, business unit managers and plant managers. This can be frustrating and consume much time. However, their buy in is critical for success.

Especially in large and complex organizations, the value of ISO 9001 certification, RBT, and risk management are fairly well understood. These organizations thrive in a very competitive environment where resources are constrained and managing quality, schedule, cost and scope performance are very critical. Any risks that hinder the achievement of performance outcomes (KRI's and KPI's) are well understood and quickly remediated.

Lesson Learned: The RBT journey is a political journey as much as a technical risk journey. Be aware of the organizational development challenges in implementing RBT.

Resource: Read 'Don't Hear What I'm Not Saying'
Http://Insights.CERMacademy.Com/2014/05/49-Dont-Hear-Im-Saying/

Is there a 'one size fits all' approach for RBT?

In the first ISO 9001 version of the standard, a company wanting to certify to ISO 9001 would find a generic quality manual off the web and tailor it to the organization. The 'one size fits all' quality manual was tailored to the organization and usually worked to secure certification.

The underlying concepts to ISO 9001:2015 make this approach more difficult. The new standard does not prescribe specific documentation. Certification evidence must be tailored to the organization.

Basically, what works for one organization regarding the risk assessment and risk-controls to assure the achievement of QMS objectives may not necessarily work for another. As well, what works for one plant may not work for a similar plant in a different country.

Bottom line: Tailor RBT and risk-controls to the organization and align with the organization's strategy.

Lesson Learned: Accreditors, CB's, certified companies, consultants, and other stakeholders are trying to understand RBT, risk assessment, and risk management. Understand RBT is also new territory for ISO standard developers.

Resource: Read 'Risk Based Thinking - No Problem'
Http://Insights.CERMacademy.Com/2014/11/67-Risk-Based-Thinking-Problem-T-Dan-Nelson/

Why do you need to scope the ISO 9001:2015 RBT and risk assessment?

This is one of the key questions in ISO 9001:2015 and it bear repeating. A key question will be how to evaluate the applicable risk areas that may inhibit meeting QMS objectives. The new standard can be scoped broadly or narrowly.

As a general observation, we advise companies to scope RBT and risk assessment narrowly for ISO 9001:2015 certification and broadly for internal improvement.

Our goal when working with client organizations is 'no surprises'. We have discovered the breadth and depth of RBT, risk assessment, or risk management should be based on organizational context, existing conditions, and known risk factors within the organization. This is a way to control scope in conducting the risk assessment and recommending a treatment or control strategy.

Lesson Learned: Keep the scope of the ISO 9001:2015 as narrow as possible. Otherwise, you will be overwhelmed by ISO risk requirements.

Resource: Read 'Building A Risk Inventory To Manage Project Risk' Http://Insights.CERMacademy.Com/2013/06/15-Building-A-Risk-Inventory-To-Manage-Project

What types of IT risk infrastructure is required for ISO 9001:2015?

Depending on the size of the ISO certified organization, product mix, locations, and other factors, the certified company may have to develop IT capabilities to track risks, treatment, and controls. Most current EQMS (enterprise Quality Management System) software does not have risk reporting capabilities.

Critical features and capabilities of IT risk infrastructure should include:

- Ability to tailor the software to different risk assessments such as those listed in ISO 31010 (see ISO 31010 list of risk assessment tools in Chapter 12).
- Ability to develop risk maps and other risk tools.
- Ability to replicate and scale its applications.
- Ability to curate and track ISO risk information.
- Ability to align with traditional eQMS software.

Lesson Learned: Identify your RBT and risk information requirements in the business case. You will be surprised how much risk data your organization and suppliers will generate.

Resource: Read 'How Secure Are Audits?'
Http://Insights.CERMacademy.Com/2014/12/73-Secure-Audits-Umberto-Tunesi/

Is there a point of diminishing return regarding investing in RBT, risk management, and ERM?

Yes. Many ISO 9001 certified organizations will be asking this question in preparation for ISO 9001:2015.

Why? The certified organization will conduct its risk assessment on the benefits and risks of certification. If the pain threshold is too high, the value proposition is too low, the cost benefit is not understood, the point of diminishing return for ISO certification will be reached quickly. When the company finds how much effort it will involve, companies may even drop their third-party certifications and self-certify to their customers.

Lesson Learned: It is critical that you develop a business case. Treat ISO 9001:2015 certification as an investment. Make sure the investment (upside risk) results in sufficient certification benefits.

Resource: Read 'Of Fires And Explosions On Trains And Boats'
Http://Insights.CERMacademy.Com/2013/07/2260/

Why should ISO 9001:2015 be project managed?

Depending on the size and complexity of the organization. ISO 9001:2015 initiative may become a major program within the enterprise. The project approach is the best way to establish project schedule, cost, and scope controls for a small company or plant level certification. Within a larger organization, we recommend setting up a Program Management Office (PMO).

If you work in a plant certified to ISO 9001, then ISO 9001:2015 certification can be project based using risk maps and other risk assessment tools to achieve certification. We usually do not recommend complex changes to certification for something that has worked well in the past. A project plan with a work breakdown may be sufficient.

On the other hand, if you work in a global, complex, integrated enterprise that has plants in many countries, then we suggest a programmatic approach to ISO 9001:2015 certification and RBT implementation.

Program or project management provides the requisite oversight, discipline, planning, and objectives for the integration of diverse RBT processes throughout the organization and into the supply chain. A Program Management Office (PMO) can ensure consistent risk taxonomy, framework, and syntax are developed. The PMO can ensure RBT, risk management, and ERM controls are consistently designed, deployed, and assured throughout the organization and supply chain. Also, risk design and deployment may be different among countries based on context, cultures, and business models, even within the same business unit.

The Program Management Office (PM0) develops the overarching risk taxonomy, framework, and syntax that will be required by the organization. To implement an operational and supply chain RBT, risk management, or ERM program, the PMO will have a number of responsibilities and accountabilities, Including:

- Supporting the ongoing efforts at the 1. Enterprise level; 2. Programmatic/Project/Process level; or 3. Product/Transactional level.
- Establishing and enforcing consistency for RBT and risk taxonomy throughout the organization.
- Project managing multiple risk initiatives within the ISO 9001:2015 certification framework.
- Operationalizing RBT within the context of an ISO 9001:2015 certification.

- Resourcing quality risk projects throughout the organization and supply chain.
- Track project risk milestones, costs, and quality implementation.

Lesson Learned: Manage your ISO 9001:2015 transition as a project or program. Develop a project plan for RBT and the transition to ISO 9001:2015. Use the plan for designing and deploying RBT in other families of ISO management system standards. Develop a business plan that includes project charter, work breakdown structure, transition risk, risk-controls, budget, schedule, and scope.

Resource: Read 'Five Rules for Project Success or Stop the Insanity' http://insights.cermacademy.com/2013/12/33-five-rules-project-success-stop-insanity-malcolm-peart/

Should the certified organization expand the focus of ISO 9001:2015 to include additional management system processes?

Depends on organizational context. The basic RBT framework described in this book can be used as the basis for deploying RBT in most management system standards.

Much discussion has appeared on the integration of ISO 14001 EMS, ISO 9001 QMS, and other management systems into an integrated business management system. Annex SL seems to be moving in that direction. This was a source of contention as ISO 9001:2015 went through its standard development process. QMS experts have advocated ISO 9001 should focus on a Business Management System as well as QMS. This still remains to be decided.

Lesson Learned: Integrate your QMS processes with other ISO management system processes. However, use common sense. If you are just starting your RBT journey, start small, stay localized, and gain success through low hanging fruit.

Resource: Read 'Basics: Project Risk Management'
Http://Insights.CERMacademy.Com/2014/12/71-Basics-Risk-Management-Rod-Farrar/

Will most companies adopt RBT to comply with ISO 9001:2015 requirements?

RBT is part of ISO 9001:2015. While we see the benefits of RBT, ISO 9001 certified companies will do the minimum to comply with ISO 9001:2015 requirements. Why? Most ISO 9001 certified companies are small to medium sized companies. They will invest in programs that are either required by contract or by statute. Anything else may be perceived as a non-value add to the organization.

In small or medium sized companies, everyone is busy and assumes different responsibilities. ISO 9001:2015 requirements may be confusing to the quality systems manager and to the organization. They will wonder about the value add and why they are pursuing registration.

Executive management must see the value in certification and the application of RBT throughout the organization. Otherwise, deployment will fail.

The benefits of ISO 9001:2015 must be clearly articulated in the business case. If management does not see its value then it will be treated like another project box that must be checked. ISO 9001:2015 benefits will not be realized.

Lesson Learned: Some quality consultants are already advocating that ISO 31000 is an ERM standard and they can move a company from RCMM Level 1 to Level 3 in six months. This is usually not possible.

Resource: Read 'Lean Risk Based Thinking'
Http://Insights.CERMacademy.Com/2014/09/57-Lean-Risk-Based-Thinking-Umberto-Tunesi/

What RBT opportunities do you foresee for the quality organization?

Bringing RBT into ISO 9001:2015 standard will create opportunities and challenges for the quality organization. Quality will have to develop a new language and processes to address RBT and risk requirements. Quality management will also have to address the following in the new ISO 9001:2015 standard:

- Develop new business policies along with its current QMS policies.
- Develop risk and RBT policies.
- Develop a risk vision, mission, and plans for the organization.
- Develop new risk knowledge, skills, and competencies within the quality organization.
- Develop new RBT reports addressing the risk of not meeting customer requirements and QMS objectives.
- Develop processes for the escalation of risks to the Board of Directors and executive management.
- Develop new problem solving methodologies to identify and assess risks.
- Develop IT systems for QMS and risk data capture, dissemination, escalation, and resolution.
- Develop performance measures such as Key Risk Indicators (KRI's).
- Develop organizational risk appetite at different levels of the organization such as 1. Enterprise level, 2. Programmatic/Project/Process level, and 3. Product/Transactional level.
- Ensure KRI's are appropriate for each business unit, process, project, and product.

- Establish risk boundaries and limits for quality throughout the organization.
- Ensure appropriate checks and balances for internal risk-controls are in place throughout the organization and supply chain but especially in high-risk areas.
- Develop the business case. Business case distills the rationale for certifying to ISO 9001:2015 and integrating risk into ISO 9001:2015 and other ISO management systems.

Lesson Learned: If possible, take the lead on the RBT and ISO 9001:2015 risk discussions. Be knowledgeable about risk. Be proactive in adopting and adapting risk to your organization. Develop risk based, problem solving and risk based, decision making methodologies in your organization. Address the above bullets in your business case.

Resource: Read 'Of Fires And Explosions On Trains And Boats'
Http://Insights.CERMacademy.Com/2013/07/2260/

What is a 'scenario test'?

A Level 2 RCMM organization is starting its risk management journey. The organization may want to know that if a black swan event occurred (low likelihood - high consequence), could the organization sustain and continue its business operations after the event? A scenario test is a process for assessing the adverse consequences of one or more possible events occurring simultaneously or serially. The event could be an earthquake that shuts down a single source supplier of a critical product. The event could be the loss of a critical customer.

Lesson Learned: Conduct a scenario test of a high risk event occurring. This will get management's attention and can be part of your business case.

Resource: Read 'Using Risk And Safety Analysis As Part Of The Requirements Process'

Http://Insights.CERMacademy.Com/2014/04/44-Using-Risk-Safety-Analysis-Part-Requirements-Process-Paul-Kostek/

What is a 'stress test'?

A Level 3 or higher RCMM organization has a mature and capable risk management system. Risk-controls and management have been in place for several years and are effective. A stress test is a process for measuring the adverse consequence if an event occurs on one or more operational factors, such as quality, supplier, design, cyber security, information technology, or people if an adverse event occurs. A stress test is similar to a scenario best to evaluate control effectiveness.

Lesson Learned: Stress testing is another great way to get management's attention. Conduct a stress test periodically on your high risk processes. If you do not have sufficient controls or risk management, reinforce your internal risk-controls.

Resource: Read 'International Quality And Risk Management'
Http://Insights.CERMacademy.Com/2014/02/40-International-Quality-Risk-Management-Julius-Hein/

Is ISO 9001:2015 RBT a change management process?

ISO 9001:2015 RBT is a change management process. Just think, RBT was not part of any management system a year ago. ISO 9001:2015 standard has a number of significant changes that will require new aptitudes and new ways of doing business.

One of the first activities the quality function will have to do is to create a process for building RBT awareness and developing buy in and acceptance of risk from quality stakeholders. Change management or sometimes called change enablement will be a significant element of your organization adopting and adapting to RBT.

Lesson Learned: Address 'hearts and minds' of critical stakeholders during the transition. This should be addressed in your business case.

Resource: Read 'Five Stages Of Engagement'
Http://Insights.CERMacademy.Com/2013/06/16-Five-Stages-Of-Engagement-John-Blakinger-Greg-Ranstrom/

CHAPTER 9:

EXECUTIVE MANAGEMENT

What is the key idea in this chapter?

The key idea in this chapter is operational risk-controls provide assurance to the Board of Directors, regulators, and financial shareholders that executive management is aware of operational (non-financial) risks and is managing them reasonably within the organization's risk appetite.

Why are you focusing on executive management and Board of Directors?

ISO 9001:2015 emphasizes the role of top management commitment to the QMS. Why? In previous versions of ISO 9001, a 'management representative' was designated to lead the QMS. When ISO was developed in 1987, this person was sometimes a director or even a vice president of quality. Over the years, this person and position has devolved sometimes into a glorified clerical function. Sad but true!

In the new ISO 9001:2015, 'top management shall demonstrate leadership and commitment' to the QMS. We read the intent is really 'executive management', who are company officers with a Vice President (VP) title or higher. Hence, we dedicated a chapter to 'Executive Management.'

The idea in ISO 9001:2015 is back to the original intent of ISO 9001, which was to have executive management actively promoting and supporting the QMS. So what does this really mean? Evidence of top management commitment can be:

- Integrating QMS into the business model and strategic plans.
- Considering QMS as a core business process.
- Accepting accountability for QMS effectiveness and appropriateness.
- Developing quality policies and quality objectives aligned with the strategic direction of the organization.
- Assuring quality policies are understood and consistently deployed.
- Assuring the alignment of QMS requirements with organizational vision, mission, and business core processes.
- Promoting the process management approach.
- Providing sufficient resources, such as people and monies, so the QMS can meet requirements and objectives.
- Promoting actively the QMS throughout the organization.
- Assuring the QMS can meet business objectives.
- Supporting continual improvement.

Lesson Learned: Executive management and executive support are absolutely essential for successful RBT deployment. Otherwise, there is a high probability the RBT journey will fail to meet its objectives.

Resource: Read 'Emperor's New Clothes Syndrome'
Http://Insights.CERMacademy.Com/2014/09/60-Emperors-New-Clothes-Syndrome-Malcolm-Peart/

Who are key quality risk stakeholders?

If you work for a large and complex organization that complies with Sarbanes Oxley or similar governance requirements, you already have robust risk management processes in operations and in supply management. You know who your risk stakeholders are.

The following stakeholder groups in your organization will be interested in RBT and how risk-controls are implemented:

- **Board of Director's Audit Committee:** Most publicly held companies have a Board level Audit Committee that provides risk oversight. Depending on the governance culture of the organization, the Audit Committee reviews material operational risks and requires assurance these risks are sufficiently controlled within the organization's risk appetite. The Audit Committee also provides input into the organization's risk appetite and sets the 'Tone at the Top' for the organization through an ERM system.

- **CEO:** CEO may chair the Board of Directors or have an independent operational role. In mature organizations, the CEO is the ultimate risk executive. This is often counter intuitive. Risk was often considered a tactical activity that was a responsibility of a lower level executive. In the new GRC framework, the CEO must consider the alignment of business objectives, identification of material risks, execution of risk-controls within the organization's risk appetite and review the suitability of risk assurance.

- **Chief Risk Officer (CRO):** This is relatively a new executive in many non-financial organizations. Banks have a CRO evaluating its overall risk position and credit risk. Since design flaws, quality recalls, and supply chain disruptions can have material impacts on the organization, CRO's will become more common in non-financial organizations.

Lesson Learned: Risk is becoming the common language of business. If you want to communicate with executive management, learn the language of risk.

Resource: Read 'Strategic Risk In The Enterprise' Http://Insights.CERMacademy.Com/2012/09/4-Strategic-Risk-At-The-Post-Office-Jim-Kline-Enterpriserisk/

What are key Risk Capability Maturity Model questions for executives?

Rarely have we seen risk-controls being applied uniformly across the enterprise. There are often pockets of risk management at various levels in the organization. Low level risk initiatives do not seem to be integrated into an enterprise framework or into enterprise strategy.

To evaluate RCMM operational effectiveness, we ask executives these 6 questions:

1. What does operational materiality mean to you?
2. What is your organization's risk appetite?
3. How do you measure risk appetite?
4. What type of operational risk assurance do you require?
5. How do you determine 'reasonable assurance' levels?
6. To whom are risks reported?

Answers to the above questions reveal quickly the operational Risk Maturity and Capability (RCMM) of the organization. The answers also indicate how effectively, how broad, and how deep the integration of operational risk management is within the enterprise.

Lesson Learned: Organizations are at different RCMM's. For most organizations, a low Level 2 RCMM should lead to ISO certification. However, understand the current RCMM of your organization because this will reveal what needs to be done to pursue the appropriate RCCM level.

Resource: Read 'Risk And Compliance' Http://Insights.CERMacademy.Com/2014/01/37-Risk-Compliance-Gary-Sikich/

What is 'governance'?

Governance is a process by which the Board of Directors reviews the decisions and actions of executive management. The purpose of good governance is to ensure applicable laws and regulations are complied with and corporate strategies are executed appropriately within the risk appetite of the organization. The hoped for result is business and QMS objectives can be achieved.

Effective corporate governance provides assurance to the investor community and other stakeholders that the organization complies with regulations, reports its performance in a fair and transparent fashion, conducts business ethically, and has a rock solid reputation. A company's reputation is reflected in its stock price. If a company's reputation is at risk, then it will diminish its brand equity and inevitably its stock price.

Lesson Learned: Governance is not a concept familiar to many operations, quality, and engineering professionals. Why? Financial governance has always been an executive or board level concern. This is now changing, as operational risks are more often a concern to the organization's executives and Board of Directors.

Resource: Read 'Governance And The Illusion Of Control' Http://Insights.CERMacademy.Com/2015/01/75-Governance-Illusion-Control-Howard-M-Wiener/

What is 'quality governance'?

Executive management is responsible for corporate risk based thinking; risk based, decision making; and risk based, problem solving. Now, QMS governance is implied with ISO 9001:2015. The standard requires more top management involvement and commitment. QMS and GRC seem to be implied and inferred throughout the standard.

Quality governance is a relatively new concept and incorporates the following key concepts:

- Board of Directors Audit Committee oversight of quality and operational issues.
- Development of enterprise quality management system and RBT policy.
- Definition of risk assurance and its implementation into the QMS.
- Executive management involvement with integrated risk management systems, which include QMS, EMS, and other management system processes.
- Development of a quality risk appetite.
- RBT support among executives and the Board.
- Top down communication of quality risk strategies and RBT tactics.

Lesson Learned: Understand concepts like GRC, ERM, RBT, and CSR since ISO will be directly or indirectly incorporating them into its families of standards over the next five years.

Resource: Read 'How to Use Strategic Imperative to Focus Corporate Risk Management'
http://insights.cermacademy.com/2014/08/55-use-strategic-imperatives-focus-corporate-risk-management-greg-carroll/

Is ISO 9001:2015 a quality governance model?

We heard this question a few months ago. We thought the Malcolm Baldrige National Quality Award (MBNQA) or the European Foundation for Quality Management (EFQM) Excellence Model would be more appropriate for a quality governance model.

Why was the question asked? In ISO 9001:2015, top management has increased responsibilities for supporting the QMS. A management representative is no longer required. Top management really cannot delegate critical QMS responsibilities.

ISO 9001 was developed to be a compliance and certification standard not an excellence or performance model. However, the ISO 9001:2015 standard implies Governance, Risk and Compliance (GRC) elements, which may be incorporated into future families of management system standards. They are already incorporated into ISO 26000, ISO's Corporate Social Responsibility standard. So, envision a future where we will have quality governance, safety governance, environmental governance, and so on.

Lesson Learned: ISO 9001:2015 may become a quality governance standard because of its incorporation of RBT and the importance of top management support.

Resource: Read 'Future Of Operations Management - GM 'Board Risk Committee'
Http://Insights.CERMacademy.Com/2014/12/71-Gm-Board-Risk-Committee-Greg-Hutchins/

What is the role of the Board of Directors regarding risk?

Most publicly listed companies whether they are on the New York Stock Exchange (NYSE) or London Stock Exchange (LSE) have an independent Board of Directors. This is often a requirement for a company to be listed on a particular exchange. The Board Audit Committee reviews the organization's policy regarding risk appetite, risk assessment, and risk-controls.

Among its responsibilities, the Board of Directors Audit Committee provides oversight over operational risk. The committee may also have a voice in expressing the requisite risk assurance and risk appetite for the organization.

Lesson Learned: If you work for a publicly listed company, then your organization has a Board of Directors Audit Committee. Understand what is critical to them in terms of material risk information about operations, suppliers, product development, or recalls. Then, align your reports and information in terms of their requirements.

Resource: Read 'GM Board Now Oversees Operational Risk' Http://Insights.CERMacademy.Com/2014/06/52-Gm-Board-Now-Oversees-Operational-Risk-Greg-Hutchins/

What does it mean to have an enterprise and business view of risk?

You are hearing the concept of ERM more often. ERM is advanced or mature RBT. ERM is becoming part of the ISO vocabulary. Global CB's are using this term in their certifications and even providing ERM certificates of conformance.

So, what is ERM? ERM is really a business and enterprise view of risks or sometimes called a portfolio view of risk management. Enterprise view of risk ensures a common approach, taxonomy, syntax, and methodology to managing risk. Why is this important to quality professionals? In a small ISO 9001:2015 certified organization, it should be fairly simple and straight forward to evaluate risks. A small organization will have common risk definitions and a standardized process for assessing risks.

The challenge with global, diversified organizations is they produce and service many products from many suppliers. Different users in the enterprise or supply chain may have different definitions of risk, risk assessment, risk - controls, and risk appetite. As well, different business units in different plants may have different business models depending on the countries in which they operate. Again variation away from a benchmark, objective, or standard is the equivalent of risk.

Lesson Learned: Understand and be able to articulate the enterprise and business view of quality, RBT, and your QMS. ISO 9001:2015 requires the QMS is aligned with the strategic direction and context of the organization.

Resource: Read 'Managing 21st Century Organizations' Http://Insights.CERMacademy.Com/2014/10/65-Managing-21st-Century-Organizations-Irm/

Why focus on the adoption of ERM in the development and deployment of ISO 9001:2015?

ERM gets executive management attention. The treatment and control of critical operational risks that are material and can impact financial reporting are a major source of concern to executive management and the Board of Directors.

Publicly held companies listed in NYSE, NASDAQ, or foreign exchanges have listing requirements. The stock exchange may strongly recommend or even require the listed company have an ERM system. If you can integrate ISO 9001:2015 and RBT into your organization's ERM system, there will be a higher inducement for executive management to approve funds for RBT and ISO 9001:2015 certification.

The underlying premise of ERM is that every enterprise, whether for profit, not for profit, or governmental body, exists to provide stakeholder value. All entities face uncertainty and the challenge for management is to determine how much uncertainty the enterprise is prepared to accept as it strives to grow stakeholder value (upside risk). Uncertainty presents both risk and opportunity, with the potential to erode or enhance value. ERM provides a framework for management to effectively deal with uncertainty and associated risk and opportunity and thereby enhance its capacity to build value.

If ISO 9001:2015 can be linked with ERM, then QMS, EMS, and other management systems can be reframed as a set of requirements or guidelines for a risk based, operational and supply management system.

Lesson Learned: RBT will move ISO management system standards toward ERM as they mature their RCMM processes. What do we mean? We may see RBT integrated into more management system standards. As certified companies mature, ERM will be part of QMS, EMS, etc.

Resource: Read 'Why Do We Fear Improvement?' Http://Insights.CERMacademy.Com/2014/06/51-Fear-Improvement-John-Dyer/

What is the Board of Directors Audit Committee?

The Board of Directors Audit Committee is interested in material risks that can impact the organization's financial statements. Quality does not normally report to the Board except dealing with regulatory compliance issues and potential exposures such as a product recall.

We are now seeing where product quality (or the lack of) can be a major risk to the organization, which can impact its reputation and brand equity. If an organization has a major recall that implies the organization cannot make quality products consistently or its products present a safety hazard. International newspapers will carry the story and speculate how a global firm with an impeccable record and strong brand equity could allow this to happen. Or in other words, it is a reflection of bad management and poor risk based, problem solving and poor risk based, decision making. The result inevitably is the loss in shareholder confidence in management's abilities, which may result in a selloff in the organization's stock. We call this brand equity dilution or market capital dilution.

The challenge for many QMS reports is they have been going to first and second level managers who may request Corrective Action or Preventive Action (CAPA). And, the reports stop at this level and specifically do not go to executive management for review.

In this book, we advocate material operational risks should be communicated to the Board of Directors Audit Committee for oversight and to executive management for discussion of possible treatment options. This is shown in the above figure.

Currently, ISO QMS reports go a Manager of System Auditing, a first or second level manager. We advocate QMS reports go solid line to the Chief Audit Executive who reports solid line to the Board of Director's Audit Committee.

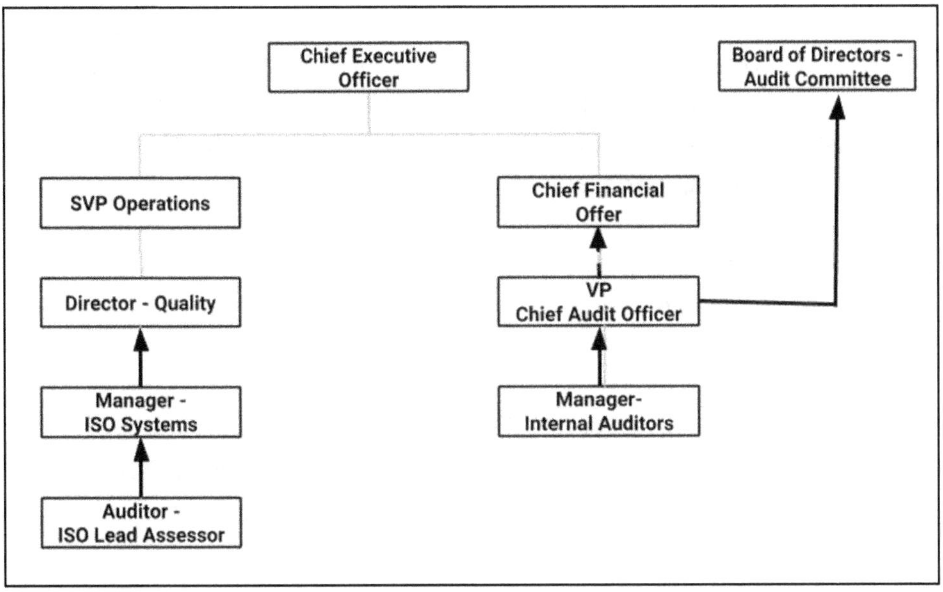

Figure 9: Reporting to Board

Lesson Learned: Frame your quality audit reports in terms of RBT, risk assessment, risk management and the organization's strategic objectives. They will go to a higher level of management and even to the Board of Directors.

Resource: Read '5 Principles That Connect CSR To The Corporate Risk Profile'
Http://Insights.CERMacademy.Com/2014/09/57-5-Principles-Connect-Csr-Th-Corporate-Risk-Profile-Kelly-Eisenhardt/

Will QMS reporting change with ISO 9001:2015?

The Board should discuss with senior quality management the state of the organization's QMS, EMS, ISMS, and other management systems. The Board does not want to be surprised by critical quality, environmental, and other types of risks. Executive management wants to know that appropriate operational risk-controls are in place and working properly within the risk appetite of the organization.

Very often, the root cause of a recurring problem is a systemic issue that can only be corrected by executive management action. Also, quality reports need to be escalated for resolution or at least communicated to executive management. The benefits of this reporting will include identification of risks; risk assessment; execution of risk treatment and controls; and the monitoring of risk performance.

Lesson Learned: Consolidate Quality Auditing with Internal Auditing so reports go to executive management and the Board of Directors. See Figure 9.

Resource: Read 'Why Risk Is Critical To Quality Management' Http://Insights.CERMacademy.Com/2014/09/60-Risk-Critical-Quality-Management-3-Functional-Ways-Paul-Leavoy/

What questions should the Board of Directors Audit Committee ask about operational risks?

The Board of the Directors Audit Committee provides oversight of risk-controls within the organization including operational and supply chain risks. Audit Committee is especially interested in:

- Assessing risks that may result from statutory noncompliance or product recall.
- Assessing supply chain risks where the supplier disruption can result in a plant shut down that may impact the company's financial statements.
- Understanding the consequences of the risk assessment and plans to mitigate process and product risks.
- Understanding the results of QMS controls and risk assessment implications to financial reporting.
- Ensuring the repeatability and scalability of the ISO RBT process.
- Assuring the alignment of ISO, QMS, and financial risk management frameworks and processes.

Lesson Learned: Review with executive management the type and extent of operational controls and QMS reporting to the Board.

Resource: Read 'Creatively Build A Risk Intelligent Culture' Http://Insights.CERMacademy.Com/2014/10/61-Creatively-Build-Risk-Intelligent-Culture-Apqc/

What are common management risk reports?

Common risk reports include:

- Environmental scan of geopolitical, social, supply chain, environmental, etc. risks.
- Value at Risk (VAR) reports of investments and potential exposures (upside risk) to the balance sheet and profit loss statements.
- Scenario analyses reviewing macro variables or inherent variables to the company's competitive situation.
- Review of business model effectiveness at the 1. Enterprise level; 2 Programmatic/Project/Process level; 3 Product/Transactional level.
- Dashboard of risks at the 3 levels identified in the previous bullet.
- Exception reporting at the three levels.
- Dashboard of enterprise risks broken down by geography, business unit, product group, market segment, etc.
- Prioritization of 2 best/worst performing investments (upside risk) and treatment plans.
- Project variance reports for scope, change orders, schedule, quality, and cost.
- Corrective Action and Preventive Action (CAPA) reporting.
- Risk assurance audits and assessment reporting.

- Review of operational improvement projects such as lean, Six Sigma, risk management, etc.

Lesson Learned: Discuss risk reporting requirements, risk appetite, and risk assurance with your management and determine what they want in terms of reporting.

Resource: Read 'Quality Executives Should Be Able To Answer These Questions'
Http://Insights.CERMacademy.Com/2013/06/19-Responses-To-Questions-Quality-Executives-Should-Answer-Greg-Hutchins/

What are key questions about risk reporting?

Most quality reporting has been to a first or second level manager. We believe the changes in ISO 9001:2015 will require new reporting relationships and reporting new types of information. The reporting of information will ensure the transparency and full disclosure of QMS control effectiveness.

A number of questions will arise including:

- Who are the risk information stakeholders?
- What types of reports do the risk stakeholders require?
- What level of data should be reported (i.e. Enterprise level; Programmatic/Process/Project level; and/or Product/Transactional level)?
- What types of risk information should be reported?
- What types of risk data from quality are available and can be gathered for reporting?
- Who should receive this information?
- How often should reports be developed?
- How will the reports be used in terms of risk treatment?

- How granular should reports be (i.e. risk-control granularity)?

Lesson Learned: Frame quality audits in terms of RBT and risk-control effectiveness. Executive management will pay more attention to quality audits and reports.

Resource: Read "The 'Risk Culture' Myth" Http://Insights.CERMacademy.Com/2014/06/52-Risk-Culture-Myth-Greg-Carroll/

What types of risk-controls does executive management require?

So, what does appropriate risk-controls mean? As a result of ISO 9001:2015, the quality organization will be establishing risk-controls and risk treatment plans similar to those found in other parts of the organization. Quality will develop processes to manage and reduce QMS risks to an acceptable level. Without a formal process, the quality organization will remain ad hoc and more reactive (low level RCMM) instead of proactive (high level RCMM) regarding controlling QMS risk across the organization.

A major challenge for quality and other operational functions will be adapting to the new requirements of ISO 9001:2015 dealing with new types of controls and broadening the scope of the standard. RBT capabilities in operations will have to be architected, designed, deployed, and assured. Risk-control capabilities will have to be defined and documented so they are repetitive, managed, and scalable.

Lesson Learned: Start discussions with executive management on QMS risk-controls, risk treatment, and risk reporting. If you understand and can satisfy executive management's requirements, they will reciprocate with QMS support and RBT commitment.

Resource: Read 'How To Use Strategic Imperatives To Focus Corporate Risk Management' Http://Insights.CERMacademy.Com/2014/08/55-Use-Strategic-Imperatives-Focus-Corporate-Risk-Management-Greg-Carroll/

Can you give examples of financial agencies requiring risk management?

Standard & Poor's (S&P) is an international rating agency. It is currently using ERM to evaluate a company's credit rating, which is its ability to handle risk. Globalization has created many challenges and risks that need to be mitigated. S&P decided to focus explicitly on ERM recognizing that accounting numbers alone do not reflect a company's credit worthiness or its profitability.

S&P currently looks at the following broad areas of ERM: 1. Strategic risk management and 2. Risk management culture. Strategic risk management involves managerial decision making and problem solving. Risk management culture involves Tone at the Top and internal control effectiveness throughout the organization.

Lesson Learned: Google and download the S&P ERM requirements and use them as a guide for your management system controls (Level 2 and 3 RCMM).

Resource: Read 'Regulations Vary Worldwide But Risk Management Is Common Denominator'
Http://Insights.CERMacademy.Com/2014/02/39-Regulations-Vary-Worldwide-Risk-Management-Common-Denominator-Cindy-Fazzi/

What is the relationship of ISO 9001:2015 with the Sarbanes Oxley Act of 2002?

Most public companies in the United States and in many parts of the world use COSO Internal Control - Integrated Framework to comply with Sarbanes Oxley or similar financial requirements. The U.S. Securities and Exchange Commission (SEC) endorses a risk based approach to evaluating Internal Control over Financial Reporting, cyber security, and operations.

There are no specific laws that require an organization to integrate ISO QMS to comply with Sarbanes Oxley Act or to comply with applicable laws and regulations. Sarbanes Oxley compliance focuses on reliable public, financial reporting to ensure investor confidence in the organization. Developing reasonable operational and supply management risk-controls should provide equivalent investor confidence in the organization.

In a number ways, ISO 9001:2015 harmonizes with Sarbanes Oxley. While Sarbanes Oxley focuses on Internal Control over Financial Reporting, ISO 9001:2015 focuses on internal control over QMS reporting.

ISO 9001:2015 can provide executive management with similar confidence and assurance that operations and supply chain internal controls are in place and effective.

Lesson Learned: Most countries have governance requirements. In the U.S., Sarbanes Oxley Act specifies requirements for financial risk reporting. Many countries have similar statutes that deal with Corporate Social Responsibility (CSR), Governance, Risk, Compliance (GRC), and Enterprise Risk Management (ERM). All of these initiatives involve risk-controls.

Resource: Read 'Dodd-Frank Conflict Minerals Reporting Deadline Nears No Escape For Retailers And Brands'
Http://Insights.CERMacademy.Com/2014/03/43-Dodd-Frank-Conflict-Minerals-Reporting-Deadline-Nears-Escape-Retailers-Brands-Kelly-Eisenhardt/

Is ERM part of good governance?

ERM (high RCMM organizations) is a critical element of good governance. ERM strengthens board oversight, ensures executive management controls over enterprise risks, and evaluates the effectiveness of internal controls to mitigate these risks.

The Board of Directors has traditionally focused on financial risks and balance sheet issues. Following Sarbanes Oxley, risk management became more strategic, specifically focusing on ERM. It first focused on the Internal Control over Financial Reporting then migrated to IT controls, which facilitated the compilation of financial information. Over the last 5 years, Internal

Control over Financial Reporting has stabilized. There are now fewer financial reporting risks. Organizational risk exposure now consists of operational, cyber, product development, and supply chain risks.

Lesson Learned: Understand how RBT controls, risk treatment, and ISO 9001:2015 certification are going to fit with your organization's financial reporting.

Resource: Read 'No One Is Really Applying ERM And I Think It's A Good Thing!'
Http://Insights.CERMacademy.Com/2014/12/73-One-Really-Applying-ERM-Think-Good-Thing-Alexei-Sidorenko/

How does ERM fit into Corporate Social Responsibility (ISO 26000)?

Customer requirements include good CSR, sustainability, ethics, and good governance throughout the extended organization and into the supply chain. The risk of exposure to bad publicity is increasing in the global marketplace. Using child or prison labor in a third-tier supplier can tarnish a company's brand equity so that social media can pick it up and stock prices will deflate 20% or 30% or more due to the unfavorable publicity. These additional responsibilities impose higher levels of due diligence for the organization, which increase the need for ERM.

CSR has a strong risk focus. The rationale for ERM is straightforward, which is to provide value to all stakeholders. Internal controls and documentation have to support the ERM system. The question then becomes how much risk can or should an organizational assume? This depends on the risk appetite and risk tolerance of the organization.

Lesson Learned: Understand how RBT will impact ISO 26000. More management system standards will incorporate RBT or some form of risk-controls.

Resource: Read '10 CSR Risks That Could Kill Your Brand' Http://Insights.CERMacademy.Com/2014/07/54-10-Csr-Risks-Kill-Brand-Kelly-Eisenhardt/

Can you provide an example of a major company that has elevated operational risk to the board level?

Many companies looked at operations, design, quality, and supply management as stable and capable processes that required little or no executive oversight. The challenge is Six Sigma, Total Quality Management, and other operational excellence initiatives leaned operations to the point where there was little flexibility or buffer. As companies leaned out, a possible disruption or slip could create additional variability because there were fewer buffers resulting in higher risks. So, many lean and Six Sigma companies must now address added risks.

Let us look at a recent story of GM. GM elevated operational risk management to the board level. General Motors in the United States had a major recall over defective ignition switches. More than 2.6 million autos were recalled. And unfortunately the defective switch was linked to accidents that may have killed at least 13 people.

As a result, the GM Board formed an operational risk committee to oversee vehicle safety, cyber security, and product quality. The GM Board committee now oversees operational risk management and product quality because it understands how the lack of adequate risk-controls can result in recalls, which can diminish the company's reputation and lower its market capitalization.

Board oversight of operational and supply risks provides risk assurance to investors and other critical stakeholders that executive management knows how to develop, protect, and sustain enterprise value. GM's oversight of operational risk-controls also helps ensure continual improvement of its operational capabilities to meet customer requirements and comply with regulations.

The value proposition of ISO 9001:2015 and RBT is they provide a management system framework, processes, and tools to effectively evaluate and ultimately manage operational uncertainties. Also, RBT ensures critical QMS risk issues are properly communicated to the right organizational level. If the Board has inadequate information and knowledge of operational and supply chain risks, the result will be lower uncertainty. The goal is to integrate RBT, risk management, and ERM into the organizational DNA, specifically into its operational and supply chain decision making and problem solving processes.

Lesson Learned: Understand your Board's requirements about reporting operational and supply chain risks. Risk management has become a core competency for all operations professionals.

Resource: Read "GM's Elephant On The Shop Floor"
Http://Insights.CERMacademy.Com/2014/08/55-Gms-Elephant-Shop-Floor-William-Levinson/

What is General Motors's Board risk charter?

The purpose of GM's risk committee is to:

> "Assist and actively advise the Board in fulfilling its oversight responsibilities with regard to a) management's identification, evaluation, and treatment of major strategic operating risks inherent in the business that could materially impact the Company's reputation and/or operating results …"[xvii]

In performing its risk oversight and review responsibilities, GM's risk committee may review with management, and take action on the following:

- "The Company's risk governance framework.
- Setting the tone and developing a culture within the Company regarding risk, promoting open risk discussion, and promoting integration of risk management into the Company's processes and goals.

- The Company's risk tolerance, risk identification, assessment and risk management practices for strategic operating risks, and the guidelines, policies and processes for risk assessment and risk management.
- The evaluation by management of strategic operating risks the Company faces including any risk concentrations, the likelihood of occurrence, the potential impact of those risks, the mitigating measures, and the types and levels of risk which are acceptable in the pursuit and protection of value.
- The strategic operating risks identified in the Risk Report, designating some or all of those risks to be subject to the Committee's oversight and reviewing them for such period of time determined by the Committee, and informing the Designated Executive of such designations.
- The Company's processes and procedures established to address the strategic operating risks identified by the Committee for oversight and review, which may include, but is not limited to, operating aspects related to ensuring vehicle development safety and security, evaluating and improving product quality, ensuring employee and other persons' health and safety at all facilities, improving Company and vehicle cyber security, protecting the Company's access to and right to use key intellectual property ("IP"), managing the supply chain, logistics and country level operating risks, managing supplier and labor relations, ensuring crisis preparedness and disaster recovery capability, and responding to any other strategic operating risk identified in the Risk Report and subject to the Committee's oversight and review.
- Management's implementation of the risk policies and procedures reviewed with management to assess their effectiveness.
- Reports and presentations received from management, including as appropriate the Designated Executive and members of the Executive Leadership Team or any other officers or other employees of the Company, independent auditors, internal auditors, legal

counsel and other outside experts regarding risks the Company faces and the Company's risk assessment and management.

- Other matters as the Chair or other members of the Committee determine relevant to the Committee's oversight of strategic operating risk assessment and management."[xviii]

Lesson Learned: Operational risk committee charters are becoming common place. ISO management system reports should go to this committee. Interestingly, GM has probably adopted COSO as its risk framework.

Resource: Read 'Bad Risk Management Decisions Made By Executives' Http://Insights.CERMacademy.Com/2013/03/Call-For-Examples-Bad-Risk-Management-Decisions-Made-By-Executives/

What is General Electric's Board risk charter?

The GE Board adopted the following risk charter:

1. "To review and discuss with management the Company's risk governance structure, risk assessment and risk management practices and the guidelines, policies and processes for risk assessment and risk management.

2. To review and discuss with management the Company's risk appetite and strategy relating to key risks, including credit risk, liquidity and funding risk, market risk, product risk and reputational risk, as well as the guidelines, policies and processes for monitoring and mitigating such risks.

3. To discuss with the Company's Chief Risk Officer, and GE Capital's Chief Risk Officer, the Company's and GE Capital's risk assessment and risk management guidelines, policies and processes, as the case may be. The committee shall meet separately at least twice a year with the Company's Chief Risk Officer and GE Capital's Chief Risk Officer.

4. To receive, as and when appropriate, reports from the Company's corporate audit staff and GE Capital's Internal Audit function on the results of risk management reviews and assessments.

5. To review the status of financial services regulatory exams relating to the Company and GE Capital, as applicable.

6. To approve the appointment and, when and if appropriate, replacement of the Company's Chief Risk Officer and GE Capital's Chief Risk Officer, each of whom shall have a reporting relationship with the committee.

7. To review disclosure regarding risk contained in the Company's Annual Report on Form 10-K and Quarterly Reports on Form 10-Q.

8. To review reports on selected risk topics as the committee deems appropriate from time to time.

9. To discharge any other duties or responsibilities delegated to the committee by the board.[xix]

Lesson Learned: Risk assessment and risk management are the responsibility of the GE's management. The Board risk committee has an oversight role to review the suitability of risk-controls.

Resource: Read 'Regulations Vary Worldwide But Risk Management Is Common Denominator'
Http://Insights.CERMacademy.Com/2014/02/39-Regulations-Vary-Worldwide-Risk-Management-Common-Denominator-Cindy-Fazzi/

Will ISO 9001:2015 improve executive management perceptions of quality?

ISO 9001:2015 specifies top management involvement. The challenge is that quality in a number of organizations is no longer an executive function. Executive management does not understand ISO 9001:2015 language and concepts. There may be exceptions, but we are reasonably sure of this assertion.

Lesson Learned: If ISO wants top management support of RBT, QMS, EMS, and other management systems then quality should understand the COSO risk management framework and learn its risk language.

Resource: Read 'Why Shifting To Conscious Leadership Supports Sustainability'
Http://Insights.CERMacademy.Com/2015/01/75-Shifting-Conscious-Leadership-Supports-Sustainability-Kelly-Eisenhardt/

How does the quality organization learn the language of executive management and the Board of Directors?

Tough question! There is no easy answer.

People and professions are resistant to change. The prevailing thinking is that 'this too shall pass.' This is simply human. People believe what has worked effectively for a number of years is fine. Why change what is working well? The quality profession believes this in terms of ISO 9001 and other management systems. Over a million companies are certified to ISO 9001. No one can argue with success.

Well, times change. Quality and ISO management systems are changing and incorporating RBT and risk. The quality organization needs to move from product level tools to the enterprise risk perspective. Hence, the reason why we advocate risk management and ERM.

Lesson Learned: Learn the language of executive management. Frame your quality, QMS, and ISO 9001 reports in terms of executive language, which is more often RBT and ERM based.

Resource: Read 'Reading The Risk Tea Leaves'
Http://Insights.CERMacademy.Com/2014/01/36-Reading-Risk-Tea-Leaves-Betty-Kildow/

What can you do if executive management does not see the value in ISO 9001:2015 certification?

For a number of years, ISO 9001 QMS has been isolated and even marginalized in some organizations. We passionately believe ISO 9001:2015 is a business management system that incorporates value added, quality and risk-control concepts.

Executive management support is critical to the effective functioning of ISO 9001. Without it, there will be the continuing discussion about the value of QMS and ISO 9001 certification. We want to move forward.

One quality consultant promotes the standard in terms of a business risk management system. This is a smart way to frame ISO 9001:2015. We believe there will be more organizational acceptance of the new ISO 9001:2015 standard if it is accepted as part of a business management system with risk-controls.

Lesson Learned: Integrate your RBT and QMS into your organization's core processes and strategic direction. If necessary, rebrand your QMS into a business management system.

Resource: Read 'Risks Of (Excessive) Quality'
Http://Insights.CERMacademy.Com/2014/05/50-Risks-Excessive-Quality-Umberto-Tunesi/

Why do you focus on executive management when it does not apply to me?

"I work for a small company. We do not have a Board of Directors. The discussion of Board of Directors does not apply to me or my organization."

ISO 9001:2015 and the new ISO management system standards now emphasize 'top management' engagement and buy in. Executive management wants to know what future events may be disastrous it terms of impacting its ability to achieve its profit and quality objectives. And if a Black Swan event occurs, how resilient and capable is the organization to ensure business continuity and customer satisfaction?

The above questions provide a powerful inducement for the organization to adopt RBT in its operations and supply chain - even in a small organization.

Lesson Learned: Tailor the business case to your organization's executive management. Their support is crucial to your success.

Resource: Read 'Selling Your Ideas Up: How To Overcome Objections And Get Your Ideas Approved'
Http://Insights.CERMacademy.Com/2014/06/52-Selling-Ideas-Overcome-Objections-Get-Ideas-Approved-Daniel-Burras/

CHAPTER 10:

NEW QUALITY ORGANIZATION

What is the key idea in this chapter?

The key idea in this chapter is the quality organization is going to be reinvented. More statutes require risk management or ERM. ISO 9001:2015 is adopting RBT. And as more companies have risk reporting requirements, quality and other operational departments will adopt risk responsibilities and accountabilities. These will require new knowledge, skills, and abilities.

Will there be resistance to the idea of a 'New Quality Organization?'

Yes. Quality Management Thinking (QMT) is the quality equivalent to RBT. QMT is an amalgam of quality control, quality assurance, and quality management. QMT has focused on consistency, customer satisfaction, and control of variation. It has worked well for more than 50 years. So, why change to RBT?

We have heard from operations and quality professionals something along the following: "We in quality have been doing risk management since the days of Deming. RBT is nothing new. It is still quality. Risk management and RBT shall pass and have no consequence on the quality profession or on me."

Lesson Learned: Be prepared. You do not have to lose your quality focus, just give risk a more prominent role. Remember, more ISO management system standards will incorporate risk.

Resource: Read 'Risk Management And Fear'
Http://Insights.CERMacademy.Com/2012/09/Risk-And-The-Boogeyman/

Why do you think there will be a new quality organization?

RBT. ERM. GRC. CSR. Each of these acronyms will add new requirements and responsibilities on the quality organization. If you have been reading this book from front to back, you will recognize these acronyms.

Many quality organizations may not accept that a new quality organization and even a new quality paradigm may have to be designed. Again, we have heard something like this: "Our quality organization has been around for years (add appropriate number here) and will continue doing what it has been doing very well. Thank you." OK.

Yes, you are right. The quality function has been efficient and effective. However, the above acronyms come with risk requirements. Just think how RBT will impact your ISO 9001:2015 direction, objectives, function, priorities, and outcomes. We are the founding writers of ASQ's 'Career Corner'. Our message from the first day is that all professions are changing and incorporating risk including quality.

We are concerned about the future of the quality profession. We believe as quality has matured, risk will become the critical element of the profession.

Lesson Learned: Plan on integrating risk into your quality function. Start with the business case discussed earlier. RBT and risk assessment in ISO 9001:2015 are just the first ISO risk drivers you will see in the next five years.

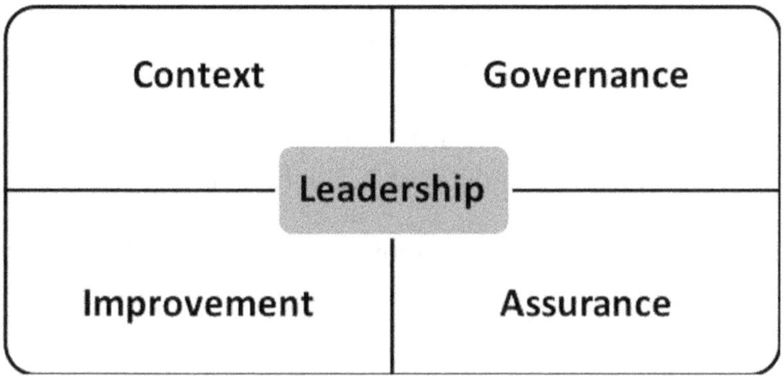

Figure 10: ***CQI Governance Model***

Resource: Read 'New Quality Management Paradigm' Http://Insights.CERMacademy.Com/2014/08/56-New-Quality-Management-Paradigm-Greg-Hutchins-Dick-Gould/

Is there a model for the new quality organization?

The UK based Chartered Quality Institute (© CQI) issued a report called 'The Quality Profession: Driving Organizational Excellence.' CQI developed a Competency Framework shown on the next page that provides an overview of the competencies required by the quality profession. This may be the model for the New Quality Organization. The framework is designed to:

- Provide benchmarks for employer and individual competence.
- Help quality professionals plan their career development.
- Help employers develop their competency framework.
- Establish requirements for CQI learning and development.
- Share with the world the competency framework.[xx]

The CQI vision for the quality profession has three critical elements:

- **Good governance.** Ensuring customer and stakeholder interests are understood and satisfied.

- **Agile assurance.** Establishing methodologies to protect and enhance a company's reputation through the treatment of risk.

- **Evaluation and improvement.** Transforming ways of working to maximize effectiveness and eliminate unnecessary cost and waste.[xxi]

Lesson Learned: Download the CQI framework at:
http://www.thecqi.org/PageFiles/11844/Competency_Framework.pdf

Resource: Read 'Five Mistakes Leaders Make When Hiring'
Http://Insights.CERMacademy.Com/2014/09/59-Five-Mistakes-Leaders-Make-Hiring-Elizabeth-Lions/

What are the key elements of the CQI Competency Framework?

The key elements of the CQI framework include:

- **Context.** Is the overarching concept to provide effective implementation of governance, assurance, and improvement.

- **Governance.** Ensures organizational resources are managed properly within the risk appetite of the organization. Board provides oversight of quality, which is where it should be.

- **Assurance.** Consists of a culture where processes, policies, and procedures are consistent with the organization's context, governance, risk-controls, and risk appetite.

- **Leadership.** Consists of behaviors to design a culture of evaluation and improvement.

- **Improvement.** Emphasizes a culture of evaluation and improvement to encourage effective, economic, efficient, and agile methods of working.

Lesson Learned: The purpose of the framework is to create a "world with quality at the heart of every organization." The UK Chartered Quality Institute (CQI) framework may point to the future of quality and other operational excellence professions.

Resource: Read 'Four Key Questions For Quality Executives' Http://Insights.CERMacademy.Com/2013/07/18-Four-Key-Questions-For-Quality-Executives-Greg-Hutchins/

What is CQI's vision of quality governance?

CQI quality governance is a relatively new concept that is implied in ISO 9001:2015. While it is not explicitly stated, it is implied in the Leadership section of the standard. Quality governance is the alignment of quality management, quality assurance, and quality control with the strategic direction of the organization.

Quality governance is a Board concept that would address CSR, ethics, and other actions that can impact the organization. Quality governance provides assurance to investors and other key stakeholders that the organization conducts its affairs with integrity, transparency, fairness, and reports its performance in a fair manner.

The Board of Directors evaluates quality governance in terms of overseeing quality decisions and actions of executive management including applicable compliance with laws and regulations that address quality.

ISO 9001:2015 seems to be adding a new level of risk assurance and scrutiny into the organization when it incorporates RBT and the achievement of QMS objectives into the standard.

Lesson Learned: Integrate the CQI concepts of quality governance into your business case for ISO 9001:2015 and RBT. Quality governance has an integral role in ISO 9001:2015 and QMS deployment.

Resource: Read 'Managing Unknown Unknowns' Http://Insights.CERMacademy.Com/2014/11/66-Managing-Unknown-Unknowns-Kiron-Bondale/

How will quality add value in the CQI framework?

According to the CQI report, the quality professional in the New Quality Organization will provide value by adopting the following leadership roles: quality advocate, stakeholder advocate, systems thinker, fact based thinker, quality planner, quality coach, quality motivator, and quality coordinator.

In terms of governance, the quality professional will represent the interests of shareholders, customers, and other stakeholders. The quality professional will provide both business (internal) and supply chain assurance (external). The quality professional will contribute to operational improvement by gathering insights, evaluating measures/results, and implementing change.

Lesson Learned: At the end of the day, quality professionals must add value. The CQI framework is a good to great vision of the quality organization that can be incorporated into your business case.

Resource: Read 'Reframing Risk' Http://Insights.CERMacademy.Com/2012/05/Reframing-In-Risk/

Are quality professionals already risk professionals?

The essence of ISO risk is the uncertainty of meeting QMS objectives. You can think of this as the variation, variance, or variability away from a QMS target, specification, or standard. This is also the basis for Statistical Process Control (SPC) and Six Sigma.

In a number of ways, quality professionals are already risk professionals at the product and transactional level. Quality professionals understand variation. Variation is a state of nature, whether in business, economic behavior, and business. Variation around a business objective, specification target, or process objective is the general condition of many management, business, quality, and project processes. Variation outside of a specification, business, or process control limits represents uncertainty and a risk event waiting to occur. In fact, variation outside of specification limits is a risk or nonconformance already occurring.

Let us look a little deeper at some risk and quality parallels:

- **Statistical Process Control (SPC) is an example of risk-control**. Variation can be detected, measured, and controlled. Risk can be defined as a variance or distance from a business objective, metric, or standard, all of which indicate risk is waiting to occur or already has occurred. For example, quality that can be specified in terms of a dimensional tolerance or a surface finish is a variable that can be risk-controlled and risk assured. If a target product dimension can be kept in the middle of the specification spread and the variation of measurements are distributed inside the specification limits and process control limits, then the risk of a hazardous event or a nonconforming product can be controlled.

- **Reliability is long term quality or risk.** Look at reliability metrics, such as Mean Time Between Failures (MTBF) and Mean Time to First Failure (MTTF), both of which can be considered probabilistic risk concepts.

- **Corrective Action and Preventive Action (CAPA) is risk oriented.** Corrective action is finding and fixing the problem at its source. Preventive action is ensuring the problem does not recur, which is a form of risk treatment.

- **Six Sigma is a risk methodology.** The Six Sigma methodology to define, measure, analyze, improve, and control (DMAIC) is fundamentally a RBT and risk management methodology.

Lesson Learned: So, think about it for a second. You are already a risk manager.

Resource: Read 'Process Approach In C Major' Http://Insights.CERMacademy.Com/2014/05/49-Process-Approach-C-Major-T-Dan-Nelson/

Should the organization incorporate risk into its QMS or the QMS into an existing risk management system?

We anticipate ISO certified organizations will be struggling with this question. The simple answer is to incorporate risk into the QMS, which is what ISO 9001:2015 calls for. One key is to build risk-controls into existing quality management, quality assurance, and quality control processes and capabilities.

A more complex answer may entail taking into account the organization's risk maturity, risk capabilities, business model, culture, risk appetite, size, complexity of products, regulatory environment, legal exposures, etc.

For smaller organizations that want to simply certify to ISO 9001:2015, they can integrate RBT into their existing quality structure, capabilities, and resources. The quality organization may develop processes to identify quality objectives, identify risks, prioritize risks, assign risk owners, analyze gaps, compare gaps to risk appetite, remediate (mitigate) risks, and monitor results.

However larger and more complex ISO 9001 certified organizations may be adopting COSO and ERM and will want RBT to be incorporated into its mature RCMM processes. This is OK. RBT is a low level RCMM. The decision between low maturity risk systems (Level 1 RCMM) and more mature risk systems (Level 3 or higher RCMM) will be a decision that may be based on the organization's risk appetite and acceptance.

Lesson Learned: Be flexible. If your organization already has an ERM system, then the smart political move is to integrate RBT into the ERM system. That is OK. We have seen this with quality and lean responsibilities. Quality is no longer the owner of quality. Manufacturing is no longer the owner of lean.

Resource: Read 'The Process Of Risk Management' Http://Insights.CERMacademy.Com/2013/08/21-The-Process-Of-Risk-Management-Linda-Westfall/

What are critical risk issues to address in developing RBT?

ISO wants ISO 9001 QMS to be mainstreamed into an organization's critical business processes. Throughout this book, we suggest this is done through some form of RBT, risk assessment, risk management, or ERM progression.

RBT needs to be architected, designed, deployed, and assured. These are common issues to be addressed:

- Ensure consistent interpretation of RBT, specifically risk based, problem solving and risk based, decision making.
- Architect the operational risk system addressing QMS processes so they are integrated with the organization's strategic risk management process.
- Integrate operational and ISO RBT and risk processes throughout the quality organization.
- Align the quality organization with ISO 9001:2015 RBT and risk objectives.
- Develop quality Key Performance Indicators (KPI's) and Key Risk Indicators (KRI's) that are designed to measure critical quality and risk performance.
- Assure RBT and risk assessment are understood and embraced by key quality managers.
- Ensure RBT and risk roles, responsibilities, and abilities are properly understood in quality.
- Design and deploy a consistent RBT and risk process in the quality

organization.

- Ensure effective documentation describes process stability, capability, and continuous improvement.
- Assure continuous monitoring of RBT and risk information within the organization.
- Escalate to decision makers the critical material risks that can impact quality objectives and public safety.

Lesson Learned: Address the above issues in a logical, effective, and efficient manner. We have seen an ad hoc approach to deploying risk. It becomes costly and ineffective. Plan is not a four letter word in this case.

Resource: Read 'Building A Reliability Culture' Http://Insights.CERMacademy.Com/2015/01/76-Building-Reliability-Culture-Fred-Schenkelberg/

What is required of the new Chief Quality Executive?

CQI Competency Framework is a good starting point to answering this question. The new quality executive will have the following attributes:

- Ability to think strategically and globally.
- Understand how RBT, risk management, and ERM can be used to compete globally.
- Excellent language skills in both the native language and other languages.
- Experience operating internationally.
- Ability to work with all levels of management and report quality risks and exposures to the Board of Directors Audit Committee.

Lesson Learned: Create a new career path for yourself and your quality organization as new ISO families adopt RBT

Resource: Read 'Quality Executives Should Be Able To Answer These Questions'
Http://Insights.CERMacademy.Com/2013/06/19-Responses-To-Questions-Quality-Executives-Should-Answer-Greg-Hutchins/

What critical risk questions should the quality organization ask?

Risk ownership, accountability, and authority are critical to the New Quality Organization. Critical questions to ask include:

- Who architects, designs, deploys, and assures the RBT management system?
- Who identifies critical 1. Enterprise level, 2. Programmatic/Project/Process, and 3. Product/Transactional risks?
- Who is the owner of RBT processes that span an organization?
- Who decides risk acceptance thresholds within quality?
- Who decides on and designs appropriate QMS risk treatment or control?
- Who monitors QMS risk effectiveness, efficiency, and economics?
- How are ISO 9001:2015 risk issues escalated and remediated?

Lesson Learned: Purchase multiple copies of this book and share them with your ISO 9001:2015 transition team. Develop questions and checklists from this book that are tailored to your organization. Pareto (think RBT) the critical issues to focus on. Address them in your business case.

Resource: Read 'Where Have All The Chief Quality Officer's Gone?'
Http://Insights.CERMacademy.Com/2013/03/Where-Have-All-The-Chief-Quality-Officers-Gone/

What is the role of the quality organization with corporate ERM?

In mature organizations, a Chief Risk Officer (CRO) will have authority over ERM and RBT. This person will be interested in the design, development, deployment, and assurance of risk-controls throughout the quality organization, operations, and the supply chain.

Most large organizations are moving to some form of operations and supply chain risk management. RBT and ISO 9001 will create opportunities for the quality organization to work with senior executives and other groups to architect, design, deploy and assure risk-controls.

For example, Quality Auditing will work closely with Internal Auditing to evaluate risk-control effectiveness in operations. Quality Auditing will work closely with Purchasing to evaluate suppliers based on operational risk, business continuity, supplier selection, contractual cost, project schedules, and quality compliance. Quality Auditing will harmonize its assurance and control evaluations based on Key Risk Indicators.

Lesson Learned: Negotiate roles, responsibilities, and authorities early with risk stakeholders. There will be multiple risk stakeholders and 'interested parties' in your organization. Many will have QMS, EMS, ISMS, OHSAS, and RBT system responsibilities.

Resource: Read 'Disagreement On Beliefs'
Http://Insights.CERMacademy.Com/2013/02/8-Disagreement-On-Beliefs-John-Blakinger/

What are 'Key Risk Indicators'?

Key Risk Indicators (KRI's) are the equivalent of quality Key Performance Indicators (KPI's). Quality often has 1. Enterprise level, 2. Programmatic/Project/Process, and 3. Product/Transactional level KPI's:

- Enterprise quality KPI's can be customer satisfaction, cost of quality, cost of recalls, social responsibility, and quality performance.

- Process KPI's can be process stability, process capability, and process improvement. Project KPI's can be schedule, cost, and scope controls.
- Product KPI's can be product nonconformances. Service or transactional quality KPI's can be up time and maintainability.

With ISO 9001:2015, quality will have to develop KRI indicators. We have seen that some quality organizations are reframing quality KPI's as KRI's. This is acceptable.

Lesson Learned: Determine your QMS KRI's at the 1. Enterprise level; 2. Programmatic/Project/Process level, and 3. Product/Transactional level.

Resource: Read 'Stop Losing Money - Implement A Human Capital Risk Management Strategy'
Http://Insights.CERMacademy.Com/2013/07/20-Youre-Losing-Implementing-A-Human-Capital-Risk-Maement-Strategy-Kristie-Evans/

What IT resources are necessary to move to ISO 9001:2015?

As a quality organization moves to RBT, operational risk management, and supply chain risk management, more information, data, and evidence will be gathered and will be consolidated into enterprise risk reporting systems. A major challenge will be to integrate risk information with the existing QMS, EMS, and other management reporting systems. Within a few years, most ISO management systems, such as quality, environmental, safety, IT, social responsibility, and other ISO management systems will integrate risk. Critical quality risk issues will have to be escalated and communicated across the enterprise.

Depending on the strategic importance and complexity of the data, we recommend that you start investigating IT risk reporting systems.

Lesson Learned: You will be surprised how much risk data you will accumulate very quickly. Develop enterprise level RBT reporting capabilities.

Resource: Read 'Cyber Security Vulnerabilities' Http://Insights.CERMacademy.Com/2014/11/69-Cyber-Security-Vulnerabilities-Mark-Bernard/

Should the new quality organization be centralized or decentralized?

This question largely depends on the Board's and executive management's view of the organization and its culture. If your organization takes a centralized risk management approach, then the portfolio or enterprise view would extend throughout the organization and into the supply chain. On the other hand, a decentralized view of RBT empowers risk owners to design, deploy, and assure the appropriate risk-controls. These alternative views for risk would have to be aligned with the enterprise view in terms of risk appetite.

This question applies to the context of the organization. If the organization produces a highly regulatory, safety related product then its risk profile would be different than an organization that produces a commodity product. So, risk may be centralized to ensure consistency of interpretation of regulations as well as consistent application of risk-controls.

The culture of the organization must also be considered. A highly regulated product dealing with user safety may require centralized risk management, while a commodity product could be decentralized

Lesson Learned: As you start your RBT journey, you will be surprised by the questions, issues, and opportunities that will arise.

Resource: Read 'Basics: Measuring Risk Management Outcomes' Http://Insights.CERMacademy.Com/2014/12/73-Basics-Measuring-Risk-Management-Outcomes-Rod-Farrar/

What are Chief Risk Officer (CRO) responsibilities?

Many large organizations have a Chief Risk Officer (CRO). This person is responsible for governance, ERM, and compliance. If the organization is small, then one person may have risk roles and responsibilities.

In a large organization, the CRO is the ERM champion. This person is key to implementation of ISO 9001:2015 and RBT. The challenge is this person may be in a different part of the organization such as operations, compliance, or legal. The CRO may not know ISO 9001:2015 requirements or ISO RBT challenges. The quality organization should initiate RBT discussions with the CRO.

A company recently advertised for a risk director. The duties provide clues as to the diversity of risk responsibilities. The following describes some of this person's responsibilities:

- "Accountable for all activities and results of a very broad functional area or multiple smaller functions. Most likely accomplished through managing the activities of Director or Senior Manager level employees. Responsible for developing and driving implementation of plans in support of strategic direction.
- Ensure that overall budget and performance standards are realistically set and attained.
- Participate with VP's in establishing a recommended organization structure for the areas managed, and developing organizational capability needed to execute strategy.
- Establish organizational procedures and plans, consistent with company policy.
- Consistently work with abstract ideas or situations across functional areas of the business. Through assessment of intangible variables, identify and evaluate fundamental issues, provide strategy and direction for major functional areas. Will require in depth knowledge of the functional area, business strategy and the company's goals in addition to industry knowledge.
- Interact internally and externally with executive level management, requiring negotiation of extremely critical matters.

- Global Vision - understands and can communicate vision and purpose beyond the short term and/or immediate organization. Set the organization's vision and mission.
- Innovate - link multiple and varied concepts to develop new and workable ideas.
- Architect and implement change successfully.
- Develop strategic and transformational leaders. Develop thought leadership.
- Actively teach strategy to senior leaders while transforming culture.
- Spend 30% of time developing people and team.
- Primary responsibility and influence is their immediate organization and respective business unit.
- Highly visible across risk and sponsors enterprise risk initiatives."[xxii]

Lesson Learned: Work closely with risk executives. The CRO may come from legal or finance and does not know operations or supply chain issues. Position the quality organization to be the information source to the CRO on operational risk-controls.

Resource: Read 'Being Anticipatory'
Http://Insights.CERMacademy.Com/2014/05/49-Anticipatory-Daniel-Burrus/

Who are today's Chief Quality Officers (CQOs)?

A few years ago, we wrote an article on CQO's from which this is derived:

> "I have been in and around quality for more than 25 years. When, I first started, most organizations did not even have a quality department. Then during the explosive growth of quality from 1980 to 2000, the quality function grew in importance to become a critical C - level function -VP or higher.

Quality went from a technical position to a first and second level manager to a director level. Many companies had VP's of quality and some even developed a position called Chief Quality Officer (CQO). This was the top quality position in our profession.

'Quality is Job #1': Remember that ad from Ford? It was Ford's mantra, its marketing tag line. Each company developed similar marketing visions and mission statements. I thought they were inspirational. I was a quality believer and evangelist for years. I wrote 4 books on quality. I gave a dozen talks on quality each year. It was an exciting and lucrative time to be a quality consulting professional. Quality professionals were at the forefront of national and organizational competitiveness. Quality professionals and consultants were in huge demand to stabilize, lean, and improve internal and supplier processes using the tools that we discussed above. Great and good times."

The good times can roll again, but with a risk theme. Take ownership of operational and supply chain RBT. If you do not, someone within your organization will.

Lesson Learned: Add risk to your job title and function. It will make you more marketable.

Resource: Read 'The Great Pretenders'
Http://Insights.CERMacademy.Com/2013/10/29-The-Great-Pretenders-Mark-Moore/

How should the quality organization work with the CRO?

Many CRO's come from compliance, legal, or finance areas. They do not know operations or quality. This person is critical to quality's success with ISO 9001:2015 in terms of providing risk approvals, direction, and resources. The quality department should be flexible and work with the CRO, specifically:

- Work with new risk stakeholders to obtain resources and establish credibility. Quality as a result of ISO 9001:2015 RBT will have additional responsibilities.

- Work with executives to establish the appropriate risk-control environment, culture and tone at the top.

- Work with other executives to establish the appropriate risk appetite for areas addressed in the ISO 9001:2015 QMS.

- Establish and communicate how ISO 9001:2015 risk requirements fit into the organizational RBT mission and ERM vision.

- Work with senior executives to define appropriate RBT roles within the ISO 9001:2015 framework.

- Reframe the role of quality management, quality assurance, and quality control to include risk.

- Work with managers and executives in other areas of the organization such as finance, internal auditing, operations, and supply chain management to integrate ISO 9001:2015 requirements with the existing risk framework, organizational strategic direction, and risk treatment processes.

- Develop new RBT and risk policies and procedures that are aligned with ISO 9001:2015 and the organization's strategy.

- Communicate ISO 9001:2015 risk goals and requirements to ensure there is a seamless integration with other organizational risk frameworks.

- Identify process, project, and product risk ownership, responsibilities, and roles. While ISO 9001:2015 primarily deals with QMS business objectives, the scope of the standard may increase to incorporate other business areas such as supply management.

- Work with other functions to address 'white space' risks. Risk ownership gaps should be identified. Ownership and responsibility gaps are risks waiting to occur so controls need to be established to close the gaps.

- Ensure risk frameworks, methodologies, tools, and techniques are aligned with the organization. A common risk vocabulary is critical for ensuring controls are in place and working effectively.

- Consult with and facilitate a consistent deployment of ISO 9001:2015 risk vision, mission, and RBT.

Lesson Learned: Do not panic! Many of the above issues can be addressed over a period of time as more ISO management system standards integrate risk and your risk processes mature.

Resource: Read 'Group Think And Unidentified Risks' Http://Insights.CERMacademy.Com/2013/06/19-Group-Think-And-Unidentified-Risks-Mark-Moore/

Why is RBT a cultural and behavioral issue?

In our experience of over 15 years of architecting, designing, deploying, and assuring risk management systems, we have learned risk management is mainly a cultural challenge not a technical challenge. The technology of risk management is fairly straightforward. The challenge is in the culture and the adoption of RBT and effective treatment of risks.

Quality has been successfully establishing QMS, EMS, and other management systems. Treating risks compared to managing, assuring, or controlling quality requires new skills and a different mindset. The quality organization needs to build RBT and risk capabilities. Issues of risk ownership, accountabilities, responsibilities, and new ways of doing business can be a challenge to people who have been hired, rewarded, and promoted for one set of skills and behaviors and now they have to adopt a new set of RBT skills and behaviors.

Lesson Learned: Remember risk is first about context and people embracing RBT. It takes longer than expected to bring folks on board, to embrace, and be passionate about RBT.

Resource: Read 'Implementing A Systems Approach To Pharmaceutical Quality Systems' Http://Insights.CERMacademy.Com/2014/02/41-Implementing-Systems-Approach-Pharmaceutical-Quality-Systems-Christine-Park/

Why is supply chain risk management critical?

Recent supply chain articles had the following headlines:

- "Quake Disrupts Key Supply Chains."
- "Stress Test for the Global Supply Chain."
- "Long Pause for Japanese Industry Raises Concerns About Supply Chain."
- "Japan Quake Likely to Affect Business Globally."

What is common to most of the above headlines? Risk is now prominent in the supply chain? Take a look at today's business model for auto, aerospace, and other companies:

- **Design products.** Design is often a core process that is retained and is done internally.
- **Outsource.** Up to 85% of the manufacturing dollar is outsourced.
- **Assemble.** Final product is assembled internally.
- **Test.** QA and QC testing to ensure quality and reliability requirements are satisfied are kept internal.
- **Manage the brand.** Branding and reputation are key issues that are retained.

Supply chain risk management (SCRM) involves the development of strategies to manage value chain Volatility, Uncertainty, Complexity, and Ambiguity (VUCA). The goal is to ensure continuity of operations.

At its simplest level, SCRM attempts to identify risks and reduce failure or vulnerable points in the supply chain. As well, supply chain points of vulnerability can be exacerbated by events such as hurricanes, supplier strikes, and acts of God. It is all about risk management.

Lesson Learned: Risk is core to today's supply management and is changing many sourcing rules.

Resource: Read 'Supplier Risks & Worker Vulnerabilities' Http://Insights.CERMacademy.Com/2014/10/63-Supplier-Risks-Worker-Vulnerabilities-Kelly-Eisenhardt/

How are supply chain rules changing?

It is all about uncertainty. The quality organization now must work in a disruptive environment, where rules are changing. The growth of supply chain risk management has created new sourcing rules such as:

- From Just in Time to Just in Case.
- From single sourcing to multiple sourcing.
- From price to risk based, supply chain decision making.
- From looking backward to looking forward.
- From supplier trust to supplier verification.
- From quality audits to risk audits.

Each of the above changes requires new knowledge, skills, and abilities from quality professionals.

Lesson Learned: Google 'Supply Risk Management' and see how risk is changing another profession, much like RBT will change the quality profession.

Resource: Read 'Finding Subcontractor Hidden Risks' Http://Insights.CERMacademy.Com/2013/10/28-Finding-Subcontractor-Hidden-Risk-John-Ayers

CHAPTER 11:

CERTIFICATION BODIES

What is the key idea in this chapter?

The key idea of this chapter is Certification Bodies, the auditors of ISO 9001 companies, were challenged by ISO 9001:2015 certification because of unanswered questions and risk based auditing.

What is more critical: 1. Certification or 2. Managing risks?

Dr. Nigel Croft, Chair of ISO TC 176/SC3, speculated:

> "ISO 9001:2015 is not about getting a certificate but rather, about managing the business, providing confidence to companies that they are doing things right and in a systematic manner particularly in managing risks."[xxiii]

This quotation sounds like the future of ISO 9001:2015 and the quality profession. It is all about RBT, risk assessment, risk assurance, and risk-control, which is the essence of this book.

Lesson Learned: ISO 9001:2015 is about smarter management, which is the objective of Risk Based Thinking. This is great for the certification community that will align CB audits with business assurance.

Resource: Read 'Certification Is A Flawed Business Model (Part 1)' Http://Insights.CERMacademy.Com/2014/09/59-Certification-Flawed-Business-Model-Arvind-Chavan/

What is a Certification Body (CB)?

CB's are independent companies that audit and assure an ISO QMS adheres to the specific requirements of the ISO 9001:2015 standard.

Certification is the equivalent to registration. In North America, CB's are often called registrars. In this book, we prefer to use the term CB's.

Lesson Learned: Talk with your CB to understand their ISO 9001:2015 certification requirements and RBT expectations following the transition.

Resource: Read 'Rethinking Sector Scheme Relationships'

Http://Insights.CERMacademy.Com/2014/10/62-Rethinking-Sector-Scheme-Relationships-T-Dan-Nelson/

What are general reasons to achieve ISO 9001 certification?

ISO 9001:2015 states customer satisfaction and meeting requirements are its main purposes. This is great. However, we want to mention the following benefits of certification:

> Profitability. Competitiveness. Operational excellence. Quality governance. Conforming products. Improving products. Risk-control system. Regulatory compliance. Contractual compliance. Business improvement. Supplier transparency. Meeting objectives. Demonstrable quality management, quality assurance, and quality control. Demonstrable process capability, control, and improvement.

Maybe all of the above? We posed this question to the quality director of a certified company. He mentioned the additional benefits of certification:

- Meet a contractual requirement.
- Satisfy a regulatory compliance requirement.
- Demonstrate a consistent ability to satisfy customers.
- Demonstrate compliant management systems.
- Demonstrate operational and/or supply chain risk-control effectiveness.
- Improve internal and supply chain operations.
- Become more competitive.
- Reduce operational and supply chain risks.
- Provide a third-party certificate to clients.

Lesson Learned: Understand the real and hidden reasons for certification. Understand and communicate the real benefits (monetized) of ISO 9001:2015 certification and RBT in your business case.

Resource: Read 'Is The Customer Always Right?'
Http://Insights.CERMacademy.Com/2014/05/50-Customer-Always-Right-T-Dan-Nelson/

What is the value of third-party certification?

Yes, we know this question is redundant. We wanted to emphasize the value of third-party certification. The value of third-party certification can be attested by the fact that more than 1.2 million companies have invested in certification. So, this question is a little different than the prior question. This question addresses the value of third-party certification, which includes:

- ISO 9001 and other ISO international standards have been incorporated and referenced in many national statutes.

- Accreditor's, peer reviews, audits, and CB's are based on similar criteria throughout the world.
- Third-party certification provides a consistent global level of assurance and value.
- Auditors have quality auditing knowledge, skills, and abilities that are validated by the CB.
- CB auditors have industry specific knowledge and abilities.
- CB auditors provide independent, third-party assessments.
- ISO conformity assessment is globally proven to be reliable, repeatable, and provides a consistent level of assurance.

Lesson Learned: ISO certifications add value and define a prescribed level of assurance to multiple stakeholders.

Resource: Read 'Value Added Certification Of An Established QMS (Part Iii)'
Http://Insights.CERMacademy.Com/2014/10/61-Value-Added-Certification-Established-Qms-Part-Ii-Arvind-Chavan/

What uncertainty do you see in ISO accreditation and certification?

We anticipate the following are ISO certification risks:

- Multiple interpretations of the requirements of new ISO standards.
- Confusion among CB's on how to verify and validate compliance to new standard with risk requirement.
- Development of sector specific risk standards that incorporate higher levels of RBT and risk assurance depending on sector requirements.

- Different risk taxonomies, frameworks, and syntax will result in additional uncertainty in ISO 9001:2015 application.

Lesson Learned: Accreditor's and CB's will face their own risks as RBT is rolled out globally to the certification community.

Resource: Read 'Future Of Assurance: BSI Statement Of Compliance For ISO 31000 ERM'
Http://Insights.CERMacademy.Com/2014/12/70-Bsi-Statement-Compliance-ISO-31000-Greg-Hutchinsw/

What critical questions will CB's face with new risk requirements?

The global CB's still have to address these questions on how to audit RBT:

- How will the accreditation bodies oversee the CB's and assure consistency?
- How will ISO risk standards and guidance documents be used to conduct risk based audits?
- How will the CB's ensure audit and auditor consistency when ISO 9001:2015 is more interpretive and discretionary than other revisions?
- Why are some CB's already evaluating clients against ISO 9001:2015?
- How will the CB's ensure or assure consistent risk based audit results?
- How will CB's monitor quality control of the audits?
- How will the CB's continue to manage the enhanced scope of the ISO 9001:2015 audits?
- How will the CB's limit exposure to conducting risk based audits?

- What will CB's do if a certified company requests a higher level of assurance beyond ISO certification?
- If a higher level of assurance is requested, what type of assurance can or will the CB provide?
- How will the CB's raise rates for the added time and liability exposure it assumes in evaluating auditee's risk assessments?
- What is the CB's exposure or liability if a public safety threat, large recall, or some other material event occurs after an ISO 9001:2015 risk based audit?
- What additional terms and conditions will be in the CB boilerplate contract to address the challenges for auditing risk in ISO 9001:2015?
- What type of written representations can or should the CB offer the auditee following the risk based audit?
- How will the CB's establish internal rules for auditability to ISO 9001:2015 because ISO 19011:2018 has loose guidelines for risk based auditing?
- What type of process will the CB's establish for scoping risk based audits?
- How will the CB's conduct integrated audits of multiple management systems, such as EMS, ISMS, etc.?
- What types of working papers will the CB's retain?

Anyway, you get the idea. Accreditation authorities and CB's must establish common protocols and proceduralize them to enforce consistency. The challenge is that RBT and risk based auditing are too new.

Lesson Learned: Understand the basis of the above questions that are critical to all CB's. You do not need specific answers to the questions, but need to understand the 'RBT' process your CB follows in its risk based audit.

Resource: Read 'Value Added By Certification Of An Established QMS' Http://Insights.CERMacademy.Com/2014/09/60-Value-Added-Certification-Established-Qms-Arvind-Chavan/

What critical questions will auditors face with ISO 9001:2015 and new risk based standards?

The following questions are a continuation from the previous question. CB auditors have to address with new risk based, ISO standards:

- Who are 'interested parties'?
- Will interested party requirements have to be addressed in terms of a risk assessment?
- How will auditors audit for effectiveness?
- How will auditors conduct process audits?
- How will auditors conduct risk based audits?
- How will auditors evaluate QMS risk-control effectiveness?
- How will auditors evaluate RBT?
- What types of additional ISO 19011:2018 auditing guidance is required by auditors?
- How will auditors address more interpretive and discretionary requirements in ISO 9001:2015 and new ISO standards?
- How will auditors determine conformance to the broader scope of ISO 9001:2015 clauses?
- How will auditors evaluate processes and risk-control effectiveness if a high level of discretion and interpretation is required?
- How will auditors scope the audit?

- How will auditors complete the audit within prescribed audit timelines?
- How will auditors conduct integrated audits of multiple management systems when the audit criteria become more discretionary?
- How will auditors be trained to conduct ISO 9001:2015 audits addressing the above issues?

The above questions deal with auditability. Over the next 3 years, this will be a critical issue for ISO, accreditors, CB's, auditors, auditees, and management system consultants.

Lesson Learned: Understand the above questions and discuss them with your CB.

Resource: Read 'Forget About The Mule - Load The Wagon' Http://Insights.CERMacademy.Com/2014/08/Forget-Mule-Load-Wagon/

What critical questions will consultants face with ISO 9001:2015?

CB auditor challenges listed in this chapter also apply to consultants. For all or most ISO consultants, the questions below are going to be a challenge. Why? Most ISO management system consultants are not risk consultants or understand RBT. RBT and risk based auditing are so new that most ISO management system consultants have not done a risk based, process, and effectiveness audit.

Consultants will have to address:

- How do consultants who have read a lot about risk management, but have little real life application provide risk advice?
- How do consultants who know ISO management system standards, learn RBT, risk assessment, and even risk management?
- How do consultants learn different risk management frameworks,

such as ISO 31000:2018, COSO, and NIST 800 - 37?

- How will consultants learn how to apply RCMM, system of controls, ISO 31000:2018, and COSO if they have never done risk?
- How will consultants learn about GRC or ERM statutes and their requirements?
- How will consultants assist a company conduct a FMEA, but do not have the enterprise, business unit, or process risk perspective?
- How will consultants learn to conduct Value Added Audits, such as Yellow Book or Red Book assessments?
- How will consultants learn new risk management paradigms beyond Deming, Crosby, Feigenbaum, etc.?
- How will consultants apply COSO or ISO 31000:2018 with ISO certified companies?
- How will ISO consultants learn the language of GRC, ERM, etc.?
- How will RBT and risk impact quality organizations?
- How will quality consultants reengineer quality organizations to RBT and higher levels of RCMM?
- How will QMS consultants apply risk treatment and control strategies, which are often more art than technology?
- How will consultants develop a business case for ISO 9001:2015 certification, when many do not understand RBT?
- How will consultants architect, design, deploy and assure risk frameworks for certified organizations?
- How will consultants who may understand the technical nature of risk assessment, understand more nuanced concepts such as materiality, reasonableness, due diligence, opinions, etc.
- How will QMS consultants with a product or transactional perspec-

tive in their quality background address 1. Enterprise level; 2. Programmatic/Project/Process level; or 3. Product/Transactional level risks?

- How will quality consultants communicate operational and supply management risks to C level executives?

Lesson Learned: Do your due diligence. Interview your ISO management systems consultants carefully since many are now risk experts. Develop a standard questionnaire and rate them based on answers to the questions. Check with their previous clients about their risk experience. If you are in doubt, keep shopping until you find the consultant that meets your requirements.

Resource: Read 'Use Creativity To Breathe New Life Into Your Products'
Http://Insights.CERMacademy.Com/2014/11/66-Use-Creativity-Breathe-New-Life-Products-Daniel-Burras/

Are all CB's the same?

Yes! CB's follow and comply with the same accreditation process, follow the same auditing protocols, and have the same structure. But, differences emerge between global CB's and smaller CB's.

Global CB's have consistent internal processes. They conduct audits with full-time auditors. They can and do scale their auditing processes globally. So an ISO audit conducted in Portland is similar to one in Poland. Global CB's have conducted risk forensics, assurance, and audits for years and a number have rebranded into risk assurance or business assurance companies.

The challenge for smaller CB's is ISO 9001 certification has become a commodity in many developed countries. There are few barriers to entry to become a CB. There are few litigation consequences for poor auditing. There are poorly trained auditors. The result is there is variation in the CB and auditor community that can result in poor certification quality.

Lesson Learned: Ask your CB how it will certify you to ISO 9001:2015? It is never too early to prepare for certification to ISO 9001:2015 and other management system standards.

Resource: Read 'Bad Quality Is Not So Funny!' Http://Insights.CERMacademy.Com/2014/09/59-Bad-Qaity-Funny-T-Dan-Nelson/

What is Gresham's Law applied to CB's?

A simplification of Gresham's Law is 'bad money drives out good money.' What does this mean? If there is too much counterfeit currency, then this will devalue the legal currency because people will not be able to differentiate between the two. The challenge is this can happen with ISO 9001:2015 auditing and certification. Confused?

Think of the quality analog: Bad auditors drive out good auditors. Good CB's and good auditors want to do their best. CB's, quality auditors, and the entire QMS structure are based on credibility and trust. Bad CB's and bad auditors do poor audits. Why? They are not trained in process, performance, and risk based auditing. They do not have time to conduct the audits. The result is lack of audit credibility and trust. The entire structure can be compromised if there is too much variation in CB's, auditors, and audit results. If QMS audit results cannot be trusted, then the entire assurance structure will collapse.

This is not good for anyone.

Lesson Learned: The type of certification assurance you want should drive your choice of CB, not lowest price. Do your CB due diligence in terms of making sure your CB understands and can answer the questions raised in this book. This is simply CB due diligence and risk management. It will save you from surprises and even potential heartburn down the road.

Resource: Read 'Gresham's Law Of ISO Certification' Http://Insights.CERMacademy.Com/2013/09/24-Greshams-Law-Of-ISO-Certification-Greg-Hutchins/

Does ISO 9001:2015 create more variability in the CB and consultant communities?

The scope of ISO 9001 since its inception in 1987 was fairly tight. The document had 'shall' procedural and process requirements. The purpose of the standard was to make auditing fairly straightforward based on clause-by-clause, conformity assessment of QMS requirements.

The scope was also limited so possible misinterpretations would not result. Loose requirements could result in varying interpretations, which could result in auditor variation, which could lower the consistency and quality of ISO audit findings.

See if the following logic makes sense. The essence of quality is consistency. The essence of QMS or any management system is standardization. The essence of any management system is proceduralization. The essence of proceduralization is process stability and capability. The essence of process stability and capability is the control of variability or risk.

ISO 9001:2015 does not require a quality manual or specific documentation. Anyway, you get the idea. ISO 9001:2015 is open to more interpretation and variability - hence more risk.

Lesson Learned: Understand the above logic and standardize your ISO certifications.

Resource: Read 'Tribal Knowledge' Http://Insights.CERMacademy.Com/2014/01/36-Tribal-Knowledge-Mark-Moore/

Are all elements of a RBT QMS the same?

No! It will be critical in ISO 9001:2015 to conduct a Pareto risk analysis to separate the critical few QMS RBT requirements from the trivial many. Otherwise, the CB will be trying to check all QMS risk requirements and will run out of time to conduct the audit.

ISO 9001:2008 required specific documentation. Aside from the required documentation, most QMS areas and requirements are treated the same in an audit. In a risk and process based assessment, the auditor will have to prioritize areas to review, test for effectiveness, and issue findings if required.

ISO 9001:2015 requires additional guidance from the International Accreditation Forum on how to conduct risk based audits. There is a precedent. The IAF introduced Advanced Surveillance and Recertification Procedures (ASRP) in 2005 for organizations with mature QMS's and EMS's. CB's could use this option to design customized and flexible risk based, audit processes. For example, critical audit areas such as corrective action, internal audit, and management review would be assessed in greater detail.

As an example, ASRP requirements for a mature certified company include the following:

- QMS and/or EMS certification for 3 years or one certification cycle.
- Demonstrable QMS and EMS performance indicators that verify products and/or services meet customer and applicable regulatory requirements.
- Continual improvement and effectiveness of the QMS and/or EMS could be validated.
- Evidence can verify continual improvement and customer satisfaction.

Lesson Learned: The IAF will have to provide CB's similar guidance for ISO 9001:2015. The CB's will have to Pareto the QMS audit based on risk very early in the ISO 9001:2015 certification audit.

Resource: Read 'Risk-Based, Quality First!' Http://Insights.CERMacademy.Com/2014/10/62-Salmonella-Isnt-Problem-Bill-Walker/

How has ISO 9001 management systems auditing evolved?

ISO 9001 auditing has evolved. CB auditors in 1987 assessed compliance to clause-by-clause 'shall' requirements. These assessments were fairly straightforward. It was a binary evaluation. The auditee did or did not comply with the clause requirement because it had or did not have the requisite QMS policy, procedure, or work instruction. A generation of QMS auditors has been trained to conduct clause-by-clause assessments.

CB auditors then evaluated processes, which involved assessing process inputs, process steps, and process outputs. The outputs had to meet customer requirements, which could be the next process owner or the ultimate customer. While most auditors understood process mechanics, they simply did not have the time or knowledge to conduct an in depth process audit. Their fall back was to conduct a clause-by-clause assessment.

CB auditors then evaluated QMS 'effectiveness.' This required a procedure as well as evidence to determine adherence to the standard. This has challenged some CB auditors. They did not know what type or extent of evidence would be required to determine adherence.

In ISO 9001:2015, CB auditors are now evaluating the effectiveness of risk-controls to assure that QMS quality objectives can be achieved. This will be an additional challenge for many of today's management system auditors.

Lesson Learned: Purchase and read **Value Added Auditing**, which is a process and risk based book. The book is available through Amazon, ASQ, or Quality + Engineering (GregH@CERMAcademy.com). The book explains how to conduct a risk based audit.

Resource: Read 'Latest ISO Certification Statistics' Http://Insights.CERMacademy.Com/2013/11/30-Iso-Trends-Greg-Hutchins/

What does ISO 9001:2015 auditability mean?

This is the #1 question for CB's with the new revision of ISO 9001:2015 standard. Most management experts acknowledge that ISO 9001:2015 is a significant change.

Auditability implies consistent outcomes from auditing management systems. If outcomes are different among CB's, then the quality of the assessment and the reliance on the outcomes may be called into question. Again, the hallmark of audit quality is consistency. If there is variability in audit outcomes then this would imply the ISO QMS audit quality could be questioned. This is the last thing that CB's, auditees, and audit customers want.

So, there are a number of critical attributes of auditability that the CB's will focus on:

- Meet the explicit and implicit requirements of ISO 9001:2015.
- Conduct the audit within prescribed time frames.
- Determine whether the audit is truly independent.
- Ensure agreement between the auditor and auditee of critical concepts such as scope of certification, RBT, critical processes, customers, requirements, interested parties, measures of effectiveness, risk based audit methodology, reporting of findings, etc.
- Determine level of risk assurance from the assessment.
- Determine the scope of the assessment.
- Ensure consistent definitions of RBT and other critical risk terms.
- Define the criteria to be used in determining findings and nonconformances.

- Ensure availability of audit evidence and consistent processes.
- Ensure accurate and sufficient evidence is acquired to form the basis of a QMS finding or nonconformance.
- Develop internal procedures to assure ISO 9001:2015 audits are reasonably consistent within sectors, across sectors and across nations.

Lesson Learned: Understand the ramifications for your organization's auditability to ISO 9001:2015, RBT, and other management system standards.

Resource: Read 'Value Added Certification Of An Established QMS (Part Iii)'
Http://Insights.CERMacademy.Com/2014/10/61-Value-Added-Certification-Established-Qms-Part-Ii-Arvind-Chavan/

How can CB's assure audit consistency?

We have reviewed several CB process and risk based auditing programs. They seem different. So, one of the challenges over the next 3 years will be to update audit standards for conducting risk based audits against ISO 9001:2015.

CB's will need auditors who can:

- Audit to different risk taxonomies, frameworks, RBT classification schemes, or risk systems/standards that may be industry specific.
- Evaluate different risk assessment methods such as those defined in ISO 31010.
- Have a breadth and depth of risk knowledge, skills, and abilities to assess the auditee's RBT and risk assessments. CB auditors will need to be sensitive to the scope of risk, nature of the risk, timing of risk, risk stakeholders, risk assessment process, risk maturity,

risk tolerance, risk appetite, risk management controls, and organizational culture.

- Be risk sensitive and make appropriate adjustments in assessing conformance to ISO 9001:2015.
- Conduct upside and downside process and risk based assessments. These will require knowledge of the sector, industry, organization, business model, operating markets, product, legal, social, political and contextual environment in which it operates.
- May need intimate knowledge of suppliers and interested parties depending on the scope of the assessment.

Lesson Learned: Ask your CB how they will audit you. What are its expectations and requirements for certification? What type of evidence will the CB require since a quality manual is no longer required. What is the CB's background in conducting risk based audits?

Resource: Read 'Value Added By Certification Of An Established QMS' Http://Insights.CERMacademy.Com/2014/09/60-Value-Added-Certification-Established-Qms-Arvind-Chavan/

What challenges do CB's face conducting risk, process and effectiveness audits?

All CB's around the world should know how to conduct process audits. This has been in the ISO 9001 standard since the 2000 revision. However, CB's are often time and resource constrained when they conduct audits of new companies. As well, we have found that clause-by-clause or 'shall' auditors have not been conducting process audits.

ISO 9001:2015 defined effectiveness as the "extent to which planned activities are realized and planned results achieved." To meet this, auditors must evaluate:

- Top management is accountable for QMS effectiveness.

- Top management provides direction to persons who contribute to QMS effectiveness.
- Organization evaluates the effectiveness of its actions.
- Organization develops personnel with appropriate competencies and evaluates the effectiveness of their actions.

Risk based audits are also new to ISO auditors. We have discussed this at length. ISO auditors must practice a higher level of due care and due diligence. ISO 9001:2015 has process changes that require interpretation and professional judgment. ISO 9001:2015 is also streamlined so now it requires more from the auditors.

Lesson Learned: Discuss the above items with your CB. It is never too early to start this conversation.

Resource: Read 'Being Anticipatory'
Http://Insights.CERMacademy.Com/2014/05/49-Anticipatory-Daniel-Bur-rus/

Why do ISO management system auditors need additional training?

ISO lead auditor training is 5 days. Certified Public Accountants (CPA's) have 4 years of accounting and a college degree in accounting. They are required to pass a 14-hour rigorous exam covering the following topics:

- Auditing and Attestation (AUD) - 4 hours.
- Business Environment and Concepts (BEC) - 3 hours.
- Financial Accounting and Reporting (FAR) - 4 hours.
- Regulation (REG) - 3 hours.

In most states, financial auditors are required to have two years of practical experience to become CPA's. Financial audits are also risk based.

Lesson Learned: If you are going to conduct management system audits, get as much RBT and risk knowledge as you can because ISO audits are moving to risk.

Resource: Read 'What Do Quality Auditors Need To Know?' Http://Insights.CERMacademy.Com/2013/02/7a-What-Do-Quality-Auditors-Need-To-Know-Greg-Hutchins/

Is training for CB auditors sufficient for the new risk based, ISO standards?

The challenge for the CB's is most lead assessor courses do not address risk based and process auditing in much depth.

Most lead assessor courses are 36 hours. This seems to be sufficient for clause-by-clause ISO management system assessments. But is this sufficient for risk based, process, and effectiveness audits? This will be a major challenge over the next 3 years.

Among the many types of audits we have conducted, this is the least number of required hours for certification that we have found in cyber security, GAGAS (Yellow Book), Internal Auditing (IIA), financial auditing, and homeland security auditing.

From early indications, the large CB's are developing training programs for their full-time auditors. The smaller CB's are relying on training providers to provide the requisite level of process and risk based auditor training.

Lesson Learned: Ask your CB how they trained their auditors to conduct risk based audits. We have evaluated ISO training products and most do not address risk based auditing in much detail.

Resource: Read 'Value Added by Certification of an Established QMS' http://insights.cermacademy.com/2014/09/60-value-added-certification-established-qms-arvind-chavan/

How long should an ISO 9001:2015 or similar certification audit take?

Great question! ISO 17023:2013, Conformity Assessment - Guidelines for Determining the Duration of Management System Certification Audits, specifies how long audits should take.

The guidelines do not provide much guidance on how long it takes to conduct risk based, process, and effectiveness audits. If the auditor conducts a checklist or compliance surveillance, then the walk through audit can be done within the specified times. If the auditor is conducting a real risk based, process, and effectiveness audit, it should take more time. This critical issue needs to be resolved.

Lesson Learned: Ask your CB how long (days) it will take to conduct a conformity assessment audit for your facility. Then inquire how they will conduct a risk based, process, and effectiveness audit. This critical issue determines how many person days the audit will take and how much your certification will cost.

Resource: Read 'Value Added Certification of an Established QMS' http://insights.cermacademy.com/2014/10/61-value-added-certification-established-qms-part-ii-arvind-chavan/

Why did some CB's conduct ISO 31000 audits?

ISO 31000:2018 is not for certification purposes. However, some CB's are offering ISO 31000:2018 conformance audits. So, what is going on?

CB's are striving to differentiate and add value to their services. The CB's have been price constrained for a number of years. The cost of ISO 9001 certification has dropped globally. Margins are squeezed. One way to differentiate from other CB's is to provide 'value added' services as part of their usual certifications. The CB's are offering 'Opportunities For Improvement' (OFI's), offering risk findings, and issuing a ISO 31000:2018 risk certificate.

This seems a little excessive and is probably part of the CB differentiation strategy. Risk based auditing will be a major value added differentiator for some CB's.

However, this creates consternation with ISO purists because:

- CB's and consultants were perceived as shamelessly promoting a standard that explicitly is not for certification.
- Critical risk auditing issues introduced in this chapter had not been resolved.
- Quality purists now resent more risk and RBT in the ISO 9001:2015 and other standards.
- ISO had not introduced definitive guidance on some issues addressed in this book.
- CB's again are still not consistent in messaging and conducting ISO 31000:2018 assessment.

Lesson Learned: If your CB has conducted an ISO 31000:2018 audit, inquire about the value proposition to you.

Resource: Read "I'm Outta Here! - Quality Auditor" Http://Insights.CERMacademy.Com/2013/02/8-How-Risk-Is-Overtaking-The-World-Of-Aerospace-Quality-Bill-Walker/

Is the new 9001:2015 standard and other risk standards a way for CB's and consultants to make more money?

We have heard this question many times. The common refrain goes something like this: "ISO 9001:2015 is a way for consultants and CB's to make more money based on risk consulting instead of improving customer satisfaction or improving product/service quality."

Yes, larger CB's will offer higher value, risk assurance services including certification, training, and consulting (through an independent arm). They will face higher risk as their reports go a higher level of management including the Board of Directors. With higher operational risks and higher levels of assurance come higher fees. But, you say this is not part of the traditional ISO QMS compliance model. Yes, you are right. ISO added RBT to its management systems standard, which provides a higher level of assurance.

The challenge in these uncertain times is that many smaller companies continue to experience financial difficulties and do not have additional resources to invest in QMS or RBT. This is a reason often offered for the decline in ISO 9001 certifications in many industrialized economies because the value proposition of ISO certification has diminished.

Lesson Learned: CB's may stratify providing a basic management system certification and also offer higher levels of risk assurance. Currently, we have global CB's that offer premium priced, assurance services. Then, we have a middle tier of national CB's that provide specialized certifications. At the lowest tier, CB's provide low priced, certifications. Global CB's will use RBT and risk management to differentiate themselves.

Resource: Read 'Certification is a Flawed Business Model'
http://insights.cermacademy.com/2014/09/59-certification-flawed-business-model-arvind-chavan/

What should the auditee expect from QMS certification?

There has been a lot of discussion about the value add of a QMS certification. Developed countries have seen flattening or even diminished number of certifications. In the developing world such as parts of Asia, South America, and Africa, ISO 9001 certifications continue to grow.

With the major changes occurring in ISO 9001:2015, we expect to see renewed examination of the value of QMS certification especially in light of the new emphasis on risk.

Continuous business improvement, achieving or surpassing customer requirements and providing conforming products were commonly stated goals of ISO 9000 QMS certification. ISO 9001:2015 is expanding the scope of controls, such as meeting quality objectives, meeting the needs and expectations of interested parties, and focusing on risk-control.

Lesson Learned: Recalibrate your expectations and reassess the benefits of ISO 9001:2015 certification and adoption of RBT. Then communicate these in your business case.

Resource: Read 'Expectation is the Root of All Heartache' http://insights.cermacademy.com/2013/04/12-expectation-is-the-root-of-all-heartache-elizabeth-lions/

Is self-certification and self-declaration to ISO 9001:2015 and to other ISO standards a realistic option?

Yes, self-certification and self-declaration are realistic and credible assurance options as long as precautions are made, limitations are disclosed, and caveats are understood.

Self-certification is the process whereby a company informs interested parties or stakeholders that it affirms the company meets the intent and letter of the management system requirements, but has not been audited by a CB. Self-declaration is a similar assertion that an ISO management system is compliant but has not been audited.

Companies self-declare because they do not want to invest in having an independent, third-party assess its management system. The company may have been audited by multiple customers (second-party audits), that may even provide a higher level of assurance and credibility than a CB audit (third-party audit).

Lesson Learned: A company may want to self-certify or self-declare it is ISO 9001:2015 compliant because it has been audited by its customers.

Resource: Read 'Remote Auditing - The Risk Of The Cyber Auditor' Http://Insights.CERMacademy.Com/2014/01/36-Remote-Auditing-Rise-Cyber-Auditor-Robert-Gibson/

Why does the certification community dismiss self-certification and self-declaration?

This is a heart burn question with many accreditors, CB's, auditors, and consultants. Why? Self-certification basically defeats the ISO recognition agreements, harmonization, accreditation, and certification logic. Companies get the benefit of ISO 9001 without the third-party validation costs.

Self-declaration or self-certification are two credible methods for providing information, credibility, and ultimately a level of assurance. Self-certification is often linked with a contractual clause that states the self-certified company meets the intent and letter of the standard. The company will provide the interested party with the requisite evidence and will be subject to a second-party audit to determine compliance or even a higher level of assurance. The self-certifying company may be held to a contract, which some may argue is a higher level of due diligence and assurance than a third-party certificate.

Lesson Learned: If a supplier self certifies or self-declares, inquire who has audited them based on ISO 9001:2015 criteria and request a copy of the audit report.

Resource: Read 'Auto Certification Principles'
Http://Insights.CERMacademy.Com/2014/08/55-Auto-Certification-Principles-Umberto-Tunesi/

What is 'Risk Based Certification'?

We believe the future of ISO certification is risk based auditing and higher levels of risk assurance. Why?

Let us look at one global CB, Det Norske Veritas also called DNV. They are a global CB. They have a registered trademark on Risk Based Certification®. The DNV marketing piece states:

"Management system certification is a great tool for any company to improve its performance as it provides a systematic way to identify, manage, and mitigate risks. ... "

Not only will our customers receive a certificate that demonstrates compliance with chosen standard(s), they will also have assurance that you have the appropriate business controls to address new areas of risk that otherwise could have impact on their business success."[xxiv]

Lesson Learned: The future of ISO certifications may be a basic QMS or EMS certification, but with enhanced risk assurance based on customer requirements.

Resource: Read 'Future Of Assurance: BSI Statement Of Compliance For ISO 31000 ERM'
Http://Insights.CERMacademy.Com/2014/12/70-Bsi-Statement-Compliance-ISO-31000-Greg-Hutchinsw/

What is the future of certification?

This is an interesting question. We think we are going to see more global CB's offering value added consulting and certification services around RBT, risk management, and ERM. For example, DNV calls its new management system certification 'Next Generation Risk Based Certification™'.

We predict the following:

- Global CB's will offer risk based certifications across a number of management system standards as part of their value added differentiation.
- Global CB's will offer differentiated levels of risk assurance.
- Global CB's will link ISO certification to Internal Control over Financial Reporting.
- Global CB's will offer forensic, assurance, and analytical services

as part of their solution offering.

- Global CB's will offer value added services such as outsourced quality, outsourced supply risk management, risk assurance, and quality forensics.

- Global CB's will offer tailored assessments based on different risk taxonomies and risk frameworks.

- CB's will take a holistic approach looking at risk and RBT across the organization's management systems.

- CB's will become more sectoral based even more than we see today. We will have CB's specializing in food safety, IT, or aerospace risk assessments.

- Certification will emphasize sustainable business performance, as well as compliance.

- ISO management system standards will evolve into business system standards.

- GRC and CSR will be incorporated into the ISO management system audits.

Lesson Learned: Ask your CB what changes they foresee over the next 3 to 5 years in ISO 9001:2015 and in the certification of management system standards. Remember: your executives do not want surprises.

Resource: Read 'Looking For A Career Transition: Consider Quality Management'
Http://Insights.CERMacademy.Com/2014/12/72-Looking-Career-Transition-Consider-Quality-Management-Greg-Peckford/

Will most companies retain their ISO 9001:2015 certification?

We predicted during transition that most companies would retain their certifications. However, we think that there may be 40% attrition in ISO certifications in developed countries. Why? There are a number of reasons:

- Companies may develop their own customer supplier requirements that are based on their sector, product, or business model.
- Sectors may adopt more definitive and prescriptive quality and risk requirements that are specific to the industry and sector.
- Mature and capable (high RCMM) may opt for ERM customer supplier requirements that are based on statutes, regulations, and rules.
- Companies may defer to internal risk programs to develop and deploy operational and supplier controls that are based on existing ERM frameworks, such as COSO.

Lesson Learned: Conduct a gap analysis of your certification options, then decide the appropriate RCMM that is right for you.

Resource: Read 'Sailing Ships And Risks What Are Your True Colors?' Http://Insights.CERMacademy.Com/2015/01/75-Sailing-Ships-Risks-True-Colors-Joe-Eads/

CHAPTER 12:

RISK BASED AUDITING

What is the key idea in this chapter?

The key idea in this chapter is risk based auditing is a new skill for ISO management system auditors. Risk based auditing requires new knowledge, skills, and abilities.

What is ISO 19011:2018?

ISO 19011:2018 is an ISO standard that describes the guidelines for conducting management system audits such as QMS and EMS audits.

The standard has a number of purposes, specifically:

- Provides explanation of the principles of ISO management system auditing.
- Defines audit terms and processes.
- Provides guidance for auditing all management systems.
- Provides guidance for evaluating auditing principles, managing an audit program, and conducting management system audits.
- Provides guidance on the professionalism and competence of auditors and audit supervision.

- Defines principles such as confidentiality and integrity that are critical to conducting audits.
- Provides guidance on the management of an audit program.
- Provides guidance on the conduct of internal or external audits.
- Provides advice on the competence and evaluation of auditors.
- Can be used for internal (first-party), customer-supplier (second-party), certification audits (third-party).

Lesson Learned: Purchase ISO 19011:2018 and become familiar with it. It is a key standard that all quality and operations professionals need to know.

Resource: Read 'Auditing Risk Auditors'
Http://Insights.CERMacademy.Com/2014/05/49-Auditing-Risk-Auditors-Umberto-Tunesi/

What does ISO 19011:2018 cover?

ISO 19011:2018 is a comprehensive standard for conducting management system certification audits. ISO 19011:2018 like most families of standards follows a cycle from managing, planning, conducting, and reporting the audit results.

Critical elements of ISO 19011:2018 include:

Foreword
Introduction

1. Scope
2. Normative references
3. Terms and definitions
4. Principles of auditing
5. Managing an audit program.
6. Conducting an audit
   6.1 General

   6.2 Initiating audit
   6.3 Preparing audit activities
   6.4 Conducting audit activities
   6.5 Preparing and distributing audit report
   6.6 Completing audit
   6.7 Conducting audit follow-
7. Competence and evaluation of auditors
   7.1 General
   7.2 Determining auditor competence
   7.3 Establishing auditor evaluation criteria
   7.4 Selecting appropriate auditor evaluation method
   7.5 Conducting auditor evaluation
   7.6 Maintaining and improving auditor competence
   Annex A (informative)
   7.7 Additional guidance for auditors planning and conducting audits

Lesson Learned: Ensure your risk based, process, effectiveness, and RBT audits are minimally based on ISO 19011:2018. This will assure audit consistency.

Resource: Read 'Risk Management: A Primer For Lean Quality Assurance'
Http://Insights.CERMacademy.Com/2014/10/65-Risk-Management-Primer-Lean-Quality-Assurance-Gian-Guido-Redden/

What is an 'audit' according to ISO 19011:2018?

In ISO 19011:2018, audit is defined as a:

> "systematic, independent and documented process for obtaining audit evidence and evaluating it objectively to determine the extent to which the audit criteria are fulfilled."[xxv]

Lesson Learned: Ensure your first-party, second-party, and third-party audits can satisfy the above definition.

Resource: Read 'White Space Risks'
Http://Insights.CERMacademy.Com/2013/04/11-White-Space-Risks-Adina-Suciu/

What are the principles of auditing according to ISO 19011:2018?

According to ISO 19011:2018, quality auditing is based on the following principles:

- **Integrity:** Basis of all audits is professionalism.
- **Fair presentation:** Auditor reports findings and conclusions accurately, truthfully, and fairly.
- **Due professional care:** Auditor exercises diligence and judgment when planning, conducting, and reporting audits.
- **Confidentiality:** Auditor protects information acquired during the audit.
- **Independence:** Auditor is independent of the party, auditee, being audited. There is no evident or appearance of conflict of interest.
- **Evidence based approach:** Auditor reaches verifiable and reproducible conclusions based on a systematic audit process.

The above principles apply to all management system audits.

Lesson Learned: Internal (first-party), customer supplier (second-party), and CB audits (third-party) will be risk based. So, develop a risk based procedure for EMS, QMS, and supplier auditing that will ensure consistent results based on the above principles.

Resource: Read 'Audit My Organization Please'
Http://Insights.CERMacademy.Com/2013/10/27-Audit-My-Process-Please-T-Dan-Nelson/

Does ISO 19011:2018 describe how to conduct an audit of ISO 9001:2015?

Yes in generic terms. The audit lead is responsible for conducting document reviews throughout the audit. Audit lead issues a report, which includes a statement on the degree to which audit criteria are fulfilled and the summary of conclusions and main audit findings.

Auditor competencies are also addressed. Auditor competencies become critical with ISO 19011:2018 due to the scope expansion of ISO 9001:2015. Attributes such as personal behavior, acting ethically, being culturally sensitive and collaborative are critical audit success factors.

Lesson Learned: Purchase ISO 19011:2018. It is a key standard in your quality arsenal.

Resource: Read 'Risk Based Auditing'
Http://Insights.CERMacademy.Com/2013/08/21-Risk Based-Auditing-Keith-Ridgeway/

Does ISO 19011:2018 address risk based auditing?

Yes, there is a little discussion on risk based auditing. However in our opinion, much more practical and how to information needs to be provided. For example, a number of the questions that ISO 9001:2015 surfaces are not addressed in ISO 19011:2018.

Lesson Learned: Value Added Auditing is the companion book to **ISO: Risk Based Thinking**. It can be purchased from ASQ, Amazon, or directly from us (GregH@CERMAcademy.com).

Resource: Read 'Risk Based Auditing'
Http://Insights.CERMacademy.Com/2013/08/21-Risk Based-Auditing-Keith-Ridgeway/

What are the biggest risks in quality auditing?

ISO 19011:2018 is the reference for auditing ISO management systems. ISO 9001, ISO 27001 and other standards are what the auditors are ensuring companies adhere to. In other words, auditors are auditing against ISO 9001 and other management system standards.

ISO 19011:2018 should be a 'how to' standard but more often reads like a broad guideline. ISO 9001:2015 and all families ISO standards are becoming more generic and more open to interpretation. Specifically, the number of 'shalls' in the standards is decreasing. Auditors must use more discretion to determine compliance and effectiveness.

Bottom Line: ISO 19011:2018 does not provide adequate guidance in many cases to conduct effectiveness, risk, RBT, and process audits to evaluate adherence against ISO 9001:2015.

Lesson Learned: Understand how quality auditing will change based on Annex SL and RBT. ISO 19011:2018 does not address many of the changes being proposed in new standards.

Resource: Read 'Time To Rethink The Checklist Audit'
Http://Insights.CERMacademy.Com/2013/10/29-Time-To-Rethink-The-Checklist-Audit-Jorge-A-Correa/

What makes a good audit management system?

A good audit management system should address 3 key questions:

- **'What'.** What should the auditor be auditing against or evaluating adherence to? These are often globally recognized standards, specifications, requirements, or other documentation. In the management system world, ISO 9001:2015 and ISO 14001:2015 are examples of 'what' documents. CB auditors evaluate adherence against these documents.
- **'How'.** How should the audit be conducted? There are subsidiary

questions and issues such as how will the audit be planned, how will the audit be conducted (field work), and how will it be reported? In ISO management systems, ISO 19011:2018 is an example of a 'how' document. Internal quality auditors follow this standard to conduct their audits.

- **'Who'.** Who will be conducting the audit? This question deals with the requisite knowledge, skills, and abilities the auditor has to ensure consistent audit outcomes. CB auditors and internal quality auditors must have adequate knowledge, skills, and abilities to conduct audits and exercise due professional care when conducting the audit.

If the above questions are answered, the audit management system is suitable, replicable, and scalable.

Lesson Learned: Determine if your audit management system (first and second-party) meets the above criteria. If not, determine what needs to be done to develop a risk based, process, and effectiveness auditing system.

Resource: Read 'Performance Excellence Models, Part 2'
Http://Insights.CERMacademy.Com/2013/01/7-Performance-Excellence-Models-Part-2-Adina-Suciu

How should audits be managed?

The management of audits may consider: characteristics of processes, products, projects, level of performance, results of previous audits, and level of maturity of the management system. The audit manager is responsible for identifying and evaluating the risks that can impact audit objectives.

The audit manager may consider the following factors: effectiveness of the audit management system, availability of information, communication technologies, and current internal and external events that may impact the audit.

The audit manager is also responsible for:

- Identifying, evaluating, and mitigating audit program risks.
- Developing procedures to mitigate these risks
- Considering risk when planning and scheduling audits.
- Safeguarding confidential information.
- Selecting appropriate sampling techniques when conducting audits.
- Providing sufficient resources to plan, conduct, and report audit results.
- Ensuring audit objectives, scope, and criteria for each audit are clearly identified.
- Evaluating the performance of the audit team.

Lesson Learned: Ask your CB who is the auditor (s) that will be certifying you? What is the person's background in risk based, process, effectiveness, and RBT auditing?

Resource: Read 'It's All About Managing Communication Risk' http://insights.cermacademy.com/2012/11/5-its-all-about-managing-communication-risks-adina-suciu-communicationsrisk/

How will CB auditor's determine conformance to the broader scope of clauses in ISO 9001:2015?

Carefully is the simple answer. This has yet to be determined by the CB's. In the broader scope either explicit or implied in the ISO 9001 standard, organizations will have to deal with the broader context of 'customer satisfaction', which may imply GRC, complying with laws, interested parties, CSR, ethical sourcing, and other moral obligations.

The challenge for the auditors will be to scope (narrow the scope) the audit to determine that critical ISO 9001:2015 requirements are being met. Also as more organizations move to value added verification of the QMS or other management systems, CB auditors will have to seek new forms of evidence and verification of the QMS. The auditors will have to make judgment calls at a higher level because there may be a lack of consistent QMS documentation. As well, auditors will be evaluating upside (opportunity) risks. This will add additional uncertainty and risk to the QMS audits.

Lesson Learned: It is important to understand how your CB will conduct a risk based, process, and effectiveness audit of customer satisfaction and other clauses open to interpretation. These are critical questions about ISO 9001:2015 auditability.

Resource: Read 'Tips On Improving Quality Auditing'
Http://Insights.CERMacademy.Com/2014/09/57-Tips-Improving-Quality-Auditing-T-Dan-Nelson/

How will auditors evaluate 'effectiveness' in ISO 9001:2015?

With ISO 9001:2015, effectiveness will have broader impacts and implications, specifically:

- **Clause 4 Context.** How effective is the organization evaluating risks within the organization's context?
- **Clause 5 Leadership.** How effective is top management commitment in supporting the QMS?
- **Clause 6 Planning.** How effective is the organization in identifying downside risks and upside opportunities?
- **Clause 8 Operations.** How effective is the organization mitigating risks and addressing opportunities?
- **Clause 9 Performance Evaluation.** How effective is the organization in monitoring, measuring, analyzing, and evaluating risk and opportunities?
- **Clause 10 Improvement.** How effective is the organization improving its ability to respond to changes in risk?

Lesson Learned: Review each of the above bullets on effectiveness and see how they relate to your processes and certification scope.

Resource: Read 'ERM Integrated Framework For Auditors' Http://Insights.CERMacademy.Com/2013/02/8-ERM-Integrated-Framework-For-Auditors-Greg-Hutchins/

How will 'interested parties' be audited?

This is still a question that results in CB variability or in other words risk.

Let us take a look at one area, specifically Corporate Social Responsibility (CSR). ISO has developed ISO 26000 guidelines for CSR. These guidelines are best management practices. The challenge is these are often open to interpretation. For example, who are stakeholders of a robust CSR program? Would potential stakeholders include end-users, retailers, first-tier suppliers, second-tier suppliers, consumers, and purchasers? Could any or all of these be considered 'customers' or 'interested parties'?

What would happen if an overzealous auditor probed the governance and ethics of the organization or interested parties? What are the limits of the auditor's scope of work? If auditors conduct ISO 9001:2015 risk audits then the auditee will have to define process controls and process outputs in many organizational areas. Will the auditor have the discretion to probe CSR artifacts and evidence?

The norms of good business behavior are also changing in many areas. ISO 9001 does not explicitly address areas of good CSR. Customer expectations are changing. What was considered customer satisfaction with the product 5 years ago has changed. In the globalized economy, products or services produced by child or prison labor or where output pollutes rivers or CO2 is put into the atmosphere are not acceptable.

Lesson Learned: As the new ISO 9001:2015 standard is written, we have played 'what if' scenarios around risk based auditing. A lot of questions still remain unanswered.

Resource: Read 'What Does 'Added Value' Really Mean?' Http://Insights.CERMacademy.Com/2014/09/59-Added-Value-Really-Mean-Umberto-Tunesi/

What is 'management system assurance'?

QMS, EMS, and other ISO management systems provide certification compliance. Compliance is a binary decision: 'yes' the company complies with ISO 9001:2015 standard requirements or it does not. In the assurance world, binary assurance is a relatively low threshold of assurance to third parties.

Lesson Learned: Management system assurance is relatively low level. Does your organization or customer require higher levels of assurance? If yes, what do they specifically want? Global CB's are ready to provide a higher level of assurance.

Resource: Read 'Why Do Corrective Actions Fail?' Http://Insights.CERMacademy.Com/2014/09/59-Correctives-Fail-Ed-Grounds/

What is 'quality assurance'?

Traditionally, quality assurance is defined as:

> "... refers to the engineering, manufacturing, supplier, and operations activities implemented in a quality system so product or service requirements can be fulfilled. It is the systematic measurement, comparison with a standard, monitoring of processes and an associated feedback loop that hopefully results in defect or error prevention."[xxvi]

Lesson Learned: The above definition has elements of risk assurance. So, integrate your quality assurance with risk assurance. It will greatly enhance your assurance to all parties.

Resource: Read 'Exposing Uncertainty About Resources In ISO DIS 9001:2015' Http://Insights.CERMacademy.Com/2014/10/63-Exposing-Uncertainty-Resources-ISO-Dis-90012015-David-Hoyle/

What is 'Business Assurance'?

There are different levels of assurance. In the early days of ISO 9001:1987, Quality Auditing was relatively straightforward. Quality auditors checked for compliance against ISO 9001 'shall' requirements. This was called a clause-by-clause quality audit. Fairly easy stuff. Low level of assurance.

ISO 9001:2015 will change the landscape of quality and risk assurance that can be provided by a CB. We will see more CB's develop advisory services similar to DNV's Business Assurance®. Business Assurance will be a value added service that specific high risk and regulatory customers may want, such as aerospace, software, oil/gas, and pharmaceutical clients.

Lesson Learned: DNV has a registered trademark on Business Assurance®. However, we are seeing more CB's use this expression. It will be interesting to see how DNV will enforce its mark.

Resource: Read 'ISO 9001:2015 Auditability' Http://Insights.CERMacademy.Com/2014/02/42-Mastering-21st-Century-Enterprise-Risk-Management-Gregory-Carroll-2/

What is 'risk assurance'?

Risk assurance is the basis for risk based auditing. It is interesting that Wikipedia does not have a reference for 'risk assurance'. However, we believe the term will have more resonance and use in the future. Risk assurance is about managing uncertainty, determining how problems are solved, and determining how decisions are made. Managers have to make decisions based on incomplete or inaccurate information, which increase decision making risk. All of which are implied in Risk Based Thinking.

ISO management system audits are moving to risk assurance with the introduction of RBT and risk in the standards. As ISO 9001:2015 incorporate risks, audit stakeholders want assurance that critical enterprise problems are solved correctly, risks are mitigated, and decisions are made within the risk appetite of the organization.

Unfortunately, ISO clause-by-clause audits are still conducted. Risk assurance is the next step from a 'check the box' compliance checklist audit to a risk based audit. Risk assurance would include:

- QMS objectives are defined and prioritized.
- Organizational 'black swan' risks are identified.
- Risks are viewed holistically at the enterprise level.
- Risk based, problem solving and risk based, decision making are emphasized.
- System of risk-controls is aligned with enterprise strategy and plans.
- Risks are properly mitigated within the risk appetite of the organization.

Lesson Learned: Introduce the concept of risk assurance and risk based auditing to your organization. It is a critical concept that will become more important as ISO 9001:2015 and RBT are institutionalized within organizations.

Resource: Read 'Risk Based Approach To Validation' Http://Insights.CERMacademy.Com/2014/04/45-Riskbased-Approach-Validation-Peter-Knauer

What is 'reasonable assurance'?

According to Generally Accepted Government Audit Standards (Yellow Book), reasonable assurance is defined as:

> "Auditors obtain reasonable assurance that evidence is sufficient and appropriate to support the auditors' findings and conclusions in relation to the audit objectives."[xxvii]

Reasonable assurance is not defined in ISO 9001:2015 or ISO 31000:2018, but it is a fundamental concept in risk management. Reasonable assurance is a level of acceptable knowledge so business objectives will be reached and known risks can be controlled. Reasonable assurance cannot anticipate uncontrollable or unknown events or the instant they can or will occur.

Sufficient and appropriate evidence is required and the testing of evidence will depend on audit objectives, findings, and conclusions. The auditor's professional knowledge and capabilities determine the sufficiency and appropriateness of evidence.

Reasonable assurance is the relative effectiveness of risk-controls that may be designed and deployed to ensure ISO 9001:2015 compliance. It is sometimes easier to say what it is not. Reasonable assurance does not mean or imply absolute or 100% assurance. Also, achieving reasonable assurance does not guarantee an organizational objective can be or is met.

Reasonable assurance is the basis for performance auditing including Yellow Book, Red Book, financial auditing, internal auditing (IIA), and quality auditing. We believe that as Internal Quality Auditing becomes harmonized with traditional Internal Auditing, reasonable assurance will become the basis for quality audit findings.

Lesson Learned: ISO 9001:2015 has inherent variability. It will be a difficult standard to certify until CB's have sufficient history to determine what is reasonable for ISO management systems assurance. Also, reasonable assurance is a critical concept for certified organizations.

When you are starting your certification and RBT journey, determine your level of reasonable assurance in terms of quantifiable information and evidence when architecting, deploying, and assuring ISO 9001:2015 risk-controls. The CB may determine this is reasonable for your organization. This key concept is not part of ISO 9001:2015 or ISO 31000:2018, but is very critical in the development of RBT and your risk treatment program.

Resource: Read 'ISO 9001:2015 Auditability' Http://Insights.CERMacademy.Com/2014/02/42-Mastering-21st-Century-Enterprise-Risk-Management-Gregory-Carroll-2/

What is an example of different levels of assurance?

Global CB's are already offering varying levels and types of assurance to their clients. As an example of varying types of assurance, some CB's are issuing certificates of conformance to their clients for ISO 31000:2018, even though it is explicitly not a conformity assessment standard. As an example of varying levels of assurance, some CB's offer the client a professional opinion or a forensics assessment, which provide a higher level of assurance to third parties than a binary or checklist assessment.

As an example, our firm (Quality + Engineering) conducts Critical Infrastructure Protection: Forensics, Assurance, Analytics® audits which offer varying levels of assurance, specifically:

- **Analytical.** Q+E engineers and scientists conduct analytical assessment following Q+E protocols evaluating IT and cyber security systems against IEEE, PMI, ISO, NIST, and AEC standards.
- **Assurance.** Q+E offers the client three levels of assurance:
    - **Compliance.** Q+E conducts a compliance audit against COBIT, NIST, or ISO standards.
    - **Assurance with opinion.** Q+E issues an opinion based on the results of a governance, risk, and compliance audit.
    - **Assurance with Department of Homeland Security Safety Act coverage.** Q+E conducts an audit and provides the requisite level of due diligence for the auditee to be covered by the Safety Act against domestic and state-sponsored terrorism.

- **Forensics.** Q+E provides all of the above levels of assurance as well as supplies a letter to a federal authority averring compliance that above criteria have been met. Critical infrastructure consists of systems and networks that if interrupted, destroyed, or disrupted will have dire national security consequences.

Lesson Learned: As one moves down the above list, the customer receives a higher level of assurance. Or another way to think of it, risk is being transferred from the auditee to the auditor as a result of risk based auditing.

Resource: Read 'Types Of Quality Risk Assessments'
Http://Insights.CERMacademy.Com/2013/09/24-Types-Of-Quality-Assessments-Greg-Hutchins/

What is the Institute of Internal Auditing (IIA)?

The Institute of Internal Auditors (IIA) is the standards development organization for the Internal Auditing profession, much like ASQ is for Quality Auditing. Both organizations have developed auditing standards. The IIA standard is called the Red Book.

The scope of Internal Auditing within an organization encompasses financial, operational, supply chain, and compliance areas. Another challenge is ISO 9001:2015 risk assessments may have to be harmonized with Internal Auditing. Why? Internal Auditing has been conducting risk based audits since the introduction of the Sarbanes Oxley Act in 2002.

Sarbanes Oxley requires risk assessments of Internal Control over Financial Reporting (ICFR) processes. The Chief Financial Officer and CEO are required to attest (sign off) on the effectiveness of risk-controls. Internal Auditors have been facilitating this process for a dozen years and reporting to the Board of Directors Audit Committee the effectiveness of risk-controls.

Lesson Learned: Internal Auditing more often is conducting operational, cyber security, supply chain, and manufacturing risk audits based on the COSO risk framework. This is a critical issue since Quality Auditing is now beginning to conduct risk based audits. Internal Auditing already has access to the Board of Director's Audit Committee and will be reporting on the effectiveness of operational and supply chain risk-controls. So, understand the structure, intent, and content of the IIA standards. IIA standards are available at www.iia.org.

Resource: Read 'Must Know Risk Facts For Quality And All Professionals'
Http://Insights.CERMacademy.Com/2013/05/13-Variation-And-The-Quality-Professional-Greg-Hutchins/

What are the core responsibilities of Internal Audit?

The Institute of Internal Auditors (IIA) has identified the following key roles for Internal Audit:

- Providing assurance on the suitability and effectiveness of organizational risk management processes.
- Providing assurance that risks are effectively evaluated within the appetite of the organization.
- Evaluating the effectiveness of risk management processes and controls.
- Reporting key risks to operations management and material risks to the Board of Directors Audit Committee.
- Reviewing the efficiency, effectiveness, and economics of key risk-controls.

Sometimes, it is easier to say what something is not. The IIA has indicated that Internal Audit should not:

- Determine the risk appetite of the organization, programs, projects, or processes.

- Determine the appropriate risk management processes for the organization.
- Serve as management's arm for implementing risk management.
- Accepting responsibility and accountability for organizational risk management.

Lesson Learned: Understand what Internal Audit does in your organization and see how you can begin working with them.

Resource: Read 'Regulations Vary Worldwide But Risk Management Is Common Denominator'
Http://Insights.CERMacademy.Com/2014/02/39-Regulations-Vary-Worldwide-Risk-Management-Common-Denominator-Cindy-Fazzi/

What is 'Internal Quality Auditing'?

Internal quality auditing is called first-party, quality auditing. Wikipedia defines Quality Auditing as:

> "The process of systematic examination of a quality system carried out by an internal or external quality auditor or an audit team. It is an important part of an organization's QMS and is a key element in the ISO quality system standard, ISO 9001." [xxviii]

The focus on Internal Quality Auditing has increased with each iteration of ISO 9001. In early iterations of ISO 9001, Internal Quality Auditing was largely compliance based reviewing 'shall' policies and procedures. Early Internal Quality Audits usually focused on compliance to documented QMS procedures.

In ISO 9001:2008, Internal Quality Auditing matured from policy adherence usually document intensive to evaluating the process effectiveness of the QMS and its results. Internal Quality Audits focused on evaluating critical QMS processes from inputs, the process, and outputs meeting requirements. Auditors would evaluate objective evidence obtained from critical processes, determine how successful the processes had been deployed, and evaluate the effectiveness of achieving defined target levels. The Internal Quality Audit reports indicated noncompliance, nonconformance, corrective action, preventive action, and opportunity for improvement.

Following the ISO 9001:2015, Internal Auditing may evolve to conducting risk based audits, specifically evaluating the effectiveness of QMS processes and internal risk-controls.

Lesson Learned: Harmonize your Internal Auditing, supplier Quality Auditing, and Quality Auditing so they are consistently focused on risk based auditing.

Resource: Read 'Emerging Risks Ii The Black Swan Syndrome' Http://Insights.CERMacademy.Com/2014/10/62-Emerging-Risks-Ii-Black-Swan-Syndrome-Greg-Carroll/

How is Internal Audit different from Quality Audit?

Both Quality Auditing and the Internal Auditing professions use the term 'internal auditing.' To avoid confusion, we usually differentiate between the two by using the terms 'Quality Auditing' and 'Internal Auditing.'

Many organizations have an Internal Audit group that focuses on internal control, specifically:

> "Internal control is broadly defined as a process, affected by an entity's Board of Directors, management and other personnel, designed to provide reasonable assurance regarding the achievement of objectives in the following categories:
>
> - Effectiveness and efficiency of operations.
> - Compliance with applicable laws and regulations.
> - Reliability of financial reporting."[xxix]

Traditional Internal Auditors follow the institute of Internal Auditor Red Book standards as well as the COSO Integrated Framework of Internal Control. Their professional designation is Certified Internal Auditor (CIA) issued by the Institute of Internal Auditors (IIA).

Quality or management system auditors focus on ISO 9001 and other quality management standards. Management system auditors follow ISO 19011:2018 as their guidance for conducting audits. Their professional designation is Certified Quality Auditor (CQA) issued by the American Society for Quality (ASQ).

Lesson Learned: Internal Quality Auditing and traditional Internal Auditing are different. Understand how they are different. Most importantly, Internal Auditors are experts in risk based auditing. So, try to integrate and align Internal Quality Audits with traditional Internal Audits. Internal audits are already risk based. They are ahead of you. There is much you can learn about risk based auditing and RBT from the Internal Audit function.

Resource: Read 'Cover Your Assets 101 and Plausible Deniability' http://insights.cermacademy.com/2013/04/11-cover-your-assets-101-ed-perkins/

What is the 'Yellow Book'?

U.S. Generally Accepted Government Auditing Standards (GAGAS) are also called the Yellow Book standards. Government Accountability Office (GAO) conducts Yellow Book audit. The Yellow Book provides an audit framework for reporting, conducting (field work), and reporting audits with competence, integrity, objectivity, and independence.

The purpose of GAGAS auditing is to provide objective and if required independent information and analysis to solve problems and make better decisions in government agencies.

GAGAS provides a framework for conducting high quality audits with due professional care following professional standards. Currently, ISO quality auditors aim for this level of independence, objectivity, and transparency

The Yellow Book can be downloaded as a free pdf from the U.S. Government Accountability Office (GAO). The Yellow Book is a good to great model for conducting risk based audits. See below **Resource** citation for download information.

Lesson Learned: Incorporate Yellow Book 'Performance Audit ' elements into your Internal Quality Audits.

Resource: Yellow Book Is Free And Can Be Downloaded At: Www.Gao.Gov/Products/Gao-12-331g

How can Quality Audit and Internal Audit provide consolidated reporting?

We have been advocating consolidated reporting of Internal Audit and Quality Audit to the Board of Directors Audit Committee for years. It is still not common. Why? The two disciplines have different taxonomies, language, perspectives, skills sets, and standards.

Joint and consolidated reporting of risks would be beneficial to the organization in a number of ways. Internal Auditing would expand its knowledge, scope, and abilities into ISO 9001:2015, supply chain assessments, and quality assurance. Quality Auditing would learn how to conduct risk based audits and effectiveness assessments. The organization and the Board of Directors would obtain the benefit of a consolidated view of operations, product development, and supply chain risks.

Internal Audit has positioned itself as the voice and assurance of risk-controls for the organization since the Sarbanes Oxley Act in 2002. Its primary focus was to validate the control effectiveness of Internal Control over Financial Reporting (ICFR). As these controls matured and become more capable, Internal Audit has extended its purview into IT, operations, supply chain, cyber security, and product development. Operations, product development, and supply chain issues have quality responsibilities. Now, Internal Audit is taking a look at them and saying there are risks in these areas that are not adequately identified, controlled, and treated.

Lesson Learned: Harmonize Quality Auditing and Internal Auditing. This is a cultural issue because each party thinks in terms of its functional vertical and may not think what is best for the organization. Defer to Internal Audit in terms of planning, reporting, and conducting risk based audits. Internal Audit has been conducting risk audits for at least 12 years. We strongly recommend that you do not get into a turf war regarding risk based audits. Quality will lose.

Resource: Read 'Risks Of Failing To Innovate'
Http://Insights.CERMacademy.Com/2014/06/51-Risks-Failing-Innovate-Gary-Gack/

Why are you making such a big deal about the reporting level of quality reports?

The level of quality reporting is an indicator of the importance of the reports. ISO 9001 QMS audit reports tend go to a second or at most a third level manager in many organizations. Internal audits go the organization's Board of Directors. Where do you think quality reports should go?

Lesson Learned: We have been strong advocates of consolidated reporting where management system audits, including EMS, QMS, and ITMS go to higher levels of management. This should be the future of quality risk based reporting.

Resource: Read 'The Risk And High Cost Of Unclear Communication'
Http://Insights.CERMacademy.Com/2014/10/62-Risk-High-Cost-Unclear-Communication-Elizabeth-Lions/

What types of quality risk reports can be generated?

Risk information facilitates RBT, CSR, ERM, and GRC. In terms of ISO 9001:2015, the impact of the standard will be to promote 1. Risk based, problem solving and 2. Risk based, decision making.

Quality reports and information can be reframed in terms of risk. The following are examples of risk reports:

- Summary of enterprise risks broken down by business units, programs, projects, and products.
- Summary of RBT, operational and/or supply chain risks.
- Summary of QMS, EMS, risks, etc.
- Operational risk reports generated for different geographies and sales channels.
- Risk register listing critical operational and supply management risks and controls.
- Summary of risk maps listing red and yellow areas and remediating controls.
- Summary of acceptable risks in different organizational areas such as business units, programs, projects, and products.
- Summary of the top and worst performing investments, whether they are capital investments, real property, etc.
- Environmental scan of potential external and internal events or emerging issues, risks, or threats that may warrant management attention.
- Details of programmatic and project variances against targets.
- Details of scope, schedule, technology, quality, and cost variances against targets.
- Operational risk reports summarizing nonconformances, exceptions, variances, breaches, threats, errors, and losses.
- Summary of Corrective Action and Preventive Action reports and current status of each.
- Summary of significant findings of internal quality audits and risk.

reviews.

Lesson Learned: Communications is an integral element of all RBT and risk management frameworks. So, start developing new RBT and risk reporting procedures that will help stakeholders and interested parties to solve problems and make better decisions.

Resource: Read 'Organization And System Failure'
Http://Insights.CERMacademy.Com/2014/01/37-Organization-System-Failure-Ian-Rosan

Should quality auditors learn how to conduct a Red Book or Yellow Book audit?

Yes. Why? U.S. government auditors conduct Yellow Book audits, which are process, effectiveness, risk, and performance based assessments. Internal auditors conduct Red Book audits, which are similarly, process, effectiveness, and risk based. Yellow Book and Red Books are risk based. Risk based auditing is an essential skill of quality auditing.

And yes, internal auditors should also learn how to conduct QMS, EMS, or ISMS audits based on ISO management system standards.

Lesson Learned: Ensure all audit stakeholders win. Quality auditors expand their professional toolbox. Internal auditors learn how to conduct management system audits. Organizations should have a consolidated view of operations.

Resource: Read '10 Strategies for Increasing Your Creativity'
http://insights.cermacademy.com/2014/01/34-10-strategies-increasing-creativity-daniel-burrus/

What do you see as the future of Quality Auditing?

Traditional Internal Audit is an objective and independent function that helps an organization meet its business objectives by evaluating and improving the effectiveness of its GRC processes.

Does this sound like a new role the quality organization may assume with ISO 9001:2015? Maybe. That is why it is critical the quality organization work closely with Internal Auditing.

The scope of Quality Auditing in ISO 9001:2015 may evolve to:

- Enhancing an organization's governance, risk, and oversight.
- Deploying enterprise risk-controls of QMS, EMS, and operations.
- Providing internal risk assurance of the effectiveness of risk-controls.
- Making recommendations on risk treatment in all management systems.
- Conducting risk audits of operational and supply chain efficiencies, effectiveness, and economics.

Lesson Learned: Learn risk based auditing. It may be the future of quality auditing.

Resource: Read 'Rethinking Sector Scheme Relationships' Http://Insights.CERMacademy.Com/2014/10/62-Rethinking-Sector-Scheme-Relationships-T-Dan-Nelson/

What do you see as the future of CB's portfolio of services?

The ISO conformity assessment landscape is rapidly changing. Global CB's are now offering a portfolio of risk consulting and risk assurance services well beyond RBT and ISO certification.

We are going to see CB's provide value added services such as risk based auditing, business assurance, and other activities that are commonly outside the scope of ISO 9001 compliance. The CB's must be independent to provide ISO 9001:2015 certification, so these value added services will be provided by independent consulting arms.

The CB's rationale for expanding their portfolio of services will be something like this. The global CB's have global clients. The global clients often want higher levels of assurance and risk-controls throughout operations. The global CB's are customer responsive providing broader and deeper levels of assurance and business risk-controls. Several global CB's have rebranded as risk organizations providing business assurance services.

Lesson Learned: Ensure the value added consulting of your CB is truly independent of your management system certification. Or, use consultants to provide the value added services to ensure there are no conflicts of interest.

Resource: Read 'Sustainable Risk Management'
Http://Insights.CERMacademy.Com/2013/03/Sustainable-Risk-Management/

CHAPTER 13:

RISK ASSESSMENT TOOLS

What is the key idea in this chapter?

The key idea in this chapter is risk assessment is the basis for RBT. Risk assessment tools emphasize risk based, problem solving and risk based, decision making.

What type of risk assessment is required by ISO 9001:2015?

ISO 9001:2015 does not require or specify any risk assessment methodology. The standard requires QMS objectives are identified and controls are in place to ensure quality objectives can be met. The identification of risk implies a risk assessment is conducted and the control of risk implies risk treatment. And depending on the context of the QMS objectives and risk-controls, this could imply the start of the RBT journey

Lesson Learned: Global CB's and ISO 31000:2018 gurus are already saying an ISO 9001:2015 risk assessment is the start of the RBT journey to some level of risk management or even enterprise risk management.

Resource: Read 'Does Anyone Really Understand Emerging Risks?' Http://Insights.CERMacademy.Com/2014/09/60-Anyone-Really-Understand-Emerging-Risks-Greg-Carroll/

What is a risk assessment?

Risk assessment according to ISO 31000:2018 includes:

- **Risk identification**. Involves identifying potential events that can positively impact the enterprise (upside opportunity) or negatively impact (downside risk) the enterprise's ability to achieve its business or QMS objectives. An organization identifies the sources of risk, areas of impacts, events, their causes, and potential consequences based on the achievement of QMS objectives.

- **Risk Analysis.** Involves determining how risks should be treated or mitigated based on the likelihood and consequence of the specific risks. An organization analyzes risk in terms of considering the causes and sources of risk, positive/negative consequences, and likelihood/probability of occurrence.

- **Risk Evaluation.** Involves making the appropriate risk decisions based on context and the risk appetite of the organization. An organization evaluates risk to assist in solving problems or in making better decisions at the 1. Enterprise level; 2. Programmatic/Project/Process level; or 3. Product/Transactional level.

Risk assessment can be a qualitative or quantitative method to evaluate risk in terms of its likelihood and consequence of a potential event occurring. RBT and risk assessment tools covered in this chapter are mainly qualitative. Why do we spend time presenting qualitative tools? Most quality organizations transitioning to ISO 9001:2015 have Level 1, ad hoc (RCMM) risk practices. They are starting their RBT journey to risk assessment.

Lesson Learned: Assess the risks that may impede achieving QMS objectives starting from a top down evaluation, specifically from the enterprise level to the product level. Keep it simple. Use a qualitative risk assessment to comply with RBT, ISO 9001:2015 and ISO 14001:2015.

Resource: Read 'Risk Assessment Lessons Learned' Http://Insights.CERMacademy.Com/2014/08/55-Risk-Assessment-Lessons-Learned-Greg-Hutchins/

Is risk assessment a process?

Yes! All commonly used risk frameworks follow a lifecycle. Each element of the lifecycle has inputs, a process, and outputs, which should satisfy a customer. Many ISO management system standards follow a cycle. The ISO 31000:2018 lifecycle process consists of the following steps:

- Communication and consultation.
- Establishing the context.
- Risk identification.
- Risk analysis.
- Risk evaluation.
- Risk treatment.
- Monitoring and review.
- Recording and reporting.

Many companies pursuing ISO 9001:2015 certification will design, deploy, and assure a risk assessment approach based on ISO 31000:2018. The above phases are described at length in the ISO 31000:2018 chapter.

Lesson Learned: Design your risk assessment framework around the ISO 31000:2018 process. It will help your CB auditors conduct the audit since it is a recognizable quality management system approach.

What is the difference between a qualitative and quantitative risk assessment?

ISO 9001:2015 risk assessments can be qualitative or quantitative or both.

Internal quality auditors, ISO consultants, and CB auditors will have to become fluent in evaluating qualitative and quantitative risk assessments.

Qualitative risk assessments are based on limited data and are often 'best guesses' or educated opinions. A heat or risk map is an example of a qualitative risk assessment. A risk map consists of severity or consequence on one axis and probability or likelihood on the other axis. A FMEA is another example of a qualitative assessment.

Quantitative risk assessments are based on extensive information or 'big' data. Quantitative data include reliability analyses and statistical process control. Qualitative risk assessments are more art than science.

The major benefit of a risk assessment is to bring people together to discuss risk based, problem solving and risk based, decision making. This RBT collaborative process may be more important than the outcome of the risk assessment because it brings people together to discuss critical issues and develop common definitions and mitigations to address risks.

Lesson Learned: Since most ISO 9001:2015 certified companies will be at the RCMM level 1, we recommend keeping the risk assessment simple. Use a risk assessment method with which you are comfortable.

Resource: Read 'How Well Do Risk Assessments Inform Decision Makers?'
Http://Insights.CERMacademy.Com/2014/06/52-Well-Risk-Assessments-Inform-Decision-Makers-Chris-Peace/

What are methods for conducting a risk assessment?

Risk assessment tools can be used for quick assessments, supporting risk management, scenario analysis, function analysis, controls assessment, and statistical analyses. Risk assessments can be qualitative and/or quantitative.

There are a number of techniques for conducting a risk assessment. In this book, we recommend ISO 9001:2015 certified companies start their

RBT journey using qualitative risk maps or even a checklist. As the company matures its RBT and risk assessment or requires a higher level of risk assurance, then we recommend selecting additional risk tools and techniques.

ISO 31010 offers the following list of risk assessment tools:

Method	Description	Application
Checklists	Simple and quick identification of possible risk uncertainties.	Used in varied ways. Checklist assessments. Low complexity. Tailored to application.
Preliminary hazard analysis.	Objective is to identify hazardous situations.	Used for threat analysis and cyber security, etc.
Structured interview and brainstorming	Objective is to collect ideas, rank, and evaluate them.	Used for risk auditing
Delphi method	System for combining expert opinions about probability and likelihood in the risk assessment.	Used for collaborative risk assessments.
Structured 'what if'	System approach used by a team to identify and assess risks.	Used in facilitated workshop.
Human reliability	Objective is to understand ergonomic and human system performance.	Used to understand human reliability and risks.
Root cause analysis	Objective is to understand root cause of a single loss.	Used in single loss analysis. Medium complexity

Scenario analysis	Identifies future scenarios through extrapolation of the present.	Used to envision future risks. Qualitative approach.
Toxicological risk assessment	Hazards are identified and analyzed including pathways.	Used to comply with regulatory requirements. Specific application.
Business impact analysis	Analysis of key disruption risks that can impact business continuity.	Used in critical applications.
Fault tree analysis	High risk events are identified and lower level risks prioritized. Mitigations are assigned to risks.	Used in many risk applications.
Event tree analysis	Inductive reasoning to translate event likelihood into possible outcomes.	Used with previous tools in multiple applications.
Cause/consequence analysis	Combination of fault tree and event tree analysis.	Used in multiple applications from first/second/third-party assessments.
Cause/effect analysis	Effect can have number of causes that are analyzed.	Often used with other assessment techniques.
Failure Mode and Effects Analysis (FMEA)	Analysis of failure modes and effects, which are then mitigated/treated.	Used mainly at the product level to ID possible design failures.

Reliability centered maintenance	Method to analyze maintainability failures, safety, availability, and operational economy.	Used mainly for operational risk assessments.
Sneak analysis	Method to identify design problems. Sneak condition refers to a latent hardware or software unwanted event.	Used mainly in product design.
Hazard and operability studies (HAZOP)	Process of risk identification of possible deviation of intended operation.	Used in operational analysis.
Hazard analysis and critical control points (HACCP)	Process to assure product quality, reliability, and safety of processes.	Used in food safety and similar areas.
Layers of protection analysis (LOPA)	Process to analyze control effectiveness.	Used in operational control effectiveness analysis.
Bow tie analysis	Visual qualitative analysis of pathways and causes of risks.	Used in product and process levels. Multiple uses.
Markov analysis	Quantitative analysis of complex systems	Used in repairable electronic and mechanical systems.
Monte Carlo analysis	Process to analyze variations in systems	Used in complex systems.
Bayesian analysis	Quantitative statistical analysis of distribution of data.	Used where sufficient data is known.

Lesson Learned: We have used most of the above risk assessment tools. They are all good, but should be used in the right application by a trained risk professional. Otherwise, it can be become a practice of 'garbage in and garbage out.'

Resource: Read 'Depend On Your QMS Tools' Http://Insights.CERMacademy.Com/2014/10/63-Depend-Qms-Tools-Mary-Mcatee/

What factors should be considered when conducting a risk assessment?

There are no set rules or factors to consider when conducting a risk assessment. It is all about context. However based on our experience, the following are factors to consider:

- Organization's context, complexity, capability, maturity, business model, core competencies, etc.
- Organization's scale, nature of products/services, and materiality of risks.
- Organizations GRC and business model.
- Regulatory nature of the sector(s) and company's products.
- Stakeholder and management's risk/reward expectations.
- Stakeholder and management's risk appetite.
- Risk interactions across and up/down the organization including the supply chain.
- Type of application of data.

Lesson Learned: Choose a few tools from the above list to conduct a risk assessment. If you choose too many, then this will result in confusion, more variability and ultimately additional risk.

Resource: Read 'Checklist Manifesto: How To Get Things Done Right' Http://Insights.CERMacademy.Com/2013/03/Checklist-Manifesto-How-To-Get-Things-Right/

What makes an effective risk-control objective?

In ISO 9001:2015, risks are always evaluated in terms being able to attain or achieve a QMS objective. Controls to mitigate risks are then developed to ensure the objective

can be reached or realized. In this book, we call these risk-control objectives, because controls are used to treat or mitigate the risks. This approach is the basis of most risk assessments. The assessment evaluates the risks in being able to attain an objective, such as a QMS objective in ISO 9001:2015.

We recommend that SMART criteria be used to develop effective control objectives. SMART is a mnemonic offering the following criteria for developing effective control objectives:

- **Specific.** Focus on a specific quality, QMS, or business control objective at the 1. Enterprise level; 2. Programmatic/Project/Process level; 3. Product/Transactional level of an organization.
- **Measurable.** Develop a control objective that is aligned with organizational strategy or tactics and is quantifiable and an indicator of continual improvement.
- **Assignable.** Specify the system, process, function, or product owners for the achievement of the control objective.
- **Realistic.** Ensure the control objective is realistic given available resources, information, etc.
- **Time.** Specify the time period when the risk-control objective should be attained. Or if the control objective is continuous for a process, then this should be specified.

Lesson Learned: Use SMART as a process to develop risk-control and QMS objectives.

Resource: Read 'When 8 Weeks Isn't Really 8 Weeks'
Http://Insights.CERMacademy.Com/2013/09/24-When-8-Weeks-Isnt-Really-8-Weeks-Mark-Moore/

What is a risk map?

The risk map is a commonly used risk assessment tool. It is a qualitative method to illustrate degrees of risk through the use of colors such as red for high risk, yellow for medium risk, and green for acceptable risk. Risk maps are also called heat maps indicating that hotter areas of the map are those with the highest risk. A heat or risk map is illustrated on the next page.

A risk map is used to identify and prioritize risks that impede achieving a business or QMS control objective. Risk maps offer a number of benefits. Risk maps are intuitive and easy to understand. Risk maps can be the basis of a common framework and language for RBT, risk assessment, risk management, and enterprise risk management. All risk maps follow a common method of evaluating likelihood or probability of the event occurring and its impact, severity or consequence.

In the risk map shown on the next page, the light gray in the lower left is green, which indicates acceptable risk. The heavier gray area in the middle is yellow, which indicates risks need to be monitored. The darkest gray area at the upper right corner is red, which indicates high risk, which indicates risks need to be mitigated or treated.

Lesson Learned: Ensure you develop a consistent framework and vocabulary for assessing risk. Otherwise, confusion may result. Then start your RBT journey with a qualitative risk assessment in a limited area of the organization. As you feel comfortable, then expand your risk assessments.

Resource: Read 'Heat Maps and Grading Project Risk'
http://insights.cermacademy.com/2013/06/15-heat-maps-and-grading-project-risk-mark-moore/

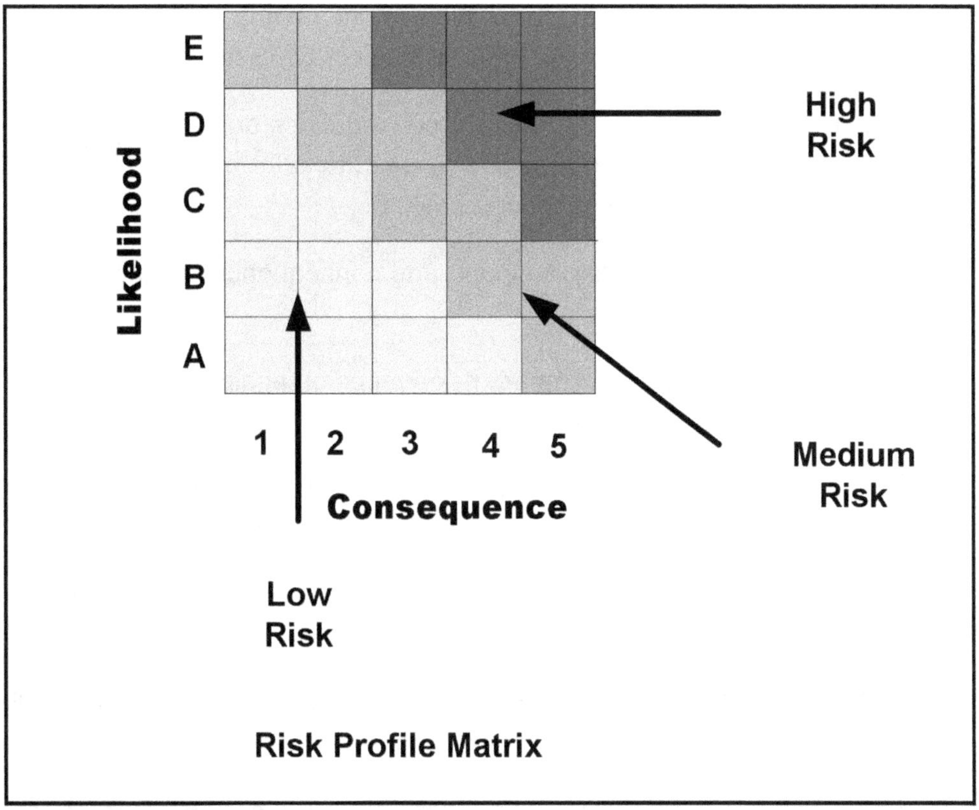

Figure 11: Heat Map

What is a typical risk assessment risk map?

On the following pages is an example of a risk or heat map template and a description on how to fill in the boxes. The following describes the boxes in the heat map template:

1. **Process/Program/Project Title.** Name or title of risk assessment.

2. **Date.** Date of risk assessment.

3. **Process/Program/Project Owner.** Name of process owner being evaluated.

4. **Risk Analyst.** Name of analyst.

5. **Control Objective:** Objective to be achieved (SMART).

6. **Risk Identification.** Description of risk, event, and/or threat that can impact achievement of a business or QMS objective.

7. **Risk Description.** Narrative of consequence or severity and probability of it occurring. Include assumptions for analysis. Calculate likelihood and consequence of risk(s).

8. **Risk Analysis.** Plot likelihood and consequence for each risk on the map.

9. **Risk Evaluation.** Compare risk evaluation against risk appetite or tolerance of the organization.

   a. **Risk Appetite/Tolerance & Action.** Determine to accept the risk or treat the risk.

10. **Choice of Risk Treatment Strategies.** Determine to avoid, accept, share or control risk.

11. **Description of Risk Treatment Application.** Describe the application of risk treatment or remediation.

12. **Post Assessment of Risk Treatment Application.** Recalculate likelihood and consequence of risk(s). Compare re-treatment against risk appetite or tolerance of the organization. Accept risk or implement additional risk treatment.

Resource: Read 'Sailing Ships And Risks - What Are Your True Colors?' Http://Insights.CERMacademy.Com/2015/01/75-Sailing-Ships-Risks-True-Colors-Joe-Eads/

What does consequence mean in a risk map?

Impact, severity, significance, or consequence are equivalent terms that are used in the risk map. The greater the impact, the higher the consequence number on the risk map. The consequence scale goes from 1 to 5 as can be seen in the above table. The highest level of consequence risk usually means there is a potential of loss of life, material loss in the business, inability to provide critical services, or inability to continue operations as a result of a major disaster and the risk.

Lesson Learned: Attempt to first control (minimize) the consequence and likelihood in a risk map before you look at other risk treatment options.

Resource: Read 'Risk Assessment: Simple Quality Example' Http://Insights.CERMacademy.Com/2013/06/18-Risk-Assessment-A-Simple-Quality-Example-Jim-Lamprecht/

Consequence or Impact Ranking		
Description	**Rank**	**Value**
Catastrophic	High	5
Critical	Medium High	4
Serious	Medium	3
Marginal	Medium Low	2
Negligible	Low	1

What does likelihood mean in a risk map?

Likelihood is one of the axes on the risk map. Likelihood is sometimes called probability. Process owners rate the severity of risk in terms of the ability to meet or achieve a business or QMS objective.

This can cause confusion. So, we often describe the severity of risk as hindrances or obstacles to the achievement of the business objective. The more obstacles or distance to achieve a business objective, the higher the risks.

Risk likelihood should be determined on the same time horizon as determining consequence. The higher the likelihood usually the higher the probability the risk will occur.

QUALITATIVE RISK ASSESSMENT/MANAGEMENT

1. Process/Program/Project Title: **2. Date:**

3. Process/Program/Project Owner: **4. Risk Analyst:**

5. Control Objective:

6. Risk Identification:

7. Risk Description:

Likelihood:

____

Consequence:

____

8. Risk Analysis:

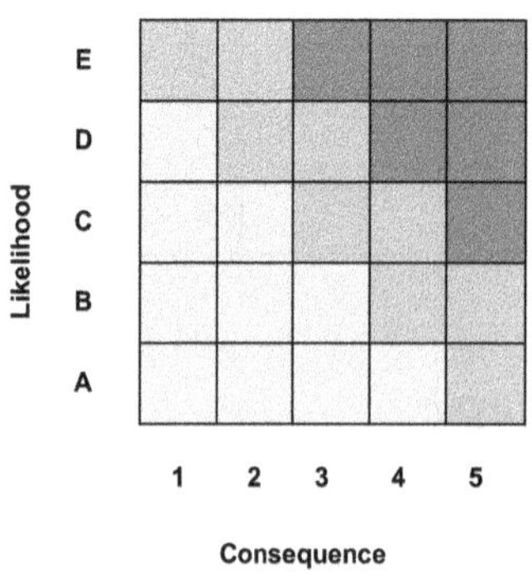

9. Risk Evaluation

High Risk – Points __

Medium Risk – Points __

Low Risk – Points __

8a. Risk Appetite/Tolerance & Action

10. Choice of Risk Treatment Strategies:

- ❑ Avoid risk
- ❑ Accept risk
- ❑ Share risk
- ❑ Control risk

11. Description of Risk Treatment Application:

12. Post Assessment Risk Treatment Application:

Likelihood: ______________________________________

Consequence: ____________________________________

Likelihood can be determined by several methods such as knowledgeable expert forecasting, best guess, expert panel, statistical methods, or group assessment.

Lesson Learned: Reduce likelihood of an event should be one of the first risk treatments to consider.

Resource: Read 'How To Calculate Project Risk' Http://Insights.CERMacademy.Com/2013/05/14-How-To-Calculate-Project-Risk-Frank-Harris/

Likelihood of Occurrence Ranking			
Description	**Probability**	**Rank**	**Value**
Highly Probable	90%	High	5
Probable	50 – 90%	Medium High	4
Sometime	50%	Medium	3
Remote	25 – 50%	Medium Low	2
Improbable	< 10%	Low	1

What are the benefits and challenges of risk maps?

Risk maps are a qualitative assessment. So, the maps are not exact and may simply be approximations of risk or even 'best initial judgments.'

The benefits of a risk map include:

- Are quick and fairly inexpensive to develop.
- Provide good visual display of enterprise, process, project, and product risks.
- Can provide an overview of organizational risks.

The challenges of a risk map include:

- Are inexact.
- Can provide a false sense of risk management and security.

Lesson Learned: The benefit of a risk map is not the map itself, but starts the process of Risk Based Thinking. Or expressed another way, the benefit is bringing the right people together for risk based, problem solving and risk based, decision making.

Resource: Read 'Unaddressed Risk' Http://Insights.CERMacademy.Com/2013/02/8-Unaddressed-Risk-Paul-Kostek/

What is the FMEA approach to an ISO 9001:2015 risk assessment?

A number of companies will use FMEA to assess risks for ISO 9001:2015. FMEA is an acronym for Failure Mode and Effects Analysis. FMEA is a logical, systematic, and documented process to identify, evaluate, and prioritize failures and their effects. The objective of a FMEA is to identify and eliminate the chance of potential failure or not being able to meet an objective.

FMEA is a tool that can be used at various organizational levels. Failure modes are the ways in which systems, processes, components, or products can fail or not perform as required. Failure effects are the outcomes of the occurrence of the failure mode on the QMS, product, or process.

Lesson Learned: Ensure you use a common FMEA in your applications. Share these with your customer and suppliers so everyone is speaking the same language. Visit the CERM Academy

Resource: Next section you will find a FMEA course that you can use as a ISO 9001:2015 risk assessment tool. Visit below to view the course: http://insights.cermacademy.com/2014/02/40-step-5-risk-based-planning-keith-ridgeway/

Resource: Read 'How To Implement A FMEA' Http://Insights.CERMacademy.Com/2014/05/48-Implement-Good-PFMEA-Carlos-E-Z-Krahembuhl

When should FMEA's be used?

FMEA is a flexible risk assessment tool. It can be used in the following:

- Early in the process improvement investigation, after a process map has been developed.
- When new systems, processes and products are being designed.
- When existing designs or processes are being changed.
- When carry over designs are used in new applications.
- After system, product, or process input and output functions have been defined, but before specific hardware is selected or released to manufacturing (ideally).

Lesson Learned: There are few hard and fast rules of what risk assessment tool to use. However, here are a few tips: Use FMEA's to evaluate mainly process and product risks. Use risk maps to evaluate enterprise, programmatic, and project risks.

Resource: Read 'Some Thoughts On FMEA's And Unknown Risks' Http://Insights.CERMacademy.Com/2014/01/36-Thoughts-FMEAs-Unknown-Risks-James-Lamprecht/

What are types of FMEA's?

The following are common types of FMEA's:

- **Strategic.** Used to develop contingency plans for new business or operating strategies. Focuses on risk elements including: markets, competition, technology, health, safety and environmental.

- **System**. Used to analyze systems and sub systems in the early concept and design stages. Focuses on potential failure modes associated with the functions of a system caused by the design.
- **Process.** Used to analyze operations. Focuses on process steps and inputs.
- **Design.** Used to analyze product designs before they are released to production. Focuses on product function.
- **Defects**. Used to error proof processes. Focuses on process steps and errors.[xxx]

Lesson Learned: Understand where and how to use FMEA's. They are a flexible quality tool for risk assessments.

Resource: Read 'FMEA: How To Find Value' Http://Insights.CERMacademy.Com/2014/12/72-FMEA-Find-Value-Fred-Schenkelberg/

What is 'inherent risk' in a risk assessment?

Inherent risk is the risk that always resides at the 1. Enterprise level; 2. Programmatic/Project/Process level; or 3. Product/Transactional level.

Some inherent risk can be controlled. However, there are a number of risks or sources of variation that are either unknown or unknowable. These result in surprises that must be mitigated after an occurrence.

Lesson Learned: Understand and write down the inherent risks in your enterprise, programs, projects, processes, products, services, and transactions. These will become a critical part of your knowledge base.

Resource: Read 'Using Risk And Safety Analysis As Part Of The Requirements Process' Http://Insights.CERMacademy.Com/2014/04/44-Using-Risk-Safety-Analysis-Part-Requirements-Process-Paul-Kostek/

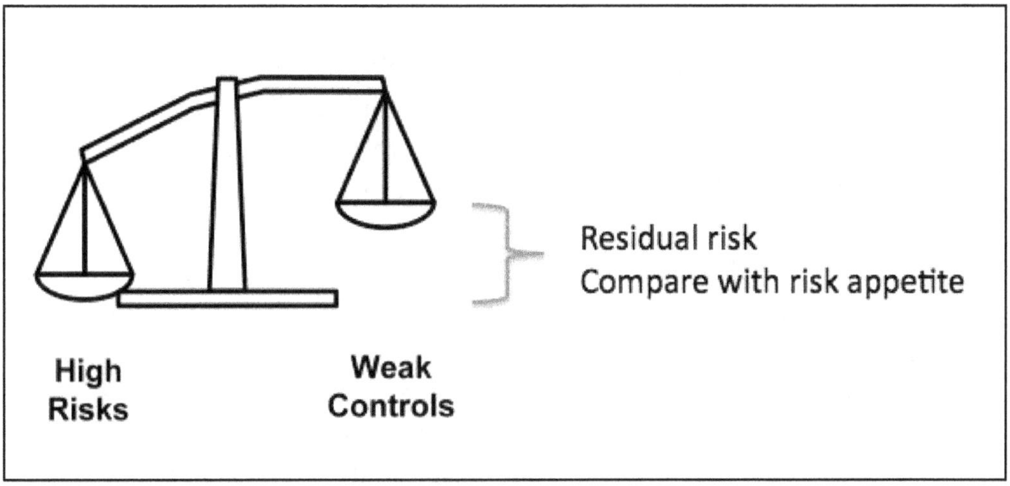

Figure 12: Residual Risk

What is 'acceptable risk' in a risk assessment?

Acceptable risk is the amount of risk that can be identified and is within the risk appetite of the organization and includes the following:

- Acceptable risk can be clarified and even quantified by time, potential loss, potential gain, cost, investment, scoping, quality, or event probability.
- Acceptable risk in a project can be defined in terms of variation in scope, quality, schedule or cost.
- Acceptable risk in a process can be defined in terms of process stability, process capability, or process improvement.

Lesson Learned: Define your acceptable risk first for achieving each QMS objective. Monetize your acceptable risk if possible.

Resource: Read 'How To Avoid Human Error in Design'
http://insights.cermacademy.com/2013/05/13-avoiding-human-error-in-design-ben-marguglio/

What is 'residual risk' in a risk assessment?

Residual risk is the risk remaining after risk mitigation or risk treatment has been applied. Residual risk can still contain unidentifiable, unknown, and unknowable risks. Residual risks are also referred to as retained risks, those retained by the organization. See Figure 12.

Let us take a look at the figure on the previous page based on a scale. There are high risks and relatively weak controls. One would think this would be unacceptable to the organization since risks are significantly higher than controls. But, it depends on the amount of residual risk. The difference or distance between the level of weak controls and level of risk is called residual risk. If the residual risk is within the risk appetite of the organization, then this would be acceptable to the organization. If the residual risk is greater than the organization's risk appetite, then this is unacceptable and additional treatment or mitigating controls would be deployed so the residual risk is within the organization's risk acceptance or risk appetite.

Lesson Learned: Understand and write down the residual risk each time you do a risk assessment.

Resource: Read 'People Are Dying Producing Your Product' Http://Insights.CERMacademy.Com/2013/12/32-People-Dying-Producing-Product-Kelly-Eisenhardt/

What are 'white space' risks in a risk assessment?

We have discussed risk in terms of not being able to meet a business or quality objective. But, a risk assessment can also be conducted of 'white space' risks.

ISO 9001:2000 and ISO 9001:2008 discuss a process based approach to conducting audits. White space risks are gaps between processes. The gaps can be vertical or horizontal. The gaps can be hand offs that are not identified or fully understood. The gaps can be hand offs that are not captured in a policy, procedure, work instruction or in a process diagram.

The consequence of these gaps is risk in terms of an elevated likelihood and probability of an unwanted event or unexpected variance.

Lesson Learned: Assess first your risks that impede the achievement of your QMS objectives. You will soon discover that many risks are in the 'white spaces' between your processes that may go into your supplier base.

Resource: Read 'Solution Aversion'
Http://Insights.CERMacademy.Com/2015/01/74-Solution-Aversion-Ed-Perkins/

How do you deal with 'whitespace' risks and their interrelationships?

Most ISO 9001 risk assessments address the ability to meet a quality objective or satisfy a customer requirement. In reality, most risks are more complex. Quite often, risks are assessed in silos, functions or processes. Many risks are often in the white spaces between silos, functions, and work between processes. These risks are often difficult to detect and to analyze. However, they are very critical to the achievement of a QMS objective.

The solution for analyzing whitespace risks and their interrelationships is to understand and map the relationships between silos, functions and processes. In the white spaces between these, there are interactions, relationships, and unknowns that should be analyzed through the use of various quality tools such as a turtle diagram and process flow charts.

The other challenge is that there may not be a causal relationship between factors. Some external and internal factors may not be related or may be difficult to separate in order to determine the core cause. Causality may not exist but correlations, which are difficult to understand. Events may also combine or interact in different ways to make a determination of likelihoods (probabilities) and consequences difficult to assess. There also may be a sequence or combination of events that make the assessment difficult as well.

However, the process of identifying, understanding, and assessing risks result in better risk based, problem solving and risk based, decision making.

Lesson Learned: 'White space' risk assessments can be difficult and time consuming. Start the process of assessing 'white space' risks by flowcharting critical QMS processes.

Resource: Read 'ALARP - As Low As Reasonably Possible' Http://Insights.CERMacademy.Com/2013/03/10-Alarp-As-Low-As-Reasonably-Possible-Paul-Kostek/

Who should conduct the risk assessment?

The risk assessment can be a first-party, second-party, or third-party engagement. The level, type, and nature of the risk assessment determine who should conduct the assessment. Some issues to consider are:

- First-party risk assessment is a self-assessment of risk. This could be part of internal auditing, self-inspection, or continuous process monitoring.
- Second-party risk assessment would involve internal auditing or quality auditing working with process risk owners to determine risks. This could be a facilitated risk assessment. There are many benefits for conducting a facilitated risk assessment with the client organization. However, a facilitated workshop requires a knowledgeable facilitator, is more expensive, and can be time consuming because knowledgeable stakeholders have to be brought into the process.
- Third-party risk assessment is an independent risk assessment. For example in a third-party engagement, an engineering firm may be retained to conduct an independent and objective risk assessment as a forensics or third-party review. Under these criteria, the firm would conduct interviews of critical process owners and risk

stakeholders. Then, the firm would evaluate independently the likelihood and consequence of the risks and define remediations to eliminate the risks.

Lesson Learned: Start the risk assessment using quality and risk professionals. Standardize (proceduralize) the risk assessment. Then, have the process owners conduct risk assessments of their processes.

Resource: Read 'Rise Of Risk Engineering'
Http://Insights.CERMacademy.Com/2013/03/The-Rise-Of-Risk-Engineering/

What is better: quantitative or qualitative risk assessment?

Qualitative risk assessments are relatively inexpensive, rapid, intuitive, and can result in great understanding of process or functional risks. However by their very nature, qualitative assessments result in only rough estimates of risk consequence and risk likelihood.

Quantitative risk assessments are often based on historical and statistical data. Quantitative assessments may also rely on Big Data. Quantitative risk assessments pose certain challenges. Quantitative risk assessments require more time and effort, which translate to higher costs. Statistical data of potential risks may not be available or are unknown. If evaluating future events, historical events may not be an indication of a Black Swan event. Statistical forecasting models may not be accurate due to poor data inputs, inadequate assumptions, or the lack of maturity of the forecasters.

Lesson Learned: Recognize the value and disadvantages of quantitative and qualitative risk assessments. Each has its value depending on the context and maturity of the organization.

Resource: Read 'Early Reliability Problems In The News'
Http://Insights.CERMacademy.Com/2014/10/64-Early-Reliability-Problems-News-Fred-Schenkelberg/

How deep and how broad should a risk assessment be?

This is a question that always confounds us as an engineering consulting firm. We make estimates and submit firm bids on our contracts as to the appropriate breadth and depth of risk assessment. Sometimes, we underestimate the amount of work that needs to be done. This is largely due to a lack of understanding of the context, technology, resources, and risks within the organization.

The appropriate level of depth and breadth of conducting the risk assessment becomes a judgment call and negotiation between the consulting firm and the client. For example, conducting a risk assessment of ISO 9001:2015 and other standards should be fairly straightforward in terms of assessing the risks to achieving management system objectives. However, the new standards seem to imply interested parties, upside risk, and even business management systems may be within the management system boundaries of the risk assessment.

Lesson Learned: Avoid scope creep in the risk assessment. Keep it simple and straightforward. Do not go too deep or too broad in your organization.

Resource: Read 'Sixty Percent (60%) Of Quality Issues Are Caused By Design Faults'
Http://Insights.CERMacademy.Com/2015/01/76-Sixty-Percent-60-Quality-Issues-Caused-Design-Faults-Roxann-Dawson/

What are common challenges of the risk assessment process?

We have conducted hundreds of risk assessments in a number of sectors from homeland security to pension funds to Parks and Recreation departments. We have a number of hard lessons learned. These are some common mistakes we have made and seen:

- **Lack of a common definition of critical risk terms.** This is probably the # 1 challenge that we have seen in conducting risk assessments. Everyone seems to have a different context, point of view, definition, and understanding of critical terms such as even basic terms of what is risk. The fix is to develop a common taxonomy, framework, and dictionary of risk, RBT, and risk assessment terms.

- **Lack of executive management support for the risk assessment.** If a risk assessment is perceived as a low level activity or special project, then these can be early indicators of failure. The key is to have executive management support and follow a top down approach to a risk assessment.

- **Lack of established ground rules for conducting the risk assessment.** Without a set of commonly accepted and understood ground rules, the risk assessment process will get bogged down in disagreements, circular arguments, positioning and posturing.

- **Lack of cultural or context understanding of the organization, function, or process being risk assessed.** We have discussed context is worth 20 IQ points. We clearly understood this expression when we were conducting risk assessments of an organization that had an opaque culture and we were wondering why our time estimates for the risk assessment were clearly wrong. We simply did not understand the organizational culture and did not include the right stakeholders in the assessment. We did not understand how the risk assessment was going to be used and the fear it engendered.

- **Lack of technical understanding of the organization, function, or process being risk assessed.** It is very difficult to establish a peer level dialogue for risk based, problem solving and risk based, decision making if the process owners do not perceive the facilitators as technical or management peers.

- **Lack of involvement of critical risk assessment stakeholders.** While we planned the risk assessment carefully using a structured framework, we did not consult with critical process owners. Critical process owners thought we were disregarding their expertise and dismissing them. Big mistake. The risk assessment took much longer than we anticipated and budgeted.

Lesson Learned: Address each of the above challenges that are relevant to your organization in the business case. This will help ensure you have a realistic expectation of what is involved in RBT and becoming a risk aware organization.

Resource: Read 'How To Scientifically Predict The Future (Well, At Least For Your Processes)' Http://Insights.CERMacademy.Com/2013/09/25-How-To-Scientifically-Predict-The-Future-Well-Least-For-Your-Processes-Angela-Montgomery/

CHAPTER 14:

RISK MANAGEMENT AND CONTROL

What is the key idea in this chapter?

The key idea in this chapter is ISO 9001:2015 requires the control and treatment of risk following the risk assessment. Risk-control is the essence of risk treatment and risk management.

Are the terms 'risk response', 'risk treatment', 'risk mitigation', and 'risk management' different?

The above terms mean pretty much the same and are often used interchangeably. ISO 9001:2015 implies the control and treatment of risk. The control of risk is the critical element of risk assessment, treatment, and mitigation.

Lesson Learned: Risk taxonomy and syntax are very critical to define early in the RBT journey. Again, this preempts confusion and ensures everyone is on the same page.

Resource: Read 'Risk Management In A Global Economy' Http://Insights.CERMacademy.Com/2014/11/67-Risk-Management-Global-Economy-Stuart-Rosenberg/

What is 'internal control'?

Internal control implies the control of risk and is the basis of the COSO risk framework. The concept is core to COSO ERM and is implied in ISO 31000:2018 and ISO 9001:2015. ISO 9001:2015 uses the term 'control' and not 'internal control'. Why? The expression internal control framework is derived from finance and accounting. To a large extent, operational control has been construed as quality control or QMS control.

Internal control forms the basis of how executive management and how the board looks at an organization. The financial concept of internal control derived from COSO is broader and more applicable for RBT, risk assessments, and management of operational and supply chain risks. So in this chapter, we emphasize the concept of internal control.

COSO defines internal control as:

> "Internal control is a process, affected by the entity's Board of Directors, management, and other personnel, designed to provide reasonable assurance regarding the achievement of objectives in the following categories:
>
> - Effectiveness and efficiency of operations.
> - Reliability of reporting.
> - Compliance with applicable laws and regulations."

While the concept of internal control is not part of ISO 9001:2015 or ISO 31000:2018:2018, it is the cornerstone of all risk assessment and enterprise risk management for a RCMM Level 2 and higher. It should also be the basis for RBT, specifically risk based, problem solving and risk based, decision making.

Lesson Learned: While the concept of 'internal control' is not specifically mentioned or required in ISO 9001:2015, the concept of control is implicit in the standard. Consider applying the concept of internal control to your

QMS and RBT if you want executive management and the Board of Directors to address ISO 9001:2015 compliance, RBT, and QMS risks.

Resource: Read 'Project Needs To Be In Control' Http://Insights.CERMacademy.Com/2012/12/6-Auditing-System-Conversions-Projects-Need-To-Be-In-Control-By-Dan-Swanson-Technologyrisk/

What are the 5 principles of effective internal control?

COSO defines the 5 critical principles of an effective risk-control environment as:

1. Commitment to integrity and ethics.
2. Oversight of internal controls by the Board of Directors, who is independent of management.
3. Structures, reporting lines, and appropriate responsibilities in the pursuit of objectives established by management and overseen by the board.
4. Commitment to attract and train competent individuals in alignment with objectives.
5. Holding individuals accountable for their internal control responsibilities in the pursuit of business objectives.[xxxi]

ISO 31000:2018 and ISO 9001:2015 use the term control but do not emphasize the control environment as much as COSO ERM does. ISO 9001:2015 uses context as an equivalent term, but this word is not part of the executive vocabulary.

We believe the above 5 principles should be incorporated into the RBT journey and ISO 9001:2015 certification. This will facilitate the harmonization of ISO 9001:2015 RBT with preexisting risk management and ERM frameworks (higher RCMM levels).

Lesson Learned: RBT should be seen as an integral part of internal control. So, integrate the ISO concept of control and RBT into the concept of 'internal control.'

Resources: Read 'Understanding The Top Drivers For Reducing Quality Risk'
Http://Insights.CERMacademy.Com/2013/09/23-Understanding-The-Top-Drivers-For-Reducing-Quality-Risk-Lns-Reserach/

What is the COSO Internal Control – Integrated Framework?

The original COSO Internal Control - Integrated Framework was published in 1992. Take a look at the COSO internal control cube on the next page. You may notice the COSO internal control framework is a subset of the COSO ERM cube that is discussed in Chapter 6.

The purpose of the framework is to design, deploy, and assure an effective system of internal control of the reporting of operational and QMS risks. COSO states the benefits of an internal control system include:

> "An effective system of internal control reduces, to an acceptable level, the risk of not achieving an objective relating to one, two, or all three categories of objectives - that is, operations, reporting, and compliance. It requires that each of the five components of internal control and relevant principles is present and functioning, and that (ii) the five components are operating together in an integrated manner."[xxxii]

> "In addition, the *Framework* can provide reasonable assurance of preparing external non-financial reports in accordance with laws, rules, regulations, standards, or other frameworks, and of internal reports to management and the Board of Directors, as deemed necessary, about the entity and its subunits."[xxxiii]

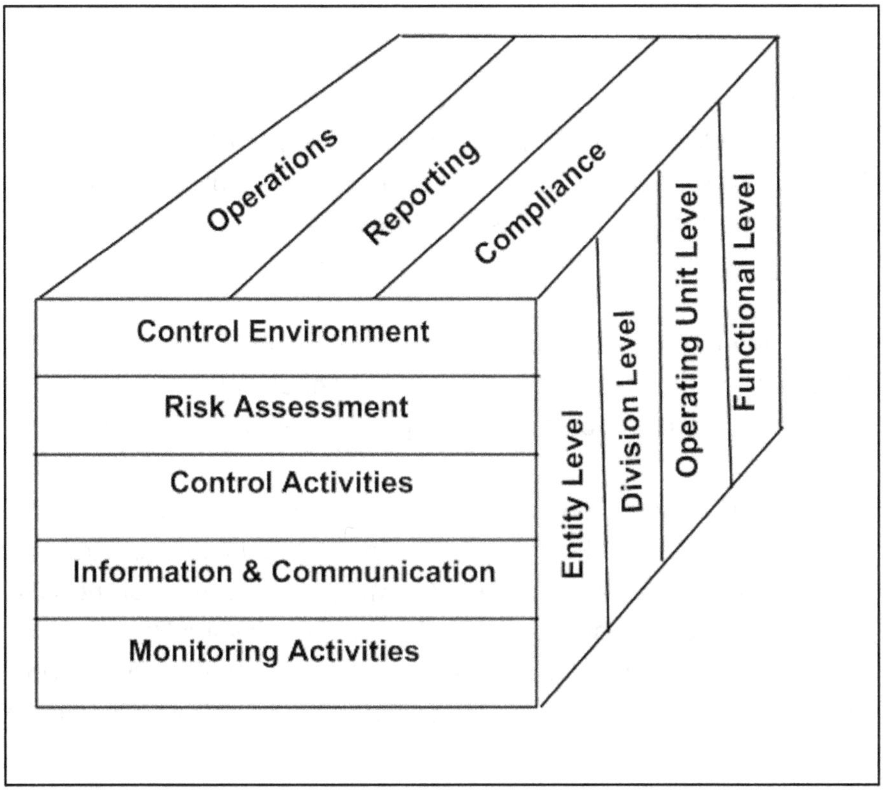

Figure 13: Control Framework

As the above figure shows, the framework consists of five components of internal control:

1. Control environment.
2. Risk assessment.
3. Control activities.
4. Information and communication.
5. Monitoring activities.

The organization's management owns and is responsible for architecting, designing, deploying, and assuring the internal control system and assessing its effectiveness. For an effective system of internal control, each of the above components should be present and functioning properly.

Architecting, designing, deploying, and assuring an internal control system in operations is difficult. In finance, there is much guidance. So, COSO recently added 'Principles' to facilitate the design of internal controls and added 'Points of Focus' to facilitate the deployment of each control element. As a company matures its RBT processes, the COSO model is an effective model and vehicle to establish controls.

The U.S. Government has incorporated the framework into its Green Book, which describes how to implement internal controls into operations. You can obtain the standard for free by going to the below **Resource**.

Lesson Learned: A challenge for some companies will be to design, deploy, and assure QMS risk-controls. Use the COSO internal control model as a guide for a Level 2 or higher RCMM. Incorporate all of the COSO principles into your internal control system and deploy the Points of Focus that are applicable to you in terms of your context, maturity, and capability. As you mature, you can incorporate additional Points of Focus to your RBT system.

Resource: Read 'Standards for Internal Control in the Federal Government.'
Http://www.gao.gov/assets/670/665712.pdf

What comprises a reasonable operational 'Control Environment'?

The control environment is sometimes called the 'internal control environment.' It is the context the company operates in, which is also key to ISO 31000 and ISO 9001:2015. The control environment includes: culture, governance, risk management, values, operating style, ethics, and ethos of the organization. Sometimes, the control environment is distilled into the expression 'Tone at the Top.'

The Principles and Points of Focus of a Control Environment are shown below:

Control Environment

	Principles	Points of Focus
1	Organization demonstrates a commitment to integrity and ethical values	Set the 'tone at the top' for senior executives and Board of Directors
		Establish appropriate standards of behavior and ethics
		Evaluate adherence to standards of behavior
		Address deviations of behavior in a timely and specified manner
2	Board of Directors demonstrates independence from management and exercises oversight of the development and performance of internal control	Establish oversight responsibilities by the Board or Chief Risk Officer
		Apply relevant expertise and knowledge
		Operate independently and objectively
		Provide oversight on Control Environment, Risk Assessment, Control Activities, Information and Communication, and Monitoring Activities in financial reporting, IT, cyber security, operations, and supply management
3	Management establishes, with board oversight, structures, reporting lines, and appropriate authorities and responsibilities in the pursuit of objectives	Consider all structures of the enterprise

		Establish reporting lines of accountability
		Define, assign, and limit authorities, accountabilities, and responsibilities
4	Organization demonstrates a commitment to attract, develop, and retain competent individuals in alignment with objectives	Establish best policies, procedures, work instructions, and practices for human resources
		Evaluate competence and address shortcomings and variances to achieving objectives
		Attract, develop, and retain human resources with appropriate knowledge, skills, and abilities
		Plan and prepare for management and key person succession
5	Organization holds individuals accountable for their internal control responsibilities in the pursuit of objectives	Enforce internal control accountability through structures, accountabilities, authorities, and responsibilities
		Establish SMART performance measures, incentives, and rewards at the 1. Enterprise; 2. Programmatic Project/Process/Project; and 3. Product/Transactional levels
		Evaluate performance measures, incentives, mentoring, and rewards for ongoing relevance and suitability
		Consider excessive risks and pressures in the pursuit of objectives
		Evaluate performance and rewards or disciplines individuals

Lesson Learned: ISO registered companies usually are not familiar with the concept of context or control environment. Depending on your RCMM requirements and context, tailor the above Principles and Points of Focus to your organization. The higher the RCMM, the more Points of Focus you will deploy or utilize in your organization.

Resource: Read 'Minimizing Litigation Risks' Http://Insights.CERMacademy.Com/2013/09/24-Minimizing-The-Risk-Of-Litigation-C-Capers-Jones/

What comprises a reasonable operational 'Risk Assessment'?

Every enterprise faces external and internal risks. Once business objectives are developed, then a risk assessment is conducted to determine risks that may inhibit or obstruct the achievement of the objective.

The Principles and Points of Focus of a Risk Assessment are shown below:

Risk Assessment

Principles	Points of Focus
6 Organization specifies objectives with sufficient clarity to enable the identification and assessment of risks relating to objectives:	
- Operations Objectives	Reflect management's choices, objectives, and expectations. Consider tolerances and appetite for risk Include operations, supply chain, IT, cyber security, and financial performance

		Develop a basis for committing resources and talent to meeting operational and supply chain objectives.
	- External Financial Reporting Objectives	Comply with applicable international accounting standards Consider financial materiality Reflect enterprise activities
	- External Non-Financial Reporting Objectives	Comply with externally established financial reporting standards and risk frameworks Consider the required level of precision and reliability Reflect enterprise activities
	- Internal Reporting Objectives	Reflect Board's and executive management's choices Consider the required level of precision and reliability
	- Compliance Objectives	Reflect enterprise activities Reflect external laws, standards, and regulations Consider tolerances and appetite for risks
7	Organization identifies risks to the achievement of its objectives across the enterprise and analyzes risks as a basis for determining how the risks should be managed	Include enterprise, subsidiary, division, operating unit, and functional levels (COSO framework)
		Analyze internal and external factors, including context Involve appropriate levels of management at the 1. Enterprise; 2. Programmatic/Project/Process; and 3. Product/Transactional levels

		Estimate significance and materiality of risks identified
		Determine how to respond and mitigate risks
8	Organization considers the potential for fraud in assessing risks to the achievement of objectives	Consider various types of fraud
		Assess incentives and pressures on business units and businesses
		Assess opportunities (upside risks)
		Assess attitudes and rationalizations for actions, expenditures, and opportunities
9	Organization identifies and assesses changes that could significantly impact the system of internal control	Assess changes in the external environment and context of operational and financial controls
		Assess changes in the business model
		Assess changes in critical leadership and management

Lesson Learned: We have discussed ISO 31010 and other tools that can be used for a risk assessment. If you are starting your RBT journey, use the risk assessment tool that meets your RCMM requirements and the Points of Focus that are applicable to your context and maturity.

Resource: Read 'Design Failure Modes And Effects Analysis' Http://Insights.CERMacademy.Com/2012/11/5-Design-Failure-Modes-And-Effects-Analysis-Paul-Kostek-Designrisk/

What comprises reasonable operational 'Control Activities'?

Control activities are policies, procedures, and other methods to ensure business objectives can be achieved. Controls or more specifically risk-controls mitigate the risks to the achievement or attainment of business objectives at the 1. Enterprise level; 2. Programmatic/Project/Process level; and 3. Product/Transactional level. Controls may include: validation, verification, approvals, authorization, separation of duties, cyber security, reconciliation, audits, and self-assessments.

The Principles and Points of Focus of Control Activities are shown below:

Control Activities

	Principles	**Points of Focus**
10	Organization selects and develops control activities that contribute to the mitigation of risks to the achievement of objectives to acceptable levels	Integrate with risk assessment
		Consider enterprise specific factors
		Determine relevant business processes at the Enterprise, Programmatic/Project/Process, and Product/Transactional levels
		Evaluate a mix of control activity types
		Consider at what level activities are applied, i.e. 1. Enterprise, 2. Programmatic/Project/Process, 3. Product/ Transactional levels
		Address segregation of duties at each organizational level
11	Organization selects and develops general control activities over technology to support	Determine dependency between the use of technology in

	the achievement of objectives	business processes and technology general controls
		Establish relevant technology infrastructure control activities, especially cyber security controls
		Establish relevant security management i.e. 1. Enterprise; 2. Programmatic/Project/Process; and 3. Product/Transactional control activities
		Establish relevant technology acquisition, development, and maintenance process control activities
12	Organization deploys control activities through policies that establish what is expected and procedures that put policies into action	Establish policies, procedures, instructions, and standards to support deployment of management's directives
		Establish responsibility and accountability for executing policies and procedures
		Perform in a timely and effective manner
		Take appropriate corrective action and preventive action (risk management)
		Perform using competent personnel with requisite resources
		Reassess policies, procedures, work instructions, and standards

Lesson Learned: Risk-controls are the key element of the internal control system. Select and deploy controls that are appropriate to your organization's context and maturity. For example if your organizational culture is participatory, design, deploy, and assure controls appropriate to the collaborative tone and culture of your organization.

Resource: Read 'Can Projects Incorporate Too Little Risk Part Ii' Http://Insights.CERMacademy.Com/2013/09/23-Can-Projects-Incorporate-Too-Little-Risk-Part-Ii-Howard-Wiener/

What comprises reasonable operational 'Information and Communication'?

Information and communication systems produce actionable and accurate reports, including control updates in the following areas: risk, quality, design, financial, compliance, governance, operational, and supply chain information. Effective information can be communicated to internal and external parties. External parties include shareholders, customers, suppliers, regulators, and banks. Internal parties include users of the information such as process owners, engineering, quality and others.

The Principles and Points of Focus of Information and Communication are shown below:

Information and Communication

	Principles	Points of Focus
13	Organization obtains or generates and uses relevant, quality information to support the functioning of other components of internal control	Identify information requirements at the enterprise
		Capture internal and external sources of data
		Process relevant data into useful information for action
		Maintain quality throughout processing of quality information

		Consider costs and benefits of acquiring quality information
14	Organization internally communicates information, including objectives and responsibilities for internal control, necessary to support the functioning of other components of internal control	Communicate internal control information throughout the organization and supply chain and with relevant stakeholders.
		Communicate with the Board of Directors
		Provide separate, independent, and objective communication lines
		Select relevant method and channels of communication
15	Organization communicates with external parties regarding matters affecting the functioning of other components of internal control	Communicate to external parties, including critical stakeholders.
		Enable inbound communications freely and without prejudice
		Communicate with the Board of Directors
		Provide separate, independent, and objective communication lines
		Select relevant method and channels of communication

Lesson Learned: Identify your interested parties and determine who needs what critical QMS and RBT reports. Reports should be actionable, accurate, suitable, and timely.

Resource: Read 'Risk And Mitigation Alarm Fatigue' Http://Insights.CERMacademy.Com/2013/06/16-Risk-And-Mitigation-Of-Alarm-Fatigue-Jim-Lamprecht/

What comprises reasonable operational 'Monitoring Activities'?

Monitoring is the process to assess the quality, suitability, and effectiveness of a company's internal control system. Ongoing monitoring includes internal auditing, control assessments, value added auditing, CAPA systems, and other processes.

The Principles and Points of Focus of Monitoring Activities are shown below:

Monitoring Activities

	Principles	Points of Focus
16	Organization selects, develops, and performs ongoing and/or separate evaluations to ascertain whether the components of internal control are present and functioning	Consider a mix of ongoing and separate evaluations for determining internal control effectiveness, efficiency, and economy
		Consider rate of change Establish baseline understanding Use knowledgeable personnel Integrate with business processes and business model Adjust scope and frequency of evaluation Objectively evaluate assurance, appetite, tolerance, and suitability

17	Organization evaluates and communicates internal control deficiencies in a timely manner to those parties responsible for taking corrective action, including executive management and the Board of Directors, as appropriate	Assess results of monitoring activities
		Communicate deficiencies, risks, and variances to parties responsible for corrective action and to executive management and the Board of Directors
		Monitor corrective actions and risk mitigations for recurrence

Lesson Learned: Monitoring activities offer risk assurance to the organization that the internal control system is effective, efficient, and economic. If the organization requires a higher level of assurance, then fine tune the monitoring based on the requisite assurance or treat the risks so they are within your risk appetite and risk assurance threshold.

Resource: Read 'Risk Management And Problem Solving Are Not Different'
Http://Insights.CERMacademy.Com/2014/12/70-Risk-Management-Problem-Solving-Different/

Why was the COSO framework updated?

While the framework has been broadly accepted in the marketplace for financial reporting, the framework was updated recently to include non-financial and operational risk reporting for the following reasons:

- Business and operating environments are globalized.

- Technology impacts on business are increasing.
- Global competition is more complex.
- Stakeholders and interested parties now require more operational information and transparency.
- Systems of Internal Control over Financial Reporting and over operational reporting are more critical.
- Stakeholders demand more risk-control and accountability.
- Board level, governance oversight is increasing.
- Laws, regulations, and standards are more complex.
- Expectations for competencies and accountabilities are increasing.

The COSO framework was updated to include non-financial reporting. What does this mean? Product development, cyber security, supply management and operations are areas of increasing organizational risk. The COSO framework can now be used to assess and report risks in areas that used to be the purview of ISO management system standards.

Lesson Learned: Integrate the above Principles and applicable Points of Focus with your ISO management systems to develop reasonable operational controls including supply chain controls based on the RCCM of your organization.

Resource: Read 'Performance Excellence Models, Part 1' Http://Insights.CERMacademy.Com/2012/12/6-Performance-Excellence-Models-Part-1-Adina-Suciu-Processrisk

Why you should consider adopting the COSO internal control framework?

The COSO framework is based on financial and non-financial risk-controls that are now migrating to operations. ISO 9001:2015 RBT was developed independently of COSO internal control framework. However, the COSO framework is well understood in the marketplace, by financial stakeholders and by executive management of large organizations. ISO 9001:2015 RBT is new and is not understood by executive management.

The COSO framework can help organizations obtain reasonable assurance of achieving their operational and supply management objectives. QMS, EMS, and other management systems have control objectives that should be part of the risk reporting to the Board.

Lesson Learned: COSO is a good model to use with ISO 31000:2018 in the RBT journey using a Risk Capability Maturity Model (RCMM). Many of the COSO Principles and Points of Focus would be at a Level 2 or Level 3 RCMM. The difference between a Level 2 and Level 3 RCMM is the extent and depth of the Points of Focus application. In other words, a Level 3 or higher RCMM would have more Points of Focus across the organization.

Resource: Read 'Can Projects Incorporate Too Little Risk' Http://Insights.CERMacademy.Com/2013/09/22-Can-Projects-Incorporate-Too-Little-Risk-Howard-Wiener/

What factors should the organization consider when evaluating the appropriate type of risk-control and risk treatment?

The type, extent, and nature of the risk assessment is driven by organizational context. Context also determines the appropriate type of risk-control and treatment.

The first item is to ensure risk treatment offers more benefits than it costs. This is critical. If the quality product attribute, process characteristic, project control, or program system is not critical, then why address it with additional costly controls or risk treatment.

Let us look at this issue a little deeper. Remember we define risk in terms of the consequence and likelihood of an event occurring that could impact the ability of meeting an objective. What should you do if there is a possibility of a 'black swan' event, specifically one with a low likelihood and very high consequence? Think of the Space Shuttle Challenger disaster with the O-ring problem. Or, you can be an organization with a critical sole source supplier or a garment maker with much of your production in developing countries. What would happen if the company did not inspect plants for child labor, safety, and working conditions? A fire at the plant or significant negative news coverage would have a negative impact on the company's reputation.

In the above cases, the 'black swan' event would justify additional risk-controls and risk treatment.

Lesson Learned: Ensure that the benefits and value of risk treatment outweigh costs. This seems to make sense, but it is amazing how often risk mitigations are so extensive that benefits seem lost.

Resource: Read 'Supplier Risks And Their Mitigation' Http://Insights.CERMacademy.Com/2013/12/32-Supplier-Risks-Mitigation-John-Ayers/

What is 'risk treatment' in ISO 31000:2018?

Both COSO and ISO 31000:2018 provide good examples of what risk treatment can involve.

ISO 31000:2018 defines risk treatment as a "process to modify risk." This can be a little confusing so ISO standard writers added a number of notes to clarify what this means.

Let us look at ISO 31000:2018 options for applying risk treatment, specifically it can involve:

- Lowering the likelihood of an event occurring.
- Lowering the consequence of an event occurring.
- Increasing the likelihood and/or consequence of an event occurring.
- Accepting the risk if it is within the risk acceptance and/or tolerance of the organization.

- Avoiding the risk by deciding not to continue or even start a project.
- Increasing the risk in order to pursue the opportunity if rewards are higher than costs.
- Removing the source of risk.
- Sharing the risk with third parties.
- Controlling the risk within the risk appetite and risk tolerance of the organization.

Lesson Learned: Determine what risk management framework you will use. If it is ISO 31000:2018, then map the risk treatment options to the risk of not being able to meet your QMS objectives.

What is 'risk treatment' in COSO and ISO 31000:2018?

COSO and ISO 31000:2018 both offer 4 strategies for risk treatment, specifically:

- Avoid risk.
- Accept risk.
- Reduce risk.
- Share risk.

We like the above 4 strategies. The COSO risk treatment strategies are similar to ISO 31000:2018. However, the COSO ERM strategies are commonly used and recognized within most organizations. See Figure 14.

Lesson Learned: Design a risk-control or treatment strategy that is based on the context, maturity, and culture of the organization. If you work for a collaborative organization, do not immediately apply a control. Seek comments and recommendations from process owners and stakeholders.

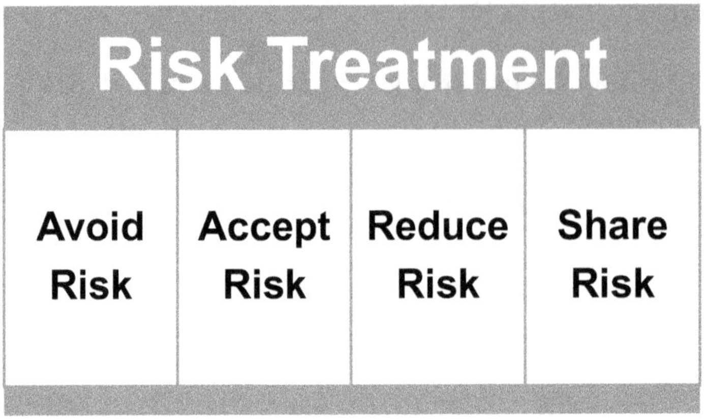

Figure 14: Types of Risk Treatment

Resource: Read 'Is Radical Improvement Worth The Risk' Http://Insights.CERMacademy.Com/2014/11/68-Radical-Improvement-Worth-Risk-John-Dyer/

What is 'risk avoidance'?

Risk avoidance is a commonly used risk treatment. The company or individual may decide to avoid the risk by not doing something, not investing in a product, or choosing a different action.

Several examples of risk avoidance include:

- Correcting a problem.
- Preventing a problem from occurring.
- Eliminating the source of variation.
- Screening products and services that do not provide the requisite return.
- Exiting markets.
- Changing products used in an assembly.

- Selecting a new supplier that is less risky.
- Redefining business objectives.
- Rebranding a product.
- Reframing issues and challenges so they are doable.

Lesson Learned: Avoiding a risk is often the result of simply good quality planning. You know what needs to be done to avoid a problem.

Resource: Read 'Mitigating Project Risk By Adopting Accelerated Delivery Techniques' Http://Insights.CERMacademy.Com/2013/06/18-Mitigating-Project-Risk-By-Adopting-Accelerated-Delivery-Techniques-Howard-Wiener/

What is 'risk acceptance'?

ISO 9001:2015 refers to upside risk or what we often call opportunity risk. This is the upside risk of a potential opportunity arising and the benefits that may result.

Companies accept risk because it is within their risk acceptance and/or risk tolerance thresholds. If risk is within these levels then no further risk treatment needs be taken.

Several examples of risk acceptance include:

- Self-insuring.
- Using lower cost parts.
- Derating products.
- Repricing products to a lower level.
- Removing risk premiums on products and services.

Lesson Learned: Remember if you decide to accept the risk, then it should be within your risk tolerance and risk appetite.

Resource: Read 'How To Manage Transportation Risks' Http://Insights.CERMacademy.Com/2013/12/33-Manage-Transportation-Risks-Stuart-Rosenberg/

What is 'risk reduction'?

Risk reduction is another term for controlling risks. Most risk treatment focuses on controlling risks. As more companies pursue this risk mitigation option, an ongoing debate is arising whether organizations are moving to control style of management.

Several examples of risk reduction include:

- Minimizing the likelihood of an event occurring.
- Minimizing the consequence of the event.
- Dispersing sources of products to reduce the risk of supply interruptions.
- Hedging decisions.
- Developing business continuity practices.
- Testing products to ensure compliance.
- Increasing operational risk capability and maturity.
- Increasing process capabilities.
- Investing in Six Sigma and lean management programs.
- Relocating suppliers to areas of less political unrest.
- Diversifying plant and supplier locations.

Lesson Learned: Several of the above examples may cross risk treatment strategies. Remember find the appropriate risk-control or reduction that fits the context or culture of your organization.

Resource: Read 'Reliability Management & Risk' Http://Insights.CERMacademy.Com/2014/06/51-Reliability-Management-Risk-Fred-Schenkelberg/

What is 'risk sharing'?

More global organizations view emerging markets as opportunities for growth and higher margins. However, developing and selling products in emerging markets can result in higher risks.

Several examples of risk sharing include:

- Outsourcing capabilities to suppliers.
- Purchasing insurance.
- Finding local partners to manufacture and sell products in emerging markets.
- Hedging risk in financial markets.
- Insuring against possible losses.
- Moving from a single source strategy to a multiple source strategy.
- Transferring risk to 3rd parties through contracts.

Lesson Learned: Monetize the cost of sharing risk against the cost of the event occurring. The value of sharing the risk should be higher than retaining the risk.

Resource: Read 'Risk Based Configuration Control' Http://Insights.CERMacademy.Com/2013/06/17-Risk Based-Configuration-Control-Linda-Westfall/

What is the minimum level of 'acceptable risk' for an ISO 9001 certified company?

This question addresses the organization's risk appetite and risk tolerance. It is one of the toughest questions a company has to address. Many companies have not addressed this question at the 1. Enterprise level; 2. Programmatic/Project/Process level; or 3. Product/Transactional level.

A company may say it meets customer requirements, service level agreements, Key Performance Indicators, Key Risk Indicators, specification limits, project variances, or process limits (Cpk's). These are great, but we advocate that an organization develop monetary limits for risk acceptance and risk tolerance. This is often difficult for organizations, because they think in terms of project variances, process capabilities, or product specifications not in terms of monetized risk appetite.

Monetary limits and acceptance levels are the language of business and ensure a common risk understanding and risk equivalency throughout the organization and with executive staff.

Lesson Learned: Ask executive management what is acceptable monetary risk to the organization. Develop a list of issues that need to be addressed and incorporate them into the business case.

Resource: Read 'How Well Does Risk Assessment Inform Decision Makers'
http://insights.cermacademy.com/2014/06/52-well-risk-assessments-inform-decision-makers-chris-peace/

Are companies going to become more control oriented due to risk-controls in ISO standards?

Many organizations are adopting some form of RBT and risk treatment. Does this mean we are moving to a control environment in many organizations? This again depends on the context and culture of the organization.

This brings up the important distinction between Theory X and Theory Y management. Theory X and Theory Y were theories of organizational behavior. Theory X assumed organizations are lax and employees are lazy. Management needed to develop additional systems and controls to manage the organization. Theory Y assumed organizations were adaptable and employees were motivated to exercise self-control.

A fundamental principle of internal control implies that process owners, project managers, and all workers are responsible for the risk-control of their operations. We hope that the focus on risk-controls will emphasize Theory Y management where process and project owners manage variation and risk through enhanced RBT.

Lesson Learned: Clarify how risk-controls are going to be designed, deployed, and assured in your organization based on culture, capability, maturity, and context.

Resource: Read 'Why Do Corrective Actions Fail?'
http://insights.cermacademy.com/2014/09/59-correctives-fail-ed-grounds/

CHAPTER 15:

FUTURE OF QUALITY: RISK®

What is the key idea in this chapter?

The key idea in this chapter is the future of quality is risk and it will require new knowledge, skills, and abilities from quality professionals.

What is the future of the development of ISO management system standards?

Annex SL describes the future of ISO management system standards. If a new series of standards is to be developed or there is a revision of existing management system standards, all ISO standards development must follow a rigorous process to:

- Ensure the new standards are based on Annex SL principles.
- Standards have market relevance in terms of meeting the needs of users and affected parties and add value.
- Are compatible with other families of management system standards.
- Have sufficient application coverage to eliminate or minimize the need for sector specific standards on the same topic.
- Are applicable to organizations in comparable sectors and cultures regardless of size.
- Are flexible in terms of assisting an organization to competitively

add to or differentiate from other organizations and to enhance their management systems beyond the minimum requirements of the standard.

- Encourage and assure the free trade or goods and services, cover the topic, are flexible, and encourage free trade.
- Encourage the use of first-party, second-party, or third-party conformity assessment.
- Ensure the user of the standard can easily use, understand, and apply the standard in different organizations and cultures.

Lesson Learned: We suspect ISO will integrate new ideas into management system standards as part of continual improvement. So, review continually new and revised management system standards that will be based on Annex SL.

Resource: Read 'The Science And Art Of Every Profession' Http://Insights.CERMacademy.Com/2014/09/58-Science-Art-Every-Profession-Daniel-Burras/

What is the future of ISO management systems?

We are not adept at reading tea leaves or forecasting the future. But, we believe that we will see the following:

- Integration of management systems into business management systems.
- Integration of RBT into all ISO families of standards.
- Integration of more rigorous risk management processes into future revisions of ISO 31000.
- Additional training of CB auditors on RBT and risk based auditing.
- Integration of quality auditing and internal auditing into a unified approach.

- Consolidated reporting of RBT and operational risk management information to the Board of Directors Audit Committee.
- Additional risk management integration into the supply chain and throughout the enterprise.
- Focus of RBT and risk management in service based industries.
- Movement to higher levels of risk maturity and capability (RCMM).

Lesson Learned: Understand the above bullets are all speculative. This is our best educated guess. This is the first time since 1987 that we have seen so many changes in thinking and application of management system standards.

Resource: Read 'How A Quality Pro Learned About Risk' Http://Insights.CERMacademy.Com/2014/12/71-Risk-Pro-Learns-Risk-Bill-Walker/

Will quality organizations adopt RBT and risk assessment?

This is a difficult question. The answer seems to reflect the culture of the organization, its size and markets, product mix, statutory requirements, context, maturity, capabilities, and other factors.

We see several possible developments:

- Quality organizations may disappear as quality responsibilities are deployed throughout the organization.
- Quality organizations will stay the course; specifically hoping what has worked in the past will work in the future.
- Quality organizations will adopt RBT and risk assessment principles along side quality and other management system principles.
- Quality organizations will rebrand into risk organizations.

Lesson Learned: Of the above options, ISO 9001:2015 and RBT can be used to move the quality organization into a new value direction. It is critical the quality vision of ISO 9001:2015 is crafted carefully. The articulation of the vision will provide a compelling view of how quality and risk will be framed, architected, organized, controlled, and assured. Also, ensure this vision is adaptable to other management systems.

Resource: Read 'RBT: It's Everywhere'
http://insights.cermacademy.com/2015/01/750-rbt-everywhere-t-dan-nelson/

Who are today's RBT and quality risk authorities?

Big problem! There are no RBT or quality risk gurus.

Twenty or so years ago, the quality profession had Philip Crosby, W. Edwards Deming, Arnold Feigenbaum and others as its quality gurus. The management world had Michael Porter, Peter Drucker, and other management gurus. Most of these folks have retired.

If the quality profession migrates to risk, then there is going to be a lot of wannabe gurus who could not spell risk two years ago.

So, we do not have any RBT gurus. Why? In the new world of risk, which is our new normal, RBT is a new discipline.

Lesson Learned: Learn as much as you can about RBT. Who knows? You may become tomorrow's RBT and quality risk guru.

Resource: Read 'Looking For A Career Transition: Consider Quality Management'
Http://Insights.CERMacademy.Com/2014/12/72-Looking-Career-Transition-Consider-Quality-Management-Greg-Peckford/

What do quality and operational professionals need to know about RBT and risk assessment?

The quality profession is maturing. Everyone is now responsible for quality and many professionals have their Six Sigma certifications. Therefore quality professionals must look at their role in the new RBT environment, assess their current skill set, determine what they need to learn to be value contributors, and make a decision of where they want to be in the future.

We all need to be career resilient and most importantly know how to add value. Quality has been very adaptable over the years. Quality body of knowledge has grown and the quality discipline has evolved from basic inspection to Six Sigma. Quality applications have expanded far beyond the manufacturing floor to providing quality in healthcare, education, and now software development. The contemporary business environment has morphed with greater expectations of quality governance.

With ISO 9001:2015, quality risk roles and responsibilities will increase. Quality is very well positioned to take the operational and supply chain risk lead. RBT, risk assessment, risk management, and ERM may be the next evolution in quality.

If you believe that risk management and quality are connected, then here are a few suggestions:

- Become career resilient and learn RBT and risk management.
- Purchase and understand ISO 9001:2015, ISO 31000:2018, ISO 31010, and additional sector specific requirements.
- Understand Sarbanes Oxley Act and its risk reporting requirements.
- Understand RBT, risk management, and ERM methodologies in RCMM.
- Understand how to conduct risk assessments and risk based audits.
- Learn how to design, deploy, and assure an internal control system

that is reportable to executive management and the Board of Directors.

Lesson Learned: The changing nature of quality and QMS may require a redesign of your career. Be career resilient.

Resource: Read 'Your New Job In 2015' Http://Insights.CERMacademy.Com/2014/12/72-New-Job-2015-Elizabeth-Lions/

RISK GLOSSARY

4P's: Trademarked business risk model representing: Proactive, Preventive, Predictive, Preemptive™ actions focused around risk management.

Adaptive leadership: Is a practical leadership and management framework to address, adapt, and thrive in today's VUCA (Volatility, Uncertainty, Complexity, and Ambiguity) business environment. Adaptive leadership is based on flexibility and risk management.

Annex SL: High-level structure, provides identical core text, and provides key definitions that will be found in future and revised management system standards

Application controls: Application controls refer to transaction processing controls, sometimes called 'input - processing - output' controls in an IT environment.

Assessment risk: Risk the organization did not identify, monitor, or root cause eliminate.

Auditee: Person or team being audited.

Auditee organization: Organization whose management system is being audited.

Auditing organization: Organization conducting the audit.

Auditor: Person or team member conducting the audit.

Audit: Engagement that provides an independent, objective, nonpartisan assessment of the stewardship, performance, or cost of an enterprise's policies, programs, or operations depending upon the type and scope of the audit.

Audit conclusion: Outcome of an audit after consideration of the audit objectives and audit findings.

Audit client: Organization or person requesting or authorizing an audit.

Audit criteria: Documents against which audits are conducted. Criteria can include policies, procedures, standards, or specifications.

Audit evidence: Records, calculations, or other documentation that are relevant to audit criteria.

Audit findings: Results of the evaluation of the collected evidence against audit criteria. Findings can indicate conformity against audit criteria or opportunities for improvement.

Audit plan: Description of activities of an audit.

Audit program: One or more audits that are directed to obtain independent and/or objective findings.

Audit risk: Result of uncertainty of achieving audit objectives. Audit risk is the uncertainty the auditor will accurately detect the effectiveness of the auditee in meeting its objectives.

Audit scope: Extent and boundaries of an audit. Scope includes physical location, organizational unit, activities, and processes.

Audit team: One or more auditors supported by technical experts that form the audit team.

Auditability: Ease, consistency, and accuracy of auditing to ISO 9001:2015 or other management system requirements.

Baldrige: Stands for Malcolm Baldrige National Quality Award.

Black Swan: Event that is high consequence and low likelihood.

Board of Directors Audit Committee: Part of an organization's Board responsible for reviewing Internal Control over Financial Reporting and operational risks.

Business assurance: New offering by Certification Bodies to provide higher levels of assurance beyond ISO conformance.

Business case: Rationale for a new project or process.

Business management system: Set of interrelated generic processes within an organization that focuses on meeting business objectives.

CRO: Acronym for Chief Risk Officer.

Certification Body: Independent companies that audit and assure an ISO QMS adheres to specific requirements of the ISO 9001:2015 standard.

CERM: Acronym for Certified Enterprise Risk Manager® certificate.

Communication: Process of sharing and obtaining risk information from stakeholders. The information relates to the existence, extent, management, control, and assurance of risk.

Competence: Ability to apply knowledge, ability, and skills to conduct the work required.

Competency framework: Model for the new quality organization. Expression was coined by UK Chartered Quality Institute.

Confidentiality: Integrity and security of information. Auditors do not disclose information.

Conformity: Also referred as a conformance. Binary decision (yes/no) to determine adherence to requirements.

Consequence: Outcome of an event that can impact business or other objectives. An event can lead to a range of circumstances. A circumstance can be certain or uncertain and can have positive or negative effects.

Consequence rating: Critical rating element and vector of risk used in assessments; risk likelihood starts at a 1 rating, which is insignificant and moves to a 5 rating, which is catastrophic.

Context: Environment in which the organization operates and achieves its business objectives

Continual improvement: Process of surpassing business objectives.

Control: Modifying or changing risk. Controls can be process, policy, device, practice, procedure, or guideline to modify risk. Control may or may not result in modifying the effect. Often referred to as risk-control.

Control environment: Includes: culture, governance, risk management, values, operating style, ethics, and ethos of the organization. Sometimes, the control environment is distilled into the expression 'Tone at the Top.'

COSO: Acronym for Committee of Sponsoring Organizations of the Treadway Commission. COSO is a joint initiative of financial organizations to provide guidance on ERM, GRC, ethics, and financial reporting.

COSO ERM: Risk management framework consisting of eight elements: 1. Internal environment; 2. Objective setting; 3. Event identification; 4. Risk assessment; 5. Risk response; 6. Control activities; 7. Information communication; 8. Monitoring.

Correction: Process or action to detect and eliminate nonconformance.

CQO: Acronym for Chief Quality Officer.

CSR: Acronym for Corporate Social Responsibility. Usually based on ISO 26000 standard.

Customer: Person (s) who receives a product or service through a value exchange.

Decision Traps: Barriers to RBT, Risk based, problem solving, and Risk based, decision making.

DIS: Acronym for Draft International Standard.

Disruptive innovation: Innovation that helps create a new market and value network, and eventually disrupts an existing market and value network.

Documented information: Controlled information to document a QMS or other management system.

Downside risk: Risk usually associated with negative consequences.

Due care: Care that a reasonable person would exercise under the circumstances; the standard for determining legal duty.

Due diligence: Effort a party makes to avoid harm to another party.

Due professional care: Application of auditing diligence and judgment.

Enhanced Risk Management: Equivalent Enterprise Risk Management term used in ISO 31000:2018.

Enterprise Risk Management (COSO): Integrated COSO framework published in 2004 defines ERM as a "...process, effected by an entity's board of directors, management, and other personnel, applied in a strategy setting and across the enterprise, designed to identify potential events that may affect the entity, and manage risk to be within its risk appetite, to provide reasonable assurance regarding the achievement of entity objectives."

Effectiveness: Ability to meet a desired result or business result.

Efficiency: Being able to meet a desired result using optimized resources.

ERM heavy: Refers to COSO risk management framework.

ERM light: Refers to ISO 31000:2018 risk management framework.

Establishing the context: Internal and external boundary conditions and scope related to managing risk, setting criteria, and defining risk management policy.

Event: Occurrence or change in a set of circumstances. An event can have one or more causes. Event is also called an incident or accident. Event with no consequences is called an incident or near miss.

Evidence based approach: Rational method for reaching reliable and reproducible audit conclusions and findings.

External audit: Conducted by independent and/or objective organizations to determine adherence against a standard or specification. CB's conduct external audits. External auditor is also called second or third-party auditor.

External context: External environment in which the enterprise operates and establishes its business objectives. External context can include: culture, social, political, legal, regulatory, financial, technological, economic, natural, and competitive criteria.

Fair presentation: Obligation to report accurately and truthfully. Audit findings reflect truthfully and accurately results of an audit.

FMEA: Acronym for Failure Mode Effects Analysis.

GAGAS: Acronym for Generally Accepted Government Auditing Standards; professional standards presented in the 2011 revision of Government Auditing Standards provide a framework for performing high quality audits.

General controls: IT controls often described in two categories: IT general controls (ITGC) and IT application controls; used in IT environment controls; other than application controls; which relate to the environment within which computer based application systems are developed, maintained, operated, and which are therefore applicable to all applications.

Governance: Process by which the Board of Directors reviews the decisions and actions of executive management.

Governance control: Usually a board level control, which includes oversight, monitoring, and determination of risk appetite.

Governance Risk Compliance (GRC): Governance, risk management, and compliance or GRC is the umbrella term covering an organization's approach across these three areas.

Gresham's Law: Simplified version is: 'Bad money drives out good money.'

Guide: Facilitator chosen by the auditee to support the audit team.

Guide 73: Common risk management definitions that will be incorporated into each management system using RBT.

IIA: Acronym for Institute for Internal Auditing.

Independence: Independence from parties whose interests might be harmed by the results of an audit.

Inherent risk: Risk that the account or financial statement note being attested to by an independent firm is materially misstated without considering internal controls due to error or fraud.

Institute of Internal Auditors: Standards development organization for the Internal Auditing profession, much like ASQ is for Quality Auditing

Integrated management system: Single management system that integrates elements of multiple management systems.

Integrity: Basis of professionalism. Includes elements of diligence, responsibility, and honesty.

Interested parties: Person or organization that can impact or be impacted by a decision. Common interested parties may include stakeholders, customers, owners, employees, suppliers, NGOs, regulators, etc.

Internal audit: Independent objective assurance and consulting activity designed to add value and improve an organization's operations; helps an organization accomplish its objectives by bringing a systematic, disciplined approach to evaluate and improve the effectiveness of risk management, control, and governance processes. Also, called first-party audit.

Internal control: Integral component of an organization's management that provides reasonable assurance that the following objectives are being achieved: effectiveness and efficiency of operations, reliability of financial reporting, and compliance with applicable laws and regulations.

Internal context: Internal environment in which the enterprise operates and establishes its business objectives. Internal context can include: governance, organizational structure, roles, accountabilities, policies, procedures, strategies, plans, tactics, capabilities, resources, perceptions, values, stakeholders, IT, relationships, standards, specifications, contracts, and culture.

Intervention risk: Risk the organization did not respond and correct the problem at the symptom and root cause levels.

ISO: Acronym for International Organization for Standardization.

ISO 9001:2015: ISO Quality Management System standard, which was finalized in Q3 of 2015.

ISO 19011:2018: Comprehensive standard for conducting management system certification audits.

ISO 31000:2018: Risk management framework or guideline used as reference for many ISO families of standards.

KRI: Acronym for Key Risk Indicator.

Level of risk: Magnitude of risk. Expressed in terms of likelihood and consequence.

Likelihood: Possibility or chance of something occurring or happening. Likelihood is also called probability or frequency.

Management control: Controlling is one of the critical managerial functions like planning, organizing, staffing and directing; important function because it helps to check the errors and to take the corrective action so that deviation from standards are minimized and stated goals of the organization are achieved in a desired manner.

Management system: Interrelated processes within an organization whose aim is to achieve business or management system objectives.

Materiality: Concept in accounting and auditing related to the importance or significance of an amount, transaction, finding, or discrepancy.

Measurement: Process to determine a value or number.

Monitoring: Continual checking, observing, and supervising the status of risk to determine changes that may affect controls or residual risk.

Non conformity: Also referred to as a non-conformance. Binary decision (yes/no) to determine adherence to requirements. In this case, an inability to conform to requirements.

Objective: Result to be secured, gained or achieved.

Observer: Person who accompanies the audit team who ensures that procedures are consistently followed.

Operational risk: Potential of loss attributable to process variation or disruption in its operations caused by internal or external factors.

Organization: Legal entity that has processes and functions that achieve business objectives.

Outsource: External organization that provides products or services.

PDCA: Acronym for Plan - Do - Check - Act.

People risk: People are the backbone and personality of a business; people are also a key source of risk, because risk management is the fundamental driver to sustainable success, understanding the various risks associated with employees must be a top priority for executive management.

Performance: Actionable or measurable output or outcome.

Preventive action: Change implemented to address a weakness in a management system that is not yet responsible for causing nonconforming product or service.

Process: Interrelated and/or interacting activities that add value to inputs to create an output.

Process risk: Probability of loss inherent in a business process; may include lack of process capability, lack of process stability, and/or lack of improvement.

Professional judgment: Standard of care that requires auditors to exercise reasonable care and diligence and to observe the principles of serving the public interest in applying professional judgment.

Project risk: Project risk involves not being able to meet project objectives or deliverables based on project scope, quality, schedule, or cost.

Quality assurance: Engineering activities implemented in a quality system so product or service requirements can be fulfilled.

Quality management: Management of quality related activities, including assurance and control.

Quality Management Thinking(QMT): Quality equivalent to Risk Based Thinking(RBT).

Quality governance: Process by which the Board of Directors reviews the RBT, quality decisions and actions of executive management.

QMS: Acronym for Quality Management System. See Business Management System and Management System.

RBT: Acronym for Risk Based Thinking. The first stage in a RCMM journey from RBT to risk assessment, risk management, to ERM.

RCMM: Acronym for Risk Capability Maturity Model, which consists of five levels from ad hoc to optimized.

Reasonable assurance: Most cost effective measures are taken in the design and implementation stages to reduce risk and restrict expected deviations to a tolerable level.

Red Book: Institute of Internal Auditors(IIA) guidelines for conducting an internal audit.

Reputational risk: Decrease in brand equity or credibility in the organization.

Requirement: Explicit or implicit needs or expectations. Customers, regulators, or interested parties can develop a requirement.

Residual risk. Risk remaining after risk treatment. Residual risk can contain unidentified risk. Residual risk is also called retained risk. Exposure to loss remaining after other known risks have been countered, factored in, or eliminated.

Review: Activity used to determine the suitability, adequacy, and effectiveness of risk-controls against established objectives.

Risk: Uncertainty on achieving a business or QMS objective. Risk is also a deviation from an objective, which can be either positive or negative. Objectives can be from the financial, quality, project, process, program, transactional, or supply chain. Qualitative risk is defined in terms of likelihood and consequence.

Risk analysis: Process to understand the nature of risk and to determine the level of risk. Risk analysis is the basis for risk evaluation and decisions about risk treatment and risk management.

Risk appetite: Level of risk that an organization is prepared to accept, before action is deemed necessary to reduce it; also sometimes called 'risk tolerance.' Amount and type of strategic risk the organization is willing to pursue and manage.

Risk assessment: Process of identifying, analyzing, and evaluating risk. Determination of quantitative or qualitative value of risk related to a concrete situation and a recognized threat (also called hazard).

Risk assurance: Ability to provide requisite level of risk-control effectiveness.

Risk attitude: Organization's approach to assess and mitigate risk. Risk management is an element of risk attitude.

Risk aversion: Attitude and policy to move away and not pursue opportunities and actions.

Risk Based Auditing: Also known as Value Added Auditing™. Red Book and Yellow Book are examples of Risk Based Auditing.

Risk Based Certification: DNV term for higher level risk certification and assurance.

Risk Based Thinking(RBT): International Organization for Standardization(ISO) tagline for ISO 9001:2015 and possibly other families of standards as they incorporate risk. ISO says that RBT has always been part of ISO standards.

Risk Based Thinking journey: Steps in risk journey from RBT to risk assessment, to risk management, to ERM.

Risk-control: Method by which firms evaluate potential losses and take action to reduce or eliminate threats. Risk-control is a technique that utilizes findings from risk assessments (identifying potential risk factors in a firm's operations).

Risk criteria: Terms against which risk is evaluated. Risk criteria are based on business objectives, external/internal context, and other criteria. Risk criteria can be based on standards, laws, policies, and other requirements.

Risk evaluation: Process of comparing the results of risk analysis against risk criteria to determine whether it is acceptable or tolerable to the enterprise. Risk evaluation is used in the decision of risk treatment. Assessing probability and consequences of individual risks, taking into account any interdependencies or other factors outside the immediate scope under investigation.

Risk event: An occurrence or change in a particular set of circumstances that usually has negative consequences.

Risk identification: Process of finding, recognizing, and describing risk. Risk identification involves identifying risk sources, events, likelihood, and possible consequences. Risk identification involves historical data, theoretical analysis, expert opinions, and stakeholder needs.

Risk inventory: List of prioritized organizational risks.

Risk likelihood rating: Critical rating element and vector of risk along with 'risk consequence'; risk likelihood starts at a 1 rating, which is a rare event and goes to a 5 rating, which is almost certain.

Risk management: Identification, assessment, and prioritization of risks (effect of uncertainty on objectives, whether positive or negative) followed by coordinated and economical application of resources to minimize, monitor, and control the probability and/or consequence of events or to maximize the realization of opportunities.

Risk management framework: Process cycle for managing risk. ISO 31000:2018 and COSO are two common risk management frameworks.

Risk management plan: Steps, procedures, approach, resources, methodology, and components applied to the management of risk.

Risk management: Also, called risk treatment or risk-control. Risk management is usually defined as the control of risk.

Risk management framework: Structure upon which to build strategy or set of controls organized in categories to reach objectives and monitor performance.

Risk management policy: Policy is the highest and strategic level intentions and organizational direction as it relates to risk management.

Risk management process: Systematic application of organizational policies, procedures, work instructions, processes, practices, and guidelines for establishing the context, analyzing, assessing, treating, monitoring, and communicating risks.

Risk map: Visual and qualitative method of laying out the risk of an event or variation; visual representation of statistics; usually consisting of red, yellow, and green elements.

Risk monitoring: Last major element of risk management framework, used to determine if the risk management plan is being followed and if internal risk-controls are working effectively.

Risk owner: Enterprise or owner with the accountability, authority, and responsibility to manage risk.

Risk profile: Description of the set of risks that can relate to the enterprise.

Risk reduction: Also called risk-control.

Risk response: Used similarly as risk treatment or risk mitigation; appropriate steps taken or procedures implemented upon discovery of an unacceptably high degree of exposure to one or more risks.

Risk source: Element(s) that have the potential that can cause risk.

Risk syntax: Use and application of risk concepts. See 'risk taxonomy.'

Risk taxonomy: Practice and science of risk classification of things or concepts plus the principles that underlie the classification

Risk tolerance: Acceptable level of variation a company or an individual is willing to accept in the pursuit of the specific objective.

Risk treatment: Process of managing risk, including: avoiding risk; increasing risk; removing the risk source; changing the likelihood; changing the consequences; sharing the risk; or retaining the risk. Risk treatment is called risk elimination, risk prevention, risk reduction, risk response, or risk management.

Sarbanes Oxley: U.S. governance and financial reporting act of 2002.

Scenario test: Process for assessing the adverse consequences of one or more possible events occurring simultaneously or serially.

SMART objectives: Acronym representing: Specific, Measurable, Assignable, Realistic, and Timely

Self-certification: Statement by an organization that it meets ISO requirements without a third-party audit.

Stakeholder: Enterprise or person that can impact or be impacted by risk.

Stress test: Process for measuring the adverse consequence on one or more quality, supplier, ISO, design, cyber security, information technology, people, or other operational factors that can impact the organization's financial condition.

Supplier: Organization or person providing a product or service as part of a value exchange.

SWOT: Acronym for Strengths - Weaknesses - Opportunities - Threats.

System: Set of interrelated and interacting activities.

Technical Committee (TC) 176: ISO committee responsible for writing QMS standard, ISO 9001:2015.

Technical controls: Example of control usually with IT and ICS systems; examples of technical control include identification and authentication.

Technical expert: Person with specific knowledge who is part of the audit team.

Technology risk: Risk that key technology processes a company uses to develop, deliver, and manage its products, services, and support operations do not meet requirements.

Top management: Same as executive management. Group that controls an organization at the highest level.

TQM: Acronym for Total Quality Management. Implies a high level of quality maturity and capability.

Upside risk: Opportunity or positive risk.

VUCA: Acronym for Volatility, Uncertainty, Complexity, and Ambiguity. Description of current business environment that requires different strategic and tactical planning models.

White space risk: Risks often in the white spaces between the silos, functions, and work between processes.

Yellow Book: Also called GAGAS or Generally Accepted Government Auditing Standards. Audit standards for public auditing in U.S. and Canada.

C

D

E

K

L

M

R

---

[i] ISO 9001:2015 'Risk Based Thinking' PPT deck, July, 2015.

[ii] ISO 9001:2015 'Risk Based Thinking' PPT deck, July, 2015.

[iii] ISO 31000, 2018, p.2.

[iv] RIMS website 2014.

[v] Distilled from ISO 31000 LinkedIn community dialog discussing 'What is the purpose of risk management?

[vi] Office of the President, OMB A-123, July 15, 2016

[vii] Baldrige Excellence Framework, 2017-2018, p. 45.

[viii] Nigel Croft, "The Next Version of ISO 9001 – What to Expect," September 2012.

[ix] ISO 19011:2018 http://insights.cermacademy.com/files/2014/01/ISO9001Risk_Based_Thinking-2.pdf

[x] ISO 31000, 2018.

[xi] ISO 31000, 2018.

[xii] COSO - Internal Control - Integrated Framework, 2002.

[xiii] ISO 31000, 1999, p.2.

[xiv] COSO, ERM: Understanding and Communicating Risk Appetite, 2012.

[xv] BSI, "ISO Revisions: Risk on the Frontline," June 2, 2014.

[xvi] Wikipedia, What is a business model? 2015.

[xvii] General Motors Company Risk Committee Charter, 2014. Web.

[xviii] General Motors Company Risk Committee Charter, 2014. Web.

[xix] GE Risk Committee Charter. Web. 2012.

[xx] Chartered Quality Institute (CQI), website, 2014.

[xxi] Chartered Quality Institute, The Quality Profession: Driving Organizational Excellence, 2014.

[xxii] PayPal description of Senior Director of ERM, 2014.

[xxiii] Nigel Croft, "ISO Malaysia Quality Conference," September 2014.

[xxiv] Next Generation Risk Certification, http://www.offshore-technology.com/downloads/whitepapers/professional/risk-based-certification/

[xxv] p1.

[xxvi] (Quality Assurance, Wikipedia, 2013)

[xxvii] Reasonable Assurance, 6.03, GAO Yellow Book, 2011, p. 124.

[xxviii] (Quality Audit, Wikipedia, 2014).

[xxix] IIA, 'What is Internal Control?' Website.

[xxx] Keith Ridgeway contributions.

[xxxi] COSO, Guidance on Internal Control, 2013.

[xxxii] COSO Internal Control – Integrated Framework FAQ, 2013.
[xxxiii] COSO Internal Control – Integrated Framework FAQ, 2013.

www.ingramcontent.com/pod-product-compliance
Lightning Source LLC
LaVergne TN
LVHW060020210926
848481LV00013B/3755
* 9 7 8 1 7 3 2 5 5 4 5 3 5 *